MW00782190

THE *THINKING CLEARLY* SERIES

Series editor: Clive Calver

The *Thinking Clearly* series sets out the main issues in a variety of important subjects. Written from a mainstream Christian standpoint, the series combines clear biblical teaching with up-to-date scholarship. Each of the contributors is an authority in his or her field. The series is written in straightforward everyday language, and each volume includes a range of practical applications and guidance for further reading.

The series has two main aims:
1. To help Christians understand their faith better.
2. To show how Christian truths can illuminate matters of crucial importance in our society.

DO YOU NEED A SPEAKER?

Many Monarch authors, including the author of this book, are willing to come and speak to groups of all sizes. To obtain a current list of authors and topics please write to: Monarch Books, Concorde House, Grenville Place, Mill Hill, London NW7 3SA

THE *THINKING CLEARLY* SERIES

Series editor: Clive Calver

Healing and Deliverance

JOHN WOOLMER

MONARCH
B O O K S

First published by Monarch Books 1999

ISBN 1 85424 444 2

Editorial Office: Monarch Books,
Broadway House, The Broadway, Crowborough,
East Sussex TN6 1HQ

British Library Cataloguing Data
A catalogue record for this book is available
from the British Library,

Designed and produced for the publishers by
Bookprint Creative Services
P.O. Box 827, BN21 3YJ, England
Printed in Great Britain.

For Jane, as we celebrate our silver wedding.

Contents

Acknowledgements

For all those who have shared their stories and have taken the risk of seeking prayer for healing.

With grateful thanks to all those from whose ministry I have learnt over the years, especially the late Fred Smith, Pastor of the New Testament Fellowship, Oxford, and Michael Green, for his encouragement and helpful critique.

With thanks to Mrs Joyce Martin and her indefatigable skill and patience in reading my handwriting and transcribing my efforts onto disk and typescript.

With thanks to Anne Goode, Hilfield Friary and Cole Manor, who have provided quiet places to write and to pray.

With thanks to all who have written on this subject, especially Francis Macnutt whose first book *Healing* I started to read while our first child was being born!

With thanks to my family, parishioners, and friends in Zambia, for their support, encouragement and patience.

With thanks to David Howell, diocesan healing advisor and other members of the Bath and Wells healing advisory group for their help and encouragement.

With thanks to Tony Collins and the staff at Monarch Books, for their unfailing courtesy, helpful criticism and hospitality.

Foreword

It is both a delight and a privilege to write this foreword to John Woolmer's new book.

It is a delight because I personally owe a great deal to this warm, godly and slightly eccentric friend. If it had not been for John Woolmer's influence at Winchester College (where I went to school), I doubt whether I would have been in any position to write this foreword today!

It was John Woolmer who, in the early 1970s, came to Winchester ostensibly with a brief to teach maths, but surreptitiously with a mandate to pray for revival. On holiday in Austria he had a strong sense that the Lord was going to bring a spiritual harvest the following term, that the work would continue, and that there would be a second revival at a subsequent date. This indeed occurred, and I was one of the many people who was soundly converted during those extraordinary days.

The story of this season of grace is told in John Woolmer's book *Thinking Clearly About Prayer*, and in my own book *Revival*. Both of these volumes are part of the series for which John has written this excellent study, *Healing and Deliverance*.

It is the excellence of this volume that makes it not only a delight but a privilege to write this foreword. I have read many books on healing, and a number on the deliverance ministry. Many of these are mediocre, some helpful, a very few outstanding. I put *Healing and Deliverance* in the category of 'outstanding'.

Why is this? First, because it is a vulnerable book. One of the things I love about John is the fact that he is not afraid to be open about the times when healing apparently did not come, or when he got things wrong. John's book is unusual in that it is triumphant without ever being triumphalistic. In other words, it inspires faith in God who heals without ever indulging in the shallow, 'name-it-and-claim-it' approach of the prosperity brigade. For that reason alone I would commend it.

A second reason why this book is so important is because it is practical. Though John has done considerable academic research as he has prepared this volume, this has not rendered the book either unreadable or inaccessible. On the one hand, there is a great deal of solid biblical scholarship as well as historical study behind the lines of this book. On the other, there is a great deal of down-to-earth advice about how to 'do the stuff' (to use John Wimber's wonderful phrase). I would want in particular to point to John's wisdom, born out of long experience, concerning the practicalities of deliverance ministry.

A third thing I like about this book is that it is humorous. There are moments when you will laugh at both the stories John tells and the distinctive way in which he tells them. Frankly, this is refreshing. There has been so much hype in the healing and deliverance ministry. John's honest, humorous retelling of certain incidents enables us to look at this subject seriously but not too seriously.

A fourth thing I enjoyed about this book is that it is balanced. John himself is an example of a balanced person. I know of no other friend who combines the mathematical logic of a Mr Spock with the spiritual openness of a Captain Kirk! Yet John does. His mathematical mentality results in a clarity of prose that is very rare these days among Christian writers. His spiritual openness means that he is no cool rationalist like B.B. Warfield but rather a 'reasonable enthusiast' like John Wesley. This combination of right and left-brain characteristics produces a mindset capable not only of *thinking clearly* but also of *thinking supernaturally*. In a postmodern culture like ours, where the scientific and the spiritual are being increasingly integrated, this is essential.

Fifthly, this book is excellent because it is courageous. Most books on healing and deliverance do a very poor job (if they attempt it at all) of answering questions like, 'Why does God sometimes *not* heal?' 'What about the healing of homosexuals?' 'What is a proper Christian attitude towards death?' 'What about territorial spirits?' John faces all of these issues, and many other tricky topics, head on. He answers them with amazing grace as well as real insight. Some may not like all of John's conclusions, but all will admire his bravery and authenticity in tackling them.

A sixth thing that makes this book attractive is that it is biblical. Some books on healing and deliverance have a far from solid foundation in the Scriptures. Their pages are full of stories – stories from the author's experience rather than stories from the Bible. John's book does not fall into this trap. What he relates from his own and other's experiences is used as an illustration of biblical principles. John does not bring the Bible in to justify his experiences. He brings his experiences to illuminate the Bible. This word-and-Spirit approach is essential to the health of the churches today.

A seventh thing that makes this book outstanding is the

fact that it is timely. Many of us believe that the fields are ripe for harvest in the UK. If that is true, then we need workers for the harvest (Matthew 9:35–38). Jesus showed that workers are people trained to preach the good news, heal the sick, and to deliver the demonised. Paul also showed that they are people equipped to demolish strongholds through militant prayer. One of the great things about *Healing and Deliverance* is its timing. To be perfectly blunt, this is one of the very few books (particularly about deliverance ministry) that I would recommend to my own people as a manual for working in the harvest and as a textbook for understanding the dynamics of spiritual warfare.

An eighth thing I welcome about this volume is the fact that it is ecumenical. Speaking as an Anglican, I love the way that John makes healing and deliverance user-friendly for Anglicans. But while John's approach is very obviously an Anglican one, his chapter on the twentieth century shows that he is very much in touch with what the Holy Spirit has been doing in the Pentecostal, Catholic, Independent and other churches. Not only is John knowledgeable about these movements, he also sounds as if he is genuinely rejoicing in them! There is a rich sense in this book not only of the grace of our Lord Jesus Christ and the love of God, but also and especially of the fellowship of the Holy Spirit. This is a sign of the 'relational' healing that is taking place in the churches today.

A ninth thing that makes this book outstanding is the fact that it is pastoral. The chapter in which John addresses FAQs (Frequently Asked Questions) shows that he is in touch with the issues that are challenging healing ministry teams on the ground. John knows from his work both in Shepton Mallet and in other parishes that there are questions which many want addressed, especially in relation to deliverance ministry. He tackles these with compassion and answers them in a way that all can understand.

A final thing I like about this book is that it is honest. In fact, it is the honesty of this book that I love most. John is honest in his descriptions of the miracles that he has witnessed. He is also honest in his descriptions of those times when people have not been visibly healed. Both types of honesty speak of a man grappling both publicly and poignantly with the paradoxes of the healing and deliverance ministry. For those of us who minister on the borders between miracle and mystery, this book will form an indispensable map, and its author an inimitable guide.

Mark Stibbe

1

Now We See Through a Glass Darkly

The opening chapter is mainly a personal account of some of the writer's experiences in healing, deliverance, and spiritual warfare.

It also begins to consider a theology of healing – facing the contrasting results of prayer in different cases and offering the view that healing is a mystery, a sign of God's gracious activity in our world, and not a right which believers can and should claim.

Now We See Through a Glass Darkly

A neighbour gazed over our back gate and smiled, wanly, at Rachel our first baby. I noticed that she had her arm in a sling. Gradually, over the next few weeks we got to know her. She was continually in pain, her right hand enlarged and deformed with fingers missing or lengthened. Apparently, her mother had contracted German Measles early in the pregnancy and this had been the result.

Our meeting with Astra seemed like an answer to prayer. I was working as a curate in a large city-centre church in Oxford, and we were living outside the parish. It wasn't easy to get to know the neighbours; the parish in which we lived was struggling and the church was facing possible closure and a bleak future.[1] Curates from successful neighbouring parishes felt somewhat alien! We had lived there about four months and were praying that Rachel might help us break the ice.

A significant healing

Astra told me about her troubles, personal and physical. The pain was so intense that she was looking for any way out, and the top specialists were mystified. I, although not a natural evangelist, told her about Jesus. Two months after Rachel's birth, Jane and I went on holiday. I encouraged Astra to go up to St Aldate's while we were away, and listen to the Bishop of Coventry preach.

Two significant things happened while we were away. I had my first decisive experience of seeing someone healed in direct answer to prayer,[2] and Astra became a Christian. She went to hear the bishop's powerful message. She was duly impressed. At the end of the service, she prepared to leave the crowded church, intending to put off making any personal response, only to find that she was sitting next to the bishop's wife! That happy coincidence made all the difference, and she responded to the challenge then and there.

Physically things did not improve, indeed they got so bad that she was admitted into hospital. Visiting her in hospital, I started to pray for her. On my second visit, Astra described my prayer as like a very strong pain-killer. Encouraged by this, I visited her and her husband each evening when she was out of hospital. The first time we prayed, in her kitchen, as I touched her hand and prayed, I felt such an excruciating pain that I had to stop after a few seconds, ask for a drink, and then continue to pray. Astra felt the pain being drawn out.

Night by night, things improved. Her hand remained deformed, but less swollen and much less painful. A few weeks later, Astra felt so much better that she took a job as a taxi driver. She and her husband started attending the local church, boosting their tiny congregation, and Astra became a member of our new healing prayer group at St Aldate's.

For three years things went quite well. Astra's faith grew, and her life improved in various ways. She and Bill moved to the edge of Oxford, and we almost lost touch. Then, one Sunday, she arrived at an evening healing service looking very grim. She had had more health troubles, been X-rayed, and then diagnosed with cancer in the liver, stomach and colon. Not surprisingly, she was given only a few months to live.

We started to pray, and each week some of the healing team travelled out to her mobile home. There was no obvious progress. At Christmas, preaching at a large carol service (with Astra's permission to share it), I told some of her story. I said that she had kept her faith, but probably wouldn't be alive next Christmas. What of the congregation? Did they believe? Were they trusting God in their much more favourable circumstances?

After Christmas, we continued to pray. Officially Astra's time was 'up', but at least she wasn't getting any worse. She was being treated with an experimental drug, and one day when we prayed, she described feeling a burning sensation in her stomach which lasted about an hour. The X-rays showed a slight improvement.

A Bible verse strengthens our faith

In March she came to see me. Before we prayed, I read her the story of the healing of the man at the pool at Bethesda (John 5:1–15). At first it didn't seem particularly significant.

Then I noticed, from verse 3, that the man had been ill for thirty-eight years. As this seemed significant, I asked Astra how old she was. 'Thirty-seven,' she replied. 'Then you, too, have been ill for thirty-eight years!' I replied. She looked puzzled, until I pointed out that she had been ill almost from conception due to her mother's German Measles. (Later we established an almost certain connection between the hand deformity and the cancer.) I smiled at her and said something that I very rarely say in such situations: 'I think you'll get better!'

I missed the grand denouement. In May, I was absent when the healing team assembled to pray. Astra felt a great fire in her stomach. This time it lasted for a week. She started to feel well, and the next X-rays showed that she was almost clear of cancer The healing continued. We both moved, and I've only seen her once or twice since. A few years ago, I was speaking in Yeovil to a group of students, and she came as a living testimony to God's healing grace. She has now been free of cancer for about twenty years.

Just before I left Oxford, a famous evangelist, David Watson,[3] came to lead a student mission. Over the years, I had got to know him quite well, and greatly admired his character, his preaching and his ability to carry on despite ill health. He suffered badly from asthma. On this occasion it was so bad that it looked as if he might have to stop preaching. With Michael Green, then the Rector of St Aldate's, we prayed for David. There was a dramatic improvement, and relatively little recurrence. We were much encouraged, and the mission went ahead.

A puzzling death

About a year later, David was diagnosed with liver cancer. Like many others, I prayed – assuming that God would heal him. We exchanged a couple of letters, and for a while things seemed quite hopeful. Many prayers were offered, a leading healing team visited him from America, prophecies were uttered and we waited for the good news.

It never came and just about a year after the original

diagnosis, David died. He was mourned by many, most of whom were puzzled as to why it had happened. I do not propose to add to the literature debating why healing was withheld, I just want to face the contrast.

The healing paradox

A world-famous evangelist, with apparently much more work to do for the kingdom, dies, unhealed physically. An unknown housewife, who, because of domestic circumstances, can do little for the kingdom, receives an apparently miraculous healing. There is the paradox. It leads to a number of reactions. The simplest is to deny the reality of healing prayer. Cases like Astra's are either misdiagnosis or spontaneous remissions. A second approach is to assert that it is always God's will to heal, but that healing grace is often blocked by sin, unbelief or whatever. A third is to accept that there is a mystery and to see healing as a 'sign' of God's gracious activity in our world, rather than as our 'right'.

The story of the healing at the Pool of Bethesda supports this third view (though other biblical stories might well be used to support the second). As far as we know, the paralysed man was the only one who received healing that day. Jesus had no word, or touch, for the remaining multitudes waiting by the pool with its five porticos.

Many people reading my two opening stories may feel that I've missed an important theological point. It is often said that 'death is the ultimate healer'. By implication, I'm wrong to regard prayer for David as a 'failure', and for Astra as a 'success'. There is, of course, a lot of truth in this objection. People are healed and like the nine lepers (Luke 17:11–19) they seem to receive no spiritual benefit.

People die having been very blessed spiritually and encourage others in the way that they handle their final illness. Arguably, David's most powerful book was written during his last illness.[4]

I've seen many people die for whom I've prayed long and hard; probably every parish priest has had this experience. All, I believe, have benefited greatly from the prayer and have been able, with their families, to face death in a much more positive way. A few have still died in pain and discomfort, most (thanks as well to the skills of modern medicine) have died peacefully. One of the saddest things is not these deaths, but the many other times where men and women are shielded from the ministry of the Church by well-meaning relatives who don't want them 'upset' by a visit from the local vicar. Death is a reality which many are not prepared to face.

In the summer of 1969 I was at theological college. It was a bad time. My mother had died at the relatively young age of fifty-seven after pioneering heart surgery. My father was showing signs of the depression from which he wouldn't recover. My uncle, in the grips of alcoholism, had written: 'I can't think why you're being ordained, your prayers didn't do your mother much good.' I had fallen in love, but circumstances dictated that what for me would ideally have been a brief courtship, was going to last five years. My choice of theological college was proving disastrous. I had been in slight rebellion after an evangelical conversion some years earlier, and had gone to a liberal college. The students were very nice and I enjoyed the sociability of the pub and the cricket field, but many seemed better suited to a career in the social services than to one in the Church. The Vice-Principal preached a sermon declaring that private prayer, except meditation, was a waste of time.

The faith of a dying lady

One weekend I was feeling particularly low. On the Sunday afternoon I was sent to take a ward service at the nearby hospital. My destination was the cancer ward. After the brief service, feeling totally depressed and spiritually inadequate, I started to talk to the patients. They all pointed to the last bed that I would visit. 'You must talk to the young lady in the corner.' When I got to her bed, she lay, obviously very ill, but radiant. Her faith shone through the darkness. It spoke to the whole ward, it spoke to me.

As I walked away, I wondered what right I had to be depressed while she was so cheerful. My depression lifted and I was given strength to cope with a very difficult four months which included changing theological colleges, seeing my new love disappear to New Guinea for eighteen months, and the deepening depression and ultimate suicide of my father.

The importance of the healing ministry

In the course of this book, I will look carefully at the biblical accounts of healing, take a brief look at Christian healing throughout the Church's history, and take notice of the steady growth of healing in churches and Christian centres in the twentieth century. But as a preliminary, I want to tackle one other question: 'Why is the healing ministry important?'

The other day, at a family christening, I was talking to Bob – a great-great uncle of the baby. He told me how one of his children had had no children after some fourteen years of marriage. A Nigerian evangelist had visited their church, and talked from the Bible about God's healing of barrenness. He had invited people to come forward for prayer. Bob's family had responded – and almost instantly they had conceived and had a healthy, much-wanted baby.

The Church's normal ministry of healing

Then I thought of Bob's late brother-in-law. Alex had been a churchwarden in our church some years earlier. He was very traditional, very straightforward and very kind. He found my predecessor difficult, and opposed his plans to modernise the church. My ideas were even worse! But we discovered a bond through the ministry of healing. Alex suffered greatly from a number of ailments; but rather to my surprise, he agreed to be prayed for and sometimes gained great benefit. We became firm friends. We disagreed about many church matters, but were able to respect each other. Prayer for healing had bridged a gap which could otherwise have caused quite a problem.

For Bob and Alex, healing prayer had opened new horizons. God was closer, more personal, more approachable. As a result, their faith seemed more practical, more real.

It is stories like that, rather than the spectacular healing of Astra, which are the backbone of the healing ministry in the parishes. Those sort of stories, very ordinary though they may seem, are highly significant. They develop faith, help spiritual growth and, like ripples when a stone is thrown into a pond, touch many other people. Everyone who is healed, or who benefits from such prayer, has a story to tell. Each story is a powerful witness, to a largely unbelieving society, of the kingdom of God. Each story is an encouragement and a challenge to those who hear to seek prayer for themselves – and above all, to seek Jesus, in whose name we all pray.

However, I quickly discovered that if you explore the healing ministry seriously you are likely to encounter darker forces. Gentle prayer for healing can erupt into violent confrontational prayer involving deliverance. In the gospel, we shall see (chapter 3) that Jesus' ministry of healing is inexorably linked with deliverance. Sometimes when healing, as in the case of the leper (Mark 1: 41), Jesus' prayer is virtually the same as an exorcism command. Many of the Early Fathers made the same connection. For many of them, including Justin, Irenaeus, Tertullian and Origen, exorcism seemed more natural, and more necessary, than healing.[5]

With the great increase of occult healing, the widespread use of tarot cards and ouija boards, we will find the same thing happening in England. We dare not separate healing and deliverance, nor must we become so obsessed by the devil and all his works that we cease to expect the blessing and protection of God.

My first experience of the need for deliverance

One Thursday evening in July 1975, Jane and I were out to dinner with a retired headmaster. Somehow, the conversation turned to the question of exorcism. There had been a very unpleasant and disastrous case of attempted exorcism reported in the papers. I felt myself, with no practical knowledge or experience, defending what I believed to be the New Testament position of the reality of evil powers and spirits. We left quite early as, theoretically, Jane was expected to go into labour that night. When we arrived home, a dishevelled couple were standing on our doorstep. What followed profoundly changed *my* thinking on the subject.[6]

'We've come to complain about the social services . . . .' Wearily, and reluctantly, I let them come in, made the inevitable cup of coffee, and listened to their story. Jane went to bed.

A baptism of fire

After a few minutes, the woman, who was doing most of the talking, suddenly said, 'My trouble is that I'm in league with the devil.' I reacted quite calmly, and suggested that she renounced the devil and all his works. The atmosphere changed. She screamed across my kitchen, 'I renounce God!' Even her partner looked a bit apprehensive. Her whole demeanour changed. She started to wander around our very small kitchen talking in the voice of an old man, walking like an old man, and becoming spiritually quite menacing. First she screamed out, 'Your wife will go into labour tonight,' to which I replied, 'No she won't. You're lying – in the name of the Lord.' (Rachel was born safely ten days later). Later, when I tried to contact Michael and Rosemary Green, my rector and his wife, she teased me, 'They're not coming, they won't come . . . .' It so happened that Michael and Rosemary were out to dinner with the only parishioners who were not on the telephone. I was totally stuck, alone, and somewhat alarmed.

Around midnight, about two hours later, Michael and Rosemary turned up. Our visitor had become more and more menacing. She started praying in a 'demonic tongue'. It was very unpleasant, and the only way I can describe it is that it sounded like Latin backwards being spat out of a machine gun. Michael commanded me to pray in tongues! I'd received this gift a few years earlier, but had always doubted its reality. This was the first time that I'd used it in public, and the effect was quite startling! For the first time in the evening, she shut up, and gradually calm was restored. Eventually everybody left, and I went to bed. Jane, still awake, asked about the old man in the kitchen. She had heard our visitor's other voice and assumed that it came from a third person.

Ministry to this lady went on over many years. Rosemary, in particular, worked with great love and determination to help her. When we began, we quickly learnt from the medical diagnosis that she had a personality disorder which meant she was not likely to be cured. We brought in the diocesan exorcist. He anointed her with oil, she leapt in the air, complaining that the oil burnt her, and threw a cup of coffee over my open Bible – scoring a direct hit on Mark 6 (where Jesus's disciples go out anointing the sick with oil!).

Michael has reminded me that on another occasion she spoke with the voice of someone called Hilda, showing marks on her arms and throat of having been tied to a stake and burnt in some previous incarnation.[7]

The next few months produced a wearisome pattern of progress and relapses. Sometimes she would come to prayer meetings and take part, then quite suddenly she would scream and totally disrupt proceedings. She went to stay with a priest and his wife, and was prepared for adult baptism the following Easter. The battle continued long after that. But gradually, healing and freedom came. I last saw her about fifteen years ago, in Rosemary's kitchen, drinking a cup of coffee and looking clothed and in her right mind.

Over the next few years, mainly during my time in Oxford, I saw many other people (none so dramatic!) who seemed to be released from evil spirits. Most were helped by quite simple ministry such as the renewal of baptism vows, a few needed several sessions, and some displayed strange psychic powers – speaking in other voices, displaying inordinate strength, wild eyes, strong negative reaction to the sacraments, sudden deafness when prayer was offered, and even the inability to join in the Lord's Prayer. Latterly, mainly in Somerset, I've had more cause to pray in disturbed buildings than with spiritually disturbed people, although three visits to Zambia have certainly reminded me of the strong spiritual forces that can control people.

Not surprisingly, as a former maths teacher in one of England's most academic schools, I often used to stop and ask myself, 'Am I being deluded? Is this really happening?'

A number of factors, which I will discuss in greater length later, have helped to convince me of both the reality and necessity of this ministry.

Deliverance justified. (1) It is scriptural

First and foremost, it is scriptural. Jesus practised it, and taught both his immediate disciples, and wider groups of followers, to do the same. Huge chunks of the Gospels and, most especially, Jesus' teaching to his disciples, have to be excised if we are to ignore this area of ministry. We shall look at this in detail in chapter 3.

Deliverance justified. (2) The power of Jesus' name

Secondly, the power of the name of Jesus is so great. Two examples will suffice. Michael and I had ministered to an American lady studying at Oxford University. She had become a strong Christian, but had become troubled by occult things that she had been involved with in the past. After some simple ministry, we thought that she was free. She wasn't. Michael takes up the story in his own words.

'David Watson and I were called in on the last night of the OICCU mission to find Barbara roaring with demonic laughter and John's night-time visitor telling her she was demonised. It was a chaotic situation. Rosemary went off to pray in the house, and Barbara confronted David and me for most of the night. She attacked us with a carving knife at one stage, with a broken glass at another, but when we made the sign of the cross she simply could not get through. Eventually, in the middle of the night, there was a break in the demonic clouds so to speak, and she called on the name of the Lord and was set free. I am in regular touch with her and she is a very powerful Christian in the Pentagon.'

In Zambia, I was working with my friend, Peter Hancock, on my first SOMA trip.[8] We had arrived with some difficulty, after travelling through a dangerous frontier road in Zaire, at the Chipili Mission Station in North Zambia. We shared a house with vast spiders, a scorpion, and the ceiling had gaping holes in which we suspected, quite correctly, that snakes could live.

An unusual church notice

Perhaps the most 'foolish' church notice that I ever heard was given, with due solemnity, by a Zambian church-warden at the end of two days' teaching on the Holy Spirit. 'Tomorrow, gentlemen, we will see signs and wonders.' Was the notice presumptuous, or a word of prophetic faith? The next day we knew. Hundreds of people flocked into the old mission church. They surged forward for prayer. We split into four teams led by Peter, Archdeacon Tobias and the local priest, Isaiah Chabala, and myself. What really surprised us all was the extraordinary reaction when we began to pray. Many crashed to the floor – shaking, screaming, even hissing, or moving like a snake. With four teams praying in quite a small area, there was pandemonium. Yet beneath it all, there was great calm. People went away smiling, feeling physically better, and spiritually free. Many seemed to be healed, many released from evil spirits, others were filled with the Holy Spirit in a new way, and some professed conversion.

I survived four hours of prayer, standing, despite a bad

hip in urgent need of replacement. Our prayers were simple and direct. Mine must have been strengthened by the intercessions of my home parish for my own suspect health and physical strength.

Towards the end of the exhausting morning, the locals said, 'There's a man in the gallery who needs prayer.' I declined to climb the rickety stairway, and asked him to be brought down. I was feeling very tired, and as he approached, he seemed to get larger and larger. He looked pretty fierce.

Something within me said, 'Ask if his father or grandfather has been a witchdoctor.' I felt rather foolish. There was a sort of snarled 'Yes'. I made the sign of the cross, and prayed aloud to cut off the power of his ancestors from him. As he was advancing close to me, he crashed to the ground. A few minutes later, he got up quite well. We all felt that we had experienced something of the power of Jesus, through the cross, over evil spirits.

Deliverance justified. (3) The gifts of healing and discernment (1 Corinthians 12:10)

Thirdly, there have been times when I've been given words of knowledge that have unlocked situations. I've very seldom been given these except in deliverance situations. Again, a few examples will suffice.

One woman asked to see me urgently. She explained that something within her was driving her to commit suicide. As she had attempted this before, I took the matter very seriously. I asked her how she was going to do the deed. She opened her bag and gave me a very large bottle of paracetamol tablets (I kept them, and they kept my family free from headaches for a considerable time!). I then asked why she felt driven (her word) to commit suicide. She said that she kept repeating a certain word, which seemed to have an evil influence on her. I asked her what it was. The word she named, Greek sounding, meant nothing to me. We agreed to meet in the evening, hopefully including Michael Green, at the church. I still wasn't quite sure how seriously to take the situation.

After she left, I searched for the word. As my concordance yielded nothing, I then tried one of my dictionaries. Eventually, I found that her word was the name of a particularly unpleasant evil spirit, found in the book of Tobit, directly inciting murder and indirectly to suicide! Somewhat shaken, I awaited the evening with some anxiety.

Fortunately, Michael was able to come. We addressed the spirit by name, and it left with such force that Michael was almost knocked over.[9] The ministry was very brief (as ideally it always should be!), authoritative, and effective. I'm sure that the woman, at that stage a fairly new believer, was as ignorant as I was of demons in the Apocrypha.

Someone at a prayer meeting saw a picture of a rose with two black spots. One person promptly interpreted this as saying that our policy on infant baptism was wrong! Knowing that this was one of his hobby horses, I rejected this interpretation. No one else had any ideas what it meant, so the picture was put on one side, and the meeting continued. This was important as otherwise the picture would have distracted us for the rest of the evening. At the end of the meeting, a young girl came up and said, 'I am the rose with the two black spots.' Apparently a radiant Christian, she had deep troubles from the past from which she needed release. A Christian Science upbringing, some exposure to occult things abroad at the time of her birth, lesbianism, and suicide attempts had left her very vulnerable to depressions and migraines.

Rather to our surprise, when we challenged anything evil within her to show itself, she manifested all the signs of demonisation. A long and very difficult deliverance followed. At one moment a spirit started to speak through her and to name itself (this should, I think, be discouraged. Jesus usually commanded silence). We couldn't identify the name. An inner voice directed me to Zechariah 2:7. Feeling somewhat foolish I read out, 'Ho! Escape to Zion, you who dwell with the daughter of Babylon'. Michael Green, who was sharing the ministry with me, leapt to his feet. 'Of course! The spirit's name is that of a Babylonian mystery religion.' Armed with this knowledge, the deliverance continued speedily. The strong biblical text, which needed both spiritual and scholastic insight, was key to unlocking her difficulties.

The story had a very happy ending. A while ago, not many years after that episode, I conducted one of the happiest wedding services I've ever taken. The Lord is good! She had married a young ordinand, whose own conversion had been partly through her radiant witness.

The spiritual battle and God's means of communication

On another occasion, we were ministering to someone who had a long and complex history of depression, which seemed to stem from involvement in levitation and the like. Ministry had proved difficult and not very successful. I met with some of the leaders of the church for one final session of prayer. The person concerned became quite restless, and kicked over a jug of water, which I had blessed. (I had by this time discovered that 'holy water' can be very efficacious. Evil powers are terrified of the cross of Christ (Colossians 2:15), and consecrated water is a reminder of baptism which is effectively linked to the cross. Michael and I discovered this when a woman mocked us, saying that we couldn't help her as we hadn't got any holy water. Michael went to the tap, blessed some Oxford water and it proved efficacious).

There was now a large damp patch on the carpet of St Aldate's parish room. An inner voice said, 'Read Exodus chapter 3.' I was puzzled – until I came to verse 5. '"Do not come any closer", God said. "Take off your sandals, for the place where you are standing is holy ground"'.

At first I couldn't quite see the point, then it clicked! The damp patch was the holy ground. We took her shoes off, and tried to place her feet in the damp patch. For a few seconds there was sheer comedy, as she walked, in a sort of trance, determinedly avoiding the damp patch. Frantically, I instructed the others to dump her in it! As her feet hit the patch, she slumped to the ground gently overpowered by the Spirit. This continued for about twenty minutes, while the rest of us prayed. When our friend awoke, there was a complete transformation. All trace of demonic activity seemed to have left, and she was completely well, able to pursue a normal life free from any spiritual oppression.

Deliverance justified. (4) The strange powers of the apparently demonised

Fourthly, there are a number of occasions where the apparently demonised people display a knowledge which it is difficult to see how they could have obtained naturally. For instance, there was a strange incident from Zambia for which I can find no rational explanation. In the midst of much ministry, and a certain amount of chaos, one apparently demonised woman spoke to me. The voice said, 'Go away, I'm not leaving this person!' Two things were particularly striking. We were in a very rural part of Zambia, and it was very unlikely that the woman would know any English. Even more startling was that she spoke in perfect Oxbridge English! Zambians speak English with a lovely soft African accent: this was spoken in harsh, authoritative BBC English! Anyway, the spirit didn't stay too long after we started to pray, and the woman disappeared into the crowd before I had the wit to ask her about her knowledge of English.

Dangers of the deliverance ministry

Of course, there are considerable problems with holding such beliefs and engaging in this sort of ministry. First, there is the serious danger of wrong diagnosis. Great damage is done by trying to exorcise non-existent evil spirits. Those prayed for can be made to feel guilty when the prayers are unsuccessful and left feeling far worse than before. Secondly, there is a related problem. Ministry may begin on the right track, perceiving and praying about a real problem, but somehow it is never quite finished. The list of 'evil spirits' grows inexorably and the person prayed for becomes trapped and far too dependent upon the group who are doing the ministry.

Thirdly, the ministry may lack authority. In the Anglican Church, most dioceses have an exorcist who should be referred to before embarking on such ministry. I have found this chain of authority very helpful, and it reminds me of the bishop's charge at an induction, 'Receive this cure which is both thine and mine.' The diocesan exorcist is the bishop's officer, and I feel greater, not less, freedom acting under his episcopal authority. Fourthly, such ministry may lack common sense. In my own case, I am conscious of inadvertently contributing to a young man's mental breakdown. He was convinced that he was possessed by demons. After doing everything that I could to explore the possibility, including a session with the diocesan exorcist who tried to reassure him, I tried to convince him that his problem wasn't demonic. But then, unthinkingly, I took him to a household where some strange psychic things were happening. This caused him to 'flip'. For a short time, he had to go into a mental hospital.

Over the next few years, he made an encouraging improvement, and was able to hold down a normal job. Nevertheless, I felt partly responsible and very guilty. Gradually, I was able to receive God's forgiveness. In particular, this involved realising that I must release to God the burden of this sort of ministry. He had to teach me that we cannot always succeed, and that we need to be released from the consequences, good and less good, of our ministry. If we give God the glory for the successes, we must allow him to bear the failure. The full reality of forgiveness for this mistake was greatly helped by the boy's father. He made it clear throughout that he didn't blame me, and continued to offer me his friendship, and to consult me about his son and other situations. I was deeply grateful to him. Others might have been less generous.

In some cases, I have heard of such strange practices in purported exorcisms that one wonders whether people have totally lost all sense of proportion and decency.

On the other hand, there is a serious danger in refusing to act. This stems from a view of Jesus' ministry which either says that he was wrong in this very fundamental area, or explains it away by saying that he was using the 'thought categories' of the day. Bishop Ryle, writing in the last century and with no actual experience of this ministry, observes in his commentary on the incident in Mark 5:5 that Africans living in equatorial forests might well doubt the existence of igloos. They would, however, be foolish to deny the possibility without first visiting the Arctic. I freely admit that, before reluctantly getting involved in such prayer, that I too would have been fairly sceptical. If the person really needs this sort of ministry, no other prayers, pills or psychiatric help will set them free. To refuse to countenance this possibility is to deny the ministry recorded of Jesus in the Gospels, and of the Apostles in the Acts. We will look at all these questions in greater detail in later chapters.

Troubled buildings and places

I will say a little more about troubled buildings in a later chapter.[10] At this stage, one example will suffice. I was asked to visit the home of a man who was critically ill. The family was very concerned because they felt that their house had an oppressive, evil atmosphere. I am not sensitive to such things, but I took with me someone who is, and she confirmed it. I was just about to pray for the man, who seemed to have a rather vague, unformed faith, when I asked him about any connections he might have had with spiritualism.

'Oh, yes,' he said, 'We had a friend who came to pray for my healing. She went into a trance and turned into a German doctor!' We prayed through the house. In one room, my prayer partner felt that further prayers were needed. When we went back downstairs to the room where the seance had taken place, I asked to see the chair on which the medium had sat. 'It's upstairs,' was the reply. It was, in fact, in the one room where the most prayer had seemed necessary – a small confirmation that we were doing something important. We finished praying through the house, prayed again for the man, and left.

I saw that man only once more. Despite his increasing weakness, he and his wife were wonderfully cheerful, and the whole house felt quite different. A few days later he died. His wife had been greatly helped by the spiritual uplift of his last week. A colleague, who knew nothing of the problems in the house, remarked to me how amazingly changed he had been in the last few days of his life. It is deeply humbling to have some small part in such ministry.

Problems in buildings

Again, it is astonishing how a few prayers said in the name of Jesus can bring peace to buildings where there has previously been so much disturbance. I've prayed in many places, including homes of Christians, deserted farm houses, stables, pubs, and one ancient house where they had even caught the poltergeist activity on closed circuit television in the midst of various strange psychical activities. The poltergeist's retort seems to have been to upset the electrics in the building to such an extent that after four hours, the South Western Electricity Board couldn't sort out the problem!

Scripture has little to say about spiritual problems in buildings, but the constant emphasis on 'destroying the high places' in the Old Testament seems to suggest that pagan and dangerous influences were liable to linger unless the places were thoroughly cleansed.

The wider spiritual battle

One last great question remains – what about territorial spirits? This is an area about which I write with little experience and some trepidation, but it is a growing issue which churches involved in any sort of prayer ministry may have to consider.

What are territorial spirits?

There has been quite a lot of recent literature on the subject.[11] The theory is that if we believe in Satan and that specific demons can inhabit individuals, then it is logical to believe in an organised spirit world, opposed to the kingdom of God. In particular, some Christians, mainly concerned with effective evangelism, believe they have identified ruling spirits which control certain towns and regions. This is obviously a serious and an important issue. No one wishes to spend hours of time praying fervently against non-existent powers; equally, if these need to be discerned before there can be effective evangelism, the more we know the better.

At a cursory reading Scripture gives little to support this view. Yet a deeper study gives a very different impression. In the next four chapters, we shall consider the underlying assumption of territorial gods in the Old Testament, explore Jesus' teaching on Satan as 'the prince of this world' (John 14:30), and look at Paul, and others, writing about the influence of 'principalities and powers' on our world.

In later chapters we shall look at the teaching of theologians of the stature of Origen and the Venerable Bede from the past, together with Michael Green and Oscar Cullmann in the present. We shall see how power battles have decisively influenced evangelism on occasions

in China, West Africa and Argentina. We shall ask what
the local church should do about this difficult, dangerous
and controversial area. Finally, we shall consider where
there is a strange synthesis between liberal theology which
sees the New Testament powers as represented by corrupt
governments, multinational companies, world debt, etc.,
and warfare theology which sees the same world problems,
but offers the theological opinion that the deeper enemy is
the dark forces that appear to control them.

It is important to realise that this is an important and
dangerous subject. The literature is full of stern warnings,[12] we should enter this field only with clear direction
from God, and supported by a strong shield of prayer.
Truly 'we see through a glass darkly', but our own caution,
and uncertainties, do not provide a sufficient excuse for
ignoring so important an area which has considerable
bearing on healing, deliverance and evangelism.

I would like to conclude this opening chapter with
another personal encounter in Zambia. In May 1992, as
part of a visit to the Luapula province in Northern
Zambia, my wife, Jane, and I, together with Martin
Cavender, administrative director of Springboard,[13] and
his son, Henry, visited Mutwe Wa Nkoko (the village of
the Severed Chicken's Head).

We arrived late one Monday evening, accompanied by
Archdeacon Tobias Kaoma,[14] and some other leading
members of the Zambian Anglican Church. En route
we paid a courtesy call to the local chief. His household
was in much disarray, with sickness and worry concerning a daughter about to give birth. We prayed for them
all. We had brought some gifts of food. About a kilometre from the village we received a traditional Zambian
welcome. Hundreds of dancing people with smiling faces.
Garlands of flowers, and endless singing of 'Sangalale,

Sangalale' (Let's be joyful!). We left our vehicle and joined in the fun. The village was quite small: a little church, a good deep well, a few houses and, in the distance, a school whose roof had been blown off eighteen months earlier.

We washed in blazing hot water in a little stockade, under the light of the Southern Cross and the other African stars. There was a camp fire, much singing and much laughter. There was a clever sketch about a man who tried to steal from his neighbour, but first he had to steal a bone to silence the dog. (All a bit safer than the fire-eater that I met in another village two years later, who sent a jet of flame towards the Bath and Wells Diocesan Missioner who, despite the most rapid evasive action, still emerged with singed eyebrows. That, apparently, was illustrating the destruction of Sodom and Gomorrah!)

The next morning, a crowd of about 500 gathered. We held a service in the open air, in front of the little church. It was all very quiet and good natured. I spoke from Isaiah 12, especially verse 3: 'With joy you will draw water from the wells of salvation.'

Their infectious joy, and their deep, clean well, were an obvious illustration. Blue Charaxes butterflies danced across from one great tree to another, providing me with a pleasant distraction. Before lunch, we started to pray for the sick. Even by the standards of ministry in the Luapula province, a ferocious battle erupted, mainly centred around the Venerable Tobias Kaoma.

The battle in Mutwe was very strong. We only had to start praying for people and many of them shook, fluttered their eyelids, collapsed on the ground (sometimes doing a passable imitation of a local snake), and screamed.

The contrast with the ministry two years earlier in Chipili was quite striking. On that occasion, despite the chaos and the screaming, we felt in control. Here the demonic forces seemed more powerful, and much less easy to shift. We returned to lunch feeling quite bruised. After a quick visit to a maize field where I was shown the devastating effect of drought on their crops, I returned to speak to the gathering crowd. Rather unexpectedly, I found myself speaking about choices. In the morning there had been an easy rapport between the crowd and the speaker, now the atmosphere seemed darkened and disturbed. Even the Charaxes butterflies seemed absent.

I challenged the congregation to choose Christ and to put away the charms, fetishes and other signs from the witch doctors. There was laughter – not the friendly laughter of the morning, but hollow, mocking laughter. I asked Tobias, who was a brilliant interpreter, what was happening. He said, 'They are saying – we have so little, and now you are asking us to give things up!' Suddenly I felt something terrible. For almost the only time in my life, I felt what seemed to be the anger of God. Even now, I find it quite awesome to write about. I spoke – I know not what – firm, hard words. It was not my normal manner. I felt that we had to publicly challenge the principalities and powers – especially Masonda, the black snake spirit, and Malenga, the water spirit. The black snake was apparently an emblem of local witchcraft. It seems probable that many of the local mothers sought for their children to have the protection of the medicine man and the baptism of the church. Hence the conflict. When I had finished, I felt quite shattered.

Like the great prophet, I would gladly have slunk away under a juniper bush (1 Kings 19:5). I felt that I had failed, going way over the top. I don't remember much about the rest of the day. We had a session with Father James, the local priest, and his healing team who were helping in the ministry. (I always insisted on having one, and preferably two or three, Zambians to help me when I was praying. It's scriptural [James 5:14], it's good for training, and it's vital to have people who know what's really going on across the barriers of language, and culture). I think that I was so shattered that Martin addressed them. Jane, my wife, had a good session with the local Mothers' Union – a spiritual tower of strength in rural Zambia.

After another hard night on a mattress on the floor, with bats above and mosquitoes and spiders alongside, I felt distinctly unenthusiastic about the arrival of Wednesday morning. At least our prayer group in Shepton Mallet would have been praying the night before. They would have received, by an expensive fax from Mansa, some nearly up-to-date information.

The next morning we began with a Eucharist in the church. This part of Zambia has a High Church Anglican tradition which means there's great dignity and order amid the freedom that the charismatic gifts can bring. I tried not to notice a substantial hornet busying itself with building a nest behind the altar. Eventually, about 300 people crowded into the small church. I struggled to preach – on Ephesians 5:15–20. I even asked the archdeacon, 'Do we need to cleanse the church after all the exorcism yesterday?' 'No,' he replied. 'The spirits left through the windows.' Then in desperation (or inspiration?) I asked Tobias Kaoma to give his testimony.

Tobias was about sixty; his wife, Prisca, had died only a month earlier at the age of forty-nine. Despite his very evident grief, Tobias had left his parish in Chipili to accompany us and act as leader and chief exorcist. His eyes lit up as he testified to his conversion, calling to the priesthood, and to the day two years earlier when he had been filled with the Spirit at a clergy conference; so much so that he had laughed and praised God for many minutes.

Seeing an angel

This testimony lifted our spirits, and as Tobias was speaking, a tall dark lady glided out of the congregation. 'Could I say something?' Her testimony was simple, its effect dramatic. Early that morning, she and friends had walked in the half-light from the village to the church. She, and one of her companions, had noticed a figure dressed in *white* following slowly along the path. She peeled off into some bushes beside the church, the figure went round the other side. She went behind the church expecting to see the person. There was no one to be seen. As she spoke, her face lit up. Everyone was deeply moved. Zambians do not wear *white*. The MU welcomed her and symbolically placed one of their turbans on her head. All of us felt that she had had a genuine experience of seeing an angel. It was the most supernatural experience of my life.

After that I preached a simple evangelistic sermon. I asked those who would like to respond to stand up and come forward. Two young men stood up, and then suddenly there was a flood. We prayed for about forty individually. Then another sixty arrived, including the local headman; more prayer and counselling.

During all this, just one demon showed up. But the person concerned was taken outside and the evil powers were released quickly and silently. Then we prayed for the leaders, and many others, to be healed, released from evil powers, and filled with the Spirit.

Lunch-time came, the Blue Charaxes courted around a

tree beside the church, and it was time to leave. We paid a return visit to the local chief. This time there was great joy. Two hours earlier his granddaughter had been safely born, the mother was well, and other members of the household were better. We prayed and gave thanks for the little girl and retreated with an honoured gift – a live chicken which entertained us, during the car journey, by pecking at Martin's trousers.

Two years later, part of a SOMA team that I was leading visited Mutwe. It was still hard going, but the lady who'd seen the angel was a very visible part of the church.

I talked to a remarkable priest in Luansha, a copperbelt mining town, who at the age of eighty was still building new churches and evangelising new areas. He said he'd had some fierce spiritual battles with demons in his younger days at Mutwe. I find this particularly significant as he probably wouldn't have been taught much about spiritual warfare in those earlier days of the Zambian church.

Clearly Mutwe is a place which lives up to its name, a place where the spiritual battle has to be taken very seriously. If I ever return there (and I hope to), I intend to engage in some serious preliminary prayer. I believe that the territorial spirits of Masonda (the snake spirit) and Malenga (the water spirit) need to be further challenged in the name of Jesus.

In this opening chapter, I have offered a small personal testimony to the reality, and importance, of prayer in the areas of healing, deliverance and spiritual warfare. Now we must look at the evidence of Scripture, and some of the evidence from differing strands of Christian history. Even if we feel that we see through a glass darkly, we must persist. This subject is of vital importance to the health of the whole Church.

Notes

1. St Matthew's, with the support of St Aldate's, later grew to be a strong, vibrant church.
2. See Chapter 8, Question 5.
3. David Watson, well-known author and evangelist, Vicar of St Michel le Belfrey, York until about two years before his death.
4. David Watson, *Fear No Evil* (Hodder and Stoughton, 1984).
5. See Chapter 6, and related literature.
6. I have included this incident at some length because it was so formative in my own, and Michael Green's, thinking. I am conscious of having lost touch with our night-time visitors. I hope they will accept, over twenty years later, that the inclusion of a few details of the encounter are important to help authenticate an important spiritual diagnosis.
7. This is not written in support of reincarnation! There is much experiential evidence that spirits can reside in families, or places, over many generations (see Exodus 20:6).
8. SOMA, Sharing of Ministries Abroad. An Anglican ministry dedicated to helping Third World churches learn about the gifts of the Holy Spirit and every-member ministry. As so often happens, those of us privileged to serve with these teams received far more than we ever were able to give.
9. I have experienced this on another occasion. (See p. 345).
10. See p. 345ff.
11. See especially, C. Wagner, *Warfare Prayer* (Monarch, 1992), *Territorial Spirits* (Sovereign World, 1991) and *Breaking Strongholds in your City* (Monarch, 1993).

12. C. Wagner, *Warfare Prayer*, especially Chapters 6 and 10.
13. Springboard is the initiative on evangelism by the Archbishops of Canterbury and York.
14. For more on Archdeacon Tobias see 7, p. 227f, and John Woolmer, *Thinking Clearly about Prayer* (Monarch, 1997), pp. 52ff and p. 110.

2

Healing and Deliverance
in the Old Testament

In this chapter, we use the Psalms as a springboard for exploring healing in the Old Testament. We discover many different aspects of healing in the Psalms. We then branch out into the more difficult questions of the source and strength of the spiritual opposition, as seen in the Old Testament, to the purposes of God. Finally, we observe the hope of the future life as it emerges in the Old Testament, realising that this will dramatically affect our spiritual vision and expectation.

Healing and Deliverance
in the Old Testament

Abimelech, Ahimelech, Adonibezek are names engraved in my memory. My first headmaster's Scripture lessons invariably began with the instruction, 'Write short notes on. . . .' We occasionally graduated to characters beginning with B, C, D, E before reverting to the confusing list of A's. However, he did give me one great piece of advice: 'Read the Psalms.' He apparently used to recite them in the bath, and certainly expected us to learn verses, usually from the Psalms, each weekend.

I am grateful for his advice; and when people come to see me in spiritual trouble, feeling abandoned by God, unable to pray, oppressed by an overwhelming burden of sin, bowed down by depression, unable to receive love and often hating themselves, assailed by evil, or whatever, I often encourage them to read the Psalms. Not just the familiar comforting Psalms, but the whole book, which I believe is some of God's finest medicine for the soul.

The Psalms – a healing prayer book

In this chapter I shall use the Psalms as the staging post from which to explore the Old Testament teaching on healing, deliverance and spiritual warfare. Superficially, we might feel that the Old Testament has little to say on these themes; but more careful study reveals an amazing depth of understanding.

To begin with, the Old Testament presents a very final view of life and death. Consequently, illness is invariably associated with sin, something that Jesus accepted in some cases and denied in others.[1] But gradually a burgeoning future hope appears which transforms the sombre picture of illness and death.

While evil spirits, Satan, and any ministry of deliverance are seldom mentioned, there is a constant theme of spiritual disobedience, followed by repentance and/or national disaster, and spiritual warfare incessantly waged against Baal worship and other sinister forces. All of this is overarched by the hope of Messiah's coming. In the great texts of Isaiah, he is seen both as suffering servant, and the bringer of much good news and healing.

When reading the Old Testament, we must always remember that its words provide the background to much of the New Testament, but that it is strangely incomplete without the cross, resurrection, and individual gift of the Spirit. We need to look at a broad canvas and beware of simplistic theologies based on a few proof texts.

The human condition: dominated by death

We begin by looking at the Old Testament view of our human destiny. There is quite a sense of frustration at the whole process of growing old. Frailty and death are all too present, inevitable and unpromising.

A fatalistic view of life and death

Psalm 88 is quite desperate, ending with words unechoed by any apostle of gloom – 'darkness is my closest friend':

> 'For my soul is full of trouble and my life draws near the grave.
> I am counted among those who go down to the pit;
> I am like a man without strength.
> I am set apart with the dead, like the slain who lie in the grave, whom you remember no more, who are cut off from your care.
> You have put me in the lowest pit, in the darkest depths.
> Your wrath lies heavily upon me;
> You have overwhelmed me with all your waves.
> You have taken from me my closest friends and have made me repulsive to them.
> I am confined and cannot escape; my eyes are dim with grief.
> I call to you, O Lord, every day; I spread out my hands to you.
> Do you show your wonders to the dead?
> Do those who are dead rise up and praise you?
> Is your love declared in the grave, your faithfulness in Destruction?
>
> (Psalm 88:3–11)

Psalm 90 has similar sentiments and paints a picture of man's limited years and failing faculties: 'The length of our days is seventy years – or eighty, if we have the strength; yet their span is but trouble and sorrow, for they quickly pass, and we fly away' (Psalm 90:10).

Psalm 103 is poignant, and realistic: 'As for man, his days are like grass, he flourishes like a flower of the field;

the wind blows over it and it is gone, and its place remembers it no more' (Psalm 103:15–16).

Psalm 115 is equally clear: 'It is not the dead who praise the Lord, those who go down to silence' (Psalm 115:17).

All this is an inevitable consequence of the fall. The terrible doom spelt out to Adam (Genesis 3: 17–19) speaks of painful toil, hard work and death. St Paul (Romans 5:12–14 and elsewhere) uses this dark canvas as the background to his wonderful, radiant message of salvation and resurrection.

Elsewhere in the Old Testament a similar picture emerges. The writer of Ecclesiastes, full of cynicism, only just holds onto the silver cord of faith, and is full of such comments: 'For the wise man, like the fool, will not be long remembered; in days to come both will be forgotten. Like the fool, the wise man too must die!' (Ecclesiastes 2:16)

Death, for the Psalmist and Ecclesiastes, is the ultimate disaster. David's famous lament for Saul and Jonathan (2 Samuel 1:17–21) offers no glimmer of comfort. When his first child by Bathsheba dies (2 Samuel 12:15–23) he adopts a fatalistic attitude: 'I will go to him, but he will not return to me', and gets on with life. This is one very important theological area where the New Testament offers a much more optimistic vision.

Throughout the Old Testament a similar view prevails except for a few fleeting visions of the resurrection and new life to be found mainly in Psalm 16, Job and Isaiah. Consumed with this view of death, the prevailing theology of much of the Old Testament is 'reward and punishment'. If you live a godly life, you will be rewarded with health and a long life, if you disobey God you, or others, will be punished.

Of course, there are shafts of light, and as we shall see,

the possibility of resurrection and life after death breaks through the gloom. Meanwhile, we note that the well-loved Psalm 23 tells of the good shepherd accompanying us even through the 'valley of the shadow of death' (v.4), and Psalm 92:14 offers the hope that the righteous 'will still bear fruit in old age'. Good news indeed amid the change and decay.

Healing prayer, in the Old Testament, especially in the Psalms

Despite the view of death expressed above, there is a powerful expectation of healing, especially in the Psalms.

> I waited patiently for the Lord; he turned to me and heard my cry.
> He lifted me out of the slimy pit, out of the mud and mire;
> he set my feet on a rock and gave me a firm place to stand.
> He put a new song in my mouth, a hymn of praise to our God.
> Many will see and fear and put their trust in the Lord.
> (Psalm 40:1–3)
> Praise the Lord, O my soul, and forget not all his benefits –
> Who forgives all your sins and heals all your diseases.
> (Psalm 103:2–3)

These verses, and others such as Psalm 107:17 and Psalm 38, emphasise the strong link that much of the Old Testament sees between sin and illness, righteousness and health. In Psalm 41, the writer confidently expects healing and restoration for those who look after the weak. He feels that God's honour is at stake if his friends and enemies can betray him and mock his illness (vv 4–12). He, too, acknowledges sin (v.4), but expects healing as a sign of God's pleasure with him.

A celebrated example of healing

King Hezekiah has a similar hope. As one of the few righteous kings, he feels aggrieved when the prophet Isaiah tells him that he is on the point of death. He is one of the few people recorded in the Old Testament who actually seems to pray for healing.

> In those days Hezekiah became ill and was at the point of death. The prophet Isaiah, son of Amoz, went to him and said, 'This is what the Lord says: Put your house in order, because you are going to die; you will not recover.' Hezekiah turned his face to the wall and prayed to the Lord, 'Remember, O Lord, how I have walked before you faithfully and with wholehearted devotion and have done what is good in your eyes.' And Hezekiah wept bitterly. Before Isaiah had left the middle court, the word of the Lord came to him: 'Go back and tell Hezekiah the leader of my people, "This is what the Lord of your father David, says: I have heard your prayer and seen your tears; I will heal you. On the third day from now you will go up to the temple of the Lord. I will add fifteen years to your life. And I will deliver you and this city from the hand of the king of Assyria. I will defend this city for my sake and for the sake of my servant David."' Then Isaiah said, 'Prepare a poultice of figs.' They did so and applied it to the boil, and he recovered.

This incident is recorded three times (see 2 Kings 20.1–7 quoted above, Isaiah 38:1–8 and 2 Chronicles 32:24–28).

Unfortunately, Hezehiah didn't use his extra years well.

The writer of Chronicles records tersely that Hezekiah's heart was proud, and 'he did not respond to the kindness shown to him'. Eventually he was warned of trouble in store for his descendants. He then produced one of the most selfish comments to be found in Scripture:

'The word of the Lord you have spoken is good,' Hezekiah replied. For he thought, 'Will there not be peace and security in my lifetime?' (2 Kings 20:19)

Such an attitude is not uncommon today as this generation destroys the environment with all too little worry for what our children and grandchildren may inherit from our selfishness.

This story is a sober warning, often repeated in the Gospels, and in pastoral experience today, that receiving God's healing does not necessarily lead people to any greater obedience or faithfulness.

Elijah (1 Kings 17:20) similarly intercedes for the widow at Zarepath's son. He clearly felt that this illness was unjust after the great kindness of the widow. The widow, characteristically, connected her son's worsening condition with her sin, real or imagined.

Sometimes there was a very strong connection between illness and sin. Miriam (see Numbers 12) was punished by the Lord for challenging Moses' position as leader. Curiously, Aaron her brother, who appears to have been equally culpable, wasn't punished, although when he saw Miriam covered with leprosy he clearly expected some human punishment from his brother Moses.

Moses, however, cried out to the Lord, 'O God, please heal her!' (Numbers 12:13), and his prayers were answered a week later when Miriam was allowed back into the camp – presumably healed of leprosy.

A healing with a New Testament significance

Soon afterwards, Moses had to intercede for the whole nation who were being bitten, and killed, by venomous snakes.

'The Lord said to Moses, "Make a snake and put it up on a pole; anyone who is bitten can look at it and live." So Moses made a bronze snake and put it up on a pole. Then, when anyone was bitten by a snake and looked at the bronze snake, he lived' (Numbers 21:8–9).

It is interesting how simple the instruction was – 'Look at it and live.' Anyone who looked at the pole, which must have seemed like a cross, would recover. A nice medieval woodcut of the incident shows the pole in the centre, the people and the snakes all around. Most are continuing to disobey. Some are trying to run away, some are praying, some are bandaging others. And all of them are in the process of being bitten. There is a certain humour (in line with some of Jesus' parables) as snakes creep up on those who are engaged in good works or religious acts. Only a few people are obeying the simple instructions and looking at the serpent. The way of salvation is too simple for most of them.

St John (John 3:14–15) sees the serpent lifted up in the wilderness as a type of the forthcoming crucifixion. There is a deep parallel in the simplicity of salvation through the cross (which men want to complicate) and the simplicity of the healing recorded in Numbers. It is interesting that Hezekiah, in the early faithful part of his reign, found it necessary to destroy the bronze serpent (2 Kings 18:4) as it was, in his time, being misused for idolatrous purposes.

Repentance, forgiveness and the consequences of sin

David, after his liaison with Bathsheba, faced the severe wrath of the Lord administered by the word of Nathan the prophet. He received both the promise of forgiveness and the punishment of the death of the child who was the fruit of his adulterous affair.

> Then David said to Nathan, 'I have sinned against the Lord.' Nathan replied, 'The Lord has taken away your sin. You are not going to die. But because by doing this you have made the enemies of the Lord show utter contempt, the son born to you will die.' After Nathan had gone

home, the Lord struck the child that Uriah's wife had borne
to David and he became ill.'

(2 Samuel 12:13–15)

Despite Nathan's words, David went into deep prayer on
behalf of the child, fasting and praying for some days. Not
surprisingly, his servants were terrified when the child
died. 'While the child was still living, we spoke to David
but he would not listen to us. How can we tell him that the
child is dead? He may do something desperate' (2 Samuel
12:18b).

David, however, was much more pragmatic. When he
discovered that the child was dead, he got up, washed,
worshipped the Lord and took food. When his servants
expressed surprise, he replied robustly, 'While the child
was still alive, I fasted and wept. I thought, "Who knows?
The Lord may be gracious to me and let the child live."
But now that he is dead, why should I fast? Can I bring
him back again? I will go to him, but he will not return to
me' (2 Samuel 12:22–23). He quickly received another son,
the famous Solomon, whom the Lord loved! It is worth
noting that although David was completely forgiven for
his sin, including the effective murder of Bathsheba's
husband Uriah, his life degenerated into chaos. Psalm
51 expresses very clearly the depth of his remorse and
repentance, and the breadth of God's forgiveness. His
sin was forgiven, but the consequences of it, within his
family and within the kingdom were very grave.

Two contrasting kings

Asa and Manasseh present almost totally opposite
spiritual stories. One is a fairly typical decline from god-
liness to apostasy; in this Asa is similar to Saul, Solomon

and others. The other, Manasseh, is a remarkable story of repentance and restoration.

Asa begins as an unusually godly monarch and the Lord was with him. Unfortunately, as his reign progressed, he lost his way spiritually and politically, and became a cruel oppressive tyrant, imprisoning the faithful seer Hanani who tried to warn him.

Healing Prayer Avoided

In the thirty-ninth year of his long reign, he suffered from a severe disease in his feet. But even in this crisis, he did not seek help from the Lord. He died within two years (see 2 Chronicles 16:12).

This story follows a familiar and rather depressing pattern. Someone begins promisingly, spiritually, but falls away, becomes ill, and declines, even in a desperate situation, to turn back and seek God's help. Clearly, the Chronicler expected him to seek God's help, and later he records with approval the unexpected repentance of Manasseh, Hezekiah's son. The unusual story of Manasseh's disobedience, punishment, repentance and restoration (2 Chronicles 33) is a powerful testimony to God's grace, and a beacon of hope for all, however desperate their circumstances. Manasseh's repentance is a forerunner of the wonderful New Testament story of the penitent thief (Luke 23:39–43). Each man knew he was punished justly, each in desperate circumstances turned to God for help.

More healing texts from the Psalms

Many of the Psalms offer models for healing prayer and spiritual protection. Psalm 40 wonderfully describes depression, particularly for the believer, with realism and hope. The writer waits patiently for the Lord, is lifted from the miry clay, rejoices and sings praises to God. He even testifies of his deliverance to the great assembly. However, all too quickly, the mood changes. In the second half, the writer reverts to depressive mode. However, the situation doesn't seem quite as bleak, and the Psalm ends with renewed prayer for help and deliverance.

Psalms which minister to depression

The pattern of the Psalm presents a familiar model to those who pray for the depressed. Release comes, and it is marvellous, only to be followed by a period of returning darkness. The hopeful thing is that the last state seems better than the first, and that the depths are not as deep as at first.[2] We may well use Psalm 40 as a model for prayer, offering hope and realism, especially to those for whom depression is a recurring problem.

Psalms 42 and 43 have a constant refrain: 'Why are you downcast, O my soul? Why are you so disturbed within me?' These Psalms are a classic statement of spiritual depression. They begin with the powerful longing to experience God, wistful remembrance of former encounters, and continue with the future hope of returning 'to the altar of God, to God my joy and my delight'.

In practice, this acknowledgement of God's former blessings,[3] and commitment to future worship, can bring a period of healing and restoration. Real spiritual thirst, as urgently expressed in Psalm 42:1, will surely be met, just as the great invitation of Isaiah 55 – 'Come to the waters' – has a wonderful promise, and 'drawing water from the wells of salvation' is a beautiful picture in Isaiah 12.

The wilderness experience

Psalm 84 is a model for how to respond in a spiritual wilderness, or the classic 'dark night of the soul'.[4] It is a pilgrim Psalm beginning with a longing for 'the courts of the Lord'. It ends with worship in the Temple and produces the beautiful sentiment 'I would rather be a doorkeeper in the house of my God than dwell in the tents of the wicked.'

In the middle, the Psalmist has to pass through the dreadful dry valley of Baca. Here true pilgrims 'make it a place of springs' (v.6); keeping calm, digging for water, or waiting for the autumn rains. The experienced pilgrim expects dry periods, and doesn't panic.

Many people experience this when they embark on praying for the sick. There is often a glorious spring when the Lord encourages their ministry with a cluster of signs and wonders, followed by a sobering period when prayers seem less fruitful and personal suffering is experienced. After a period of testing, the pilgrim emerges with a more mature, realistic faith, more compassionate, and more able to absorb the hurts of others.

So many people today seem to suffer from a deep lack of self-worth. They cannot love themselves, and often try to compensate for this by frantically working to help others. Yet if we cannot love ourselves, we cannot truly fulfil the great command of Luke 10:27 (based on Deuteronomy 6:5 and Leviticus 19:18): 'Love the Lord your God with all your heart and with all your soul and with all your strength and with all your mind; and, love your neighbour as yourself.'

Self-rejection and the need for inner healing

Often this seems to stem from unwanted conception, rejection by the mother in the womb, a difficult birth, a stormy or abused childhood, or a disastrous marriage. Psalm 139:1–18 speaks deeply to this condition. The Psalmist has a wonderful insight into the all-seeing nature of God, and better still, the certainty of God's gracious involvement in *our* creation: 'For you created my inmost being; you knit me together in my mother's womb. I praise you because I am fearfully and wonderfully made; your works are wonderful, I know that full well' (Psalm 139:13–14).

Self-rejection is a devastating spiritual condition rendering many Christians incapable of enjoying worship and receiving love, and making them overwork to win approval. In extreme cases it leads to them humiliating themselves, thereby deepening the vicious circle of increasing isolation and rejection.[5]

This Psalm is a model for healing prayer and can be used effectively to help someone see their true worth to God. We shall return to the whole question of inner healing on pp. 258ff and 336ff.

Psalms which express the need for quietness and meditation

Psalm 8, with its glorious assertion of humanity's special place in creation, is another fine theological answer to self-rejection. We need to affirm our special place in God's scheme of things, rejoicing in the manhood of Christ, and that we are co-heirs with him (Romans 8:17).

Psalm 62 tells of the need for a quiet, ordered lifestyle. Psalm 119, especially vv.91–104, takes the same line. Activism, especially in Christian ministry (and the healing ministry can be very tiring), leads to burn-out, which quickly becomes physical illness and depression. *Satan hampers more ministries in this way than by temptation to sin, or direct attack.*

Speaking personally, the advice of a thoughtful layman to set aside time each week to escape from the parish for prayer, preparation and writing has been a godsend, and a transforming instruction.

Only in silence and rest will we begin to hear God's silent

voice. Only as we hear God's silent voice will we be made whole, and be able effectively to pray for others. The more[6] we serve others, the more we *must* allow God to serve and refresh us! It is only spiritual pride and ambition, the sin by which angels fell,[7] that make us think otherwise.

Praying for the stiff-necked

Pride, the deadliest spiritual state, is addressed firmly in Psalm 75 (especially vv.4–5). The people of God, when proud or disobedient, are often addressed as 'stiff-necked'. Psalm 3 offers a useful antidote: 'But you are a shield around me, O Lord, my Glorious One who lifts up my head.'

I remember praying for a young man with a very stiff neck. We saw no improvement until one of my prayer partners gently addressed the question of his family pride. Dr Kenneth McAll, the well-known author of *Healing the Family Tree* (see Chapter 8), taught me to pray for stiff necks by gently placing my hands under someone's chin and lifting, easing the pressure on the neck, while praying for healing. It often proved effective – just as pride can literally cause a stiff neck, so the prayerful lifting of the head can bring release.

Praying against fear

Fear is another deep-seated emotion addressed in the Psalms. Fear of people, and fear of failure, paralyse many of us. Even great prophets like Moses and Jeremiah were affected. Psalm 27, with its emphasis on worship and the beauty of the Lord, realises that if 'the Lord is my light and salvation – whom shall I fear?' (v.1).

A deep fear, particularly in Third World households, is the prospect of childlessness. The Psalmist addresses this fear. 'He settles the barren woman in her home as a happy mother of children. Praise the Lord' (Psalm 113:9).

Prayers for children

There are, of course, many biblical stories which relate the healing of this problem, none more poignant than the suffering prayer of Hannah (1 Samuel 1:13), so misunderstood by Eli. This is an area of prayer where I've had encouragements and disappointments (pp. 323, 331, 335). One new member of our church quickly became pregnant after years of trying, and an adoption. When asked by a New Age colleague if she had done anything different, she replied, 'Yes, I've become a Christian!'

A long time ago, Jane and I prayed for a childless couple. The wife, Pat, had been diagnosed with severely damaged fallopian tubes. She had been offered an operation, but with little realistic prospect of success. Jane had a great sense of expectation and prayed with great confidence for the release of the problem.

Pat decided to go for the operation. The surgeon was very surprised when he operated. Expecting to find furred up fallopian tubes, he found them blocked by what he described as a simple clip which he removed without difficulty. Soon afterwards, Pat conceived the first of her two children.

Other good Christian people have had to accept their childless situation. One couple, whom I greatly admire, exercise a dual ministry enhanced both in quality and availability by their childlessness; nevertheless, it must seem a big price to pay.

Righteous generations

A particularly Christian hope is that our children will grow up to follow the Lord. Psalm 103:17 offers this hope. 'But from everlasting to everlasting the Lord's love is with those who fear him, and his righteousness with their children's children.' I believe we should use this to pray not only for our children, but their (unborn) descendants. We need to pray for future generations, and that Christian families will be established over many generations. This does happen, and is a splendid witness in an age of such fragmentation of family life. I, personally, believe that this is a way in which the Lord will bring healing to our nation. Splendid work is being done in many places in bringing children to a mature faith.[8]

One of my friends tells a lovely story of her grandmother's conversion at the age of eighty. She asked the evangelist what she should do with the rest of her life. 'Pray – for your children and grandchildren' was his reply. She certainly brought forth fruit in old age (Psalm 92:14). Her prayers were particularly for her grandson, Alfredo, a potential late-teenage disaster. Travelling around Spain, amid the hippy culture, he had an overwhelming sense of God near Avila. He became a remarkable evangelist, and led most of his grandmother's family to faith in Christ. The old lady, then aged ninety, was able to attend his ordination shortly before she died.

The oil of gladness

The Psalms have another lovely phrase – 'anointing you with the oil of joy' (Psalm 45:7). This is also one of the great promises of Isaiah 61:1–4.[9] Joy (or gladness) has a great healing quality. Joy is infectious, and helps the faith of others. Another great prophetic poem (Isaiah 35) gives a picture of a wilderness rejoicing as it bursts into flower, with the lame and the dumb rejoicing as they are healed. The redeemed walk along the king's highway singing for joy as they approach Zion.

Oil, in the New Testament, is a symbol of the Holy Spirit (Matthew 25:1–10). I believe a wider use of anointing would prove valuable.[10] How our worship would change if we were all anointed with joy! Such worship would almost certainly bring spontaneous physical and emotional healing to many of those who participate.

Psalms and forgiveness

Receiving forgiveness is a deeply healing experience. David's great Psalms on this theme are 32 and 51. Psalm 51 (see p. 56), traditionally associated with the Bathsheba incident, is very powerful. The very writing of it must have been therapeutic, and helped David to see hope for the future. Psalm 32 shows the importance of confession, here it brings both physical and spiritual restoration.

Finally, in this section, we might note that rather often the Psalms have a violent, vengeful streak. The end of the marvellous Psalm 139 is an obvious example. For those troubled by this (and that probably includes all of us) C.S. Lewis has some powerful and helpful words.[11] The idea of forgiving others, a necessary preliminary to release from bitterness, and hence to some physical healing, is strangely absent from the Psalms and, indeed, from the Old Testament. Jesus more than compensated for this with many references to this, not only in the Lord's Prayer, but also in the context of the prayer of faith (see Mark 11:22–25).

Old Testament – deliverance and Satan

The Psalms have a special verse about spiritual protection. 'The angel of the Lord encamps around those who fear him, and he delivers them' (Psalm 34:7).

One esteemed colleague, when first involved in praying for deliverance, felt that there hadn't been a proper encounter if he, his household and even his dog, didn't suffer some form of spiritual counter-attack. This seemed unnecessary to me, and the discovery and application of

Psalm 34:7 proved efficacious. Psalm 91, especially vv.11 and 12, famously misapplied by Satan (Matthew 4:6), provides similar protection.

Psalm 118, v.12 – 'They swarmed around me like bees, but they died out as quickly as burning thorns; in the name of the Lord I cut them off' gives a powerful picture of a person's enemies swarming around them. The Psalmist cuts them off and is free. This gives a promising prayer model which is particularly useful (see p. 261ff) when praying for someone facing either spiritual oppression or troubles handed down from previous generations (Exodus 20:5).

The Old Testament has little to say about evil spirits, although King Saul is plagued by them. As we have already seen,[12] a particularly unpleasant one features in the Apocrypha, in the book of Tobit.

The role and limitations of Satan

Satan appears first in the guise of a snake, as architect of the fall, and his origins are partly explained, in veiled language, in Ezekiel 28 (especially v.12 ff). He is prominent in the book of Job, provokes David to his fateful sin of numbering the people (1 Chronicles 21:1),[13] and appears in the book of Zechariah.

As the opening chapters of the great drama of Job make clear, Satan only operates within God's permission. 'The Lord said to Satan, "Very well, then, everything he has is in your hands, but on the man himself do not lay a finger"' (Job 1:12).

> On another day the angels came to present themselves before the Lord, and Satan also came with them to present himself before him. And the Lord said to Satan, 'Where have you come from?' Satan answered the Lord, 'From roaming through the earth and going to and in it.'

Then the Lord said to Satan, 'Have you considered my servant Job? There is no-one on earth like him, he is blameless
and upright, a man who fears God and shuns evil. And he
still maintains his integrity, though you incited me to ruin him
without any reason.'

'Skin for skin!' Satan replied 'A man will give all he has for
his own life. But stretch out your hand and strike his flesh and
bones, and he will surely curse you to your face.'

The Lord said to Satan, 'Very well, then, he is in your
hands; but you must spare his life.'

(Job 2:1–6)

We are here dealing with a great mystery which we shall
discuss more fully in the next chapter.[14]

In Zechariah 3, Satan appears, as in Revelation 12:10,
as the accuser. He is quickly despatched and doesn't play
any significant part in the drama. His true significance is
not apparent until the confrontations with Jesus recorded
in the Gospels.

Spiritual warfare in the Old Testament

At a personal level, the Israelites were given many warnings
against all forms of occult practice. At a national level, they
were warned to avoid all contact with the seductive attractions of other religions and to destroy all signs of their
presence. These commands were seldom obeyed. Behind
all this lurks a deep spiritual battle which is touched upon
in a few rather tantalising passages of Scripture.

Spiritual instructions and warnings

'The sorrows of those will increase who run after other
gods. I will not pour out their libations of blood or take
up their names on my lips' (Psalm 16:4).

This verse expresses the consequences, and 'the book of the Law' makes it even clearer:

> These are the decrees and laws you must be careful to follow in the land that the Lord, the God of your fathers, has given you to possess – as long as you live in the land. Destroy completely all the places on the high mountains and on the hills and under every spreading tree where the nations you are dispossessing worship their gods. Break down their altars, smash their sacred stones and burn their Asherah poles in the fire; cut down the idols of their gods and wipe out their names from those places. You must not worship the Lord your God in their way.
>
> (Deuteronomy 12:1–4)

There were two main reasons for Israel's constant disobedience in this area. The first stemmed from the opportunism of Jeroboam, the son of Nebat (1 Kings 12 ff). Jeroboam was given a prophecy (1 Kings 11:29 ff) that he would be given a large part of the kingdom as a result of Solomon's disobedience. Having become king of the ten tribes, Jeroboam faced an awkward decision. He realised that if the people went up to Jerusalem to sacrifice to Yahweh they would quickly revert to his rival Rehoboam (Solomon's unpleasant son who was king of Judah). He devised a neat solution. He built some golden calves (cf Aaron, Exodus 32), and set them up for worship in two centres.

Golden calves have spiritual power

This apostasy ran right through the history of Israel until the destruction of Samaria many centuries later. A constant theme of the writers of Kings is that Israel's rulers were following the way of 'Jeroboam, the son of Nebat, who caused Israel to sin.' Jeroboam's golden calves opened the way for Jezebel, and others, to bring their own religion into Israel. Despite their apparent powerlessness, which was mocked by Elijah on Mount Carmel, they had both a moral and spiritual force which sapped the strength of the nation.

The attraction of other cults

The second reason was that these foreign, or false, cults were superficially much more attractive than the austere worship of Yahweh. Just as the New Age cults of today present an enticing and attractive alternative to the often staid Church, so the cults of Old Testament times offered ritual sex, exciting festivals and occult experiences.[15] Even godly kings like Jehoshaphat and Hezekiah didn't completely eliminate the spiritual opposition. It was left to the boy king Josiah (2 Kings chapters 22–23) to destroy all remnants of Jeroboam's altar at Bethel.

The instruction against occult practices is equally clear.

> When you enter the land the Lord your God is giving you, do not learn to imitate the detestable ways of the nations there. Let no-one be found among you who sacrifices his son or daughter in the fire, who practises divination or sorcery, interprets omens, engages in witchcraft, or casts spells, or who is a medium or spiritist, or who consults the dead. Anyone who does these things is detestable to the Lord, and because of these detestable practices the Lord your God will drive out those nations before you. You must be blameless before the Lord your God.
>
> (Deuteronomy 18:9–13)

Clear texts forbidding occult activity

Such clear warnings are strengthened by other passages such as Leviticus 19:31, Leviticus 20:6, 2 Kings 16:3 (child sacrifice), 2 Kings 21:6 (some of the sins of Manasseh before his repentance), Isaiah 8:19, Isaiah 44:25, Isaiah

47:5–13 and, of course, the celebrated encounter between King Saul, the Witch of Endor, and the purported spirit of Samuel (1 Samuel 28:8–25).

The problem with such practices is not their absurdity, but their potential power. This is well illustrated by the story of Moab's rebellion against Israel recorded in 2 Kings 3. The Old Testament leaves us with the impression of a powerful victory, rather reluctantly engineered by the good offices of Elisha. As a last resort, the King of Moab, like the Israelite King Ahaz, practised child sacrifice – slaying his eldest son and using the unfortunate boy as a burnt offering.

The writer of the book of Kings rather quaintly records the Israelite response: 'The fury of Israel was great and they withdrew and returned to their own land.' The archeological discovery of the Moabite stone paints a slightly fuller picture.[16] It suggests that the Moabite god, Chemosh, granted them victory, something just hinted at by the rather inexplicable Israelite withdrawal.

Spiritual warfare can be waged both by Yahweh and by his opponents. Ultimately, the great biblical claim is that all operate within Yahweh's permissive will: 'I form the light and create darkness, I bring prosperity and create disaster, I, the Lord, do all these things' (Isaiah 45:7).

Cyrus, the Persian king (Isaiah 45:1–6) is seen as a mere tool for Yahweh's divine purposes, though he was presumably unaware that his humanitarian actions towards the Jewish people had a deeper purpose and were part of a divine plan.

Territorial powers

It comes as quite a surprise to discover the power, and varied nature, of the spiritual opposition.

The healing of Naaman (2 Kings 5) tells us something important about the very ground on which we live and pray. It also illustrates a lot about territorial powers.

First, Naaman's servant tells him of the exceptional powers of the prophet in Israel. Then the king of Israel panics when asked to heal him, but Elisha intervenes. Naaman is furious at being sent to wash in the lowly river Jordan, obviously feeling that his own larger rivers should have greater healing power. After learning a lesson in humility, Naaman is healed and promises to worship the Lord. He makes the fascinating request:

Please let me, your servant, be given as much earth as a pair of mules can carry, for your servant will never again make burnt offerings and sacrifices to any god but the Lord. But may the Lord forgive your servant for this one thing: When my master enters the temple of Rimmon to bow down and he is leaning on my arm and I bow there also – when I bow down in the temple of Rimmon, may the Lord forgive your servant for this.

(2 Kings 5:17,18).

He will take some Israelite earth so that he has the right 'territory' on which to worship the Lord, but wishes to be forgiven when his military duties make it essential for him to enter and bow down in the temple of Rimmon. Elisha is satisfied with this.

The importance of territorial control

If all this seems surprising, read chapter 14 of Wagner's book on territorial spirits[17] where Paul Long, a Presbyterian missionary, in Congo describes how he was completely overwhelmed when trying to preach on what the locals called 'the devil's territory'. Later, he preached with exceptional freedom on land where a chapel had once been built. As a result, the locals decided to rebuild the Lord's house. Despite this great victory, the devil's turf remained a no-go area and he learnt never to invade it without clear orders from the Lord.

Daniel's insights into spiritual warfare

The prayers of Daniel give us a glimpse into some of the deeper battlefields of Scripture. Daniel (see especially chapter 10 and chapter 12, verse 1) is often deep in prayer. For three weeks he prays and abstains from wine and meat, and uses no lotions to cleanse his body. Eventually he receives a remarkable vision of a powerful angelic being. Amazingly this messenger has been delayed, for three weeks, by the 'prince of Persia' – an angelic being in powerful rebellion against God. Only the intervention of the Archangel Michael releases help for Daniel and allows the stream of visions and prophecies to continue.

These texts strongly support the idea that there are territorial spirits who have great power and influence over specific geographical regions. We should note that Daniel didn't take part directly in the spiritual battle. His part was to fast and to pray. There are great dangers if we try to get involved at a depth to which we haven't been called.

By contrast, Nehemiah, whose opening prayer (Nehemiah 1:5-11) is very similar to Daniel's great prayer on behalf of his nation (Daniel 9:4–19), meets opposition which is distinctly earthbound. Sanballat and Tobiah (Nehemiah 2:10 and throughout) use every form of trickery to frustrate his work. While they fail to prevent the rebuilding of the wall, social injustices (Nehemiah 5) cause a real delay, and national repentance

(Nehemiah 9) is needed before the great work is truly complete.

We should learn from Nehemiah and Daniel that opposition to the building of God's kingdom takes many forms. It would be naïve, and against the balance of Scripture, to think that the battles that Daniel witnessed are typical, but it would be equally unwise to ignore them. Modern examples strongly suggest that understanding in this whole area is often necessary if there is to be effective spiritual advance.[18]

We get the same varied picture from the battles of Israel and Judah. The godly King Josiah foolishly tries to stop Pharoah (2 Kings 23:29 ff) and is killed. But elsewhere, Jerusalem is miraculously protected from Sennacherib (2 Kings 19); Jehoshaphat (2 Chronicles 20) and Elisha (2 Kings 6:8ff) win remarkable victories by spiritual means.

To complete our brief tour of the Old Testament, we must look at the Old Testament glimpses into the future life – something which will radically alter and enlarge our spiritual vision.

Old Testament view of death and resurrection

We began the chapter with some sombre references to death. We conclude with a very different viewpoint. But first, we must look at another Psalm famous for its reso-nances of the crucifixion.

> My God, my God, why have you forsaken me?
> All who see me mock me; they hurl insults, shaking their heads:
> He trusts in the Lord; let the Lord rescue him, since he delights in him.

I am poured out like water, and all my bones are out of joint.
My heart has turned to wax; it has melted away within me.
They divide my garments among them and cast lots for my
    clothing.

                          (Psalm 22:1a,7–8,14,18)

Although the Psalm ends in triumph, the abiding impression is of spiritual disaster, separation from God, including intense physical and mental suffering. Together with Isaiah 52:13–53:12, it forms the great prophetic base for the Calvary sacrifice. As we shall see in the New Testament, Matthew 8:17 connects this suffering with the healing ministry of the Messiah. There is an alternative reading of Isaiah 53:4 (RSV) – 'Surely he has borne our griefs [sicknesses] and carried our sorrows [pains]' which makes the link more clearly. Later (p. 96ff, p. 292ff), we shall consider whether this means that there is healing in the atonement, or that the healing ministry is part of the pain and hardship which Isaiah foresaw for the 'servant of the Lord'.[19]

Finally, Psalm 16 ends with a wonderful blaze of resurrection light which makes all illness and suffering much more possible to bear.

Therefore my heart is glad and my tongue rejoices;
my body also will rest secure,
because you will not abandon me to the grave,
nor will you let your Holy One see decay.
You have made known to me the path of life;
you will fill me with joy in your presence,
with eternal pleasures at your right hand.

                            (Psalm 16:9–11)

Isaiah 25:6–8 gives a fabulous picture of the future kingdom of God. Isaiah 65:17–25, echoed in Revelation 21, shows us the new Jerusalem – full of joy and peace. These great Old Testament prophecies seem much closer to fulfilment after Jesus' death and resurrection, but in the interim they must have offered great hope to the frequently oppressed, and often faithless, Jewish people.

Summary of Old Testament teaching on healing and deliverance

Reading the Old Testament, and we have only touched the surface, we see that there is a wonderful kaleidoscope of teaching and experience. The Psalms have had a special place in our understanding, speaking to many conditions and situations that are prevalent today. Physical healing is relatively rare, and illness is often associated with sin.

While deliverance and exorcism are non-existent, evil spirits lurk, mediums and spirits (eg Isaiah 8:19) whisper and mutter in the background. Spiritual warfare is a constant factor in the history of the period; loyalty to God, and purity of religious practice are, even among God's chosen people, strangely lacking.

All this creates a wonderful and varied landscape, a great mosaic; but it is a picture with a cross-shaped piece missing. Without this, the spiritual battles of the Old Testament cannot be fully understood; without this it is sometimes unclear who are the winners and who are the losers; without this the king of Moab can sacrifice his son to Chemosh with apparent impunity. The great prophet Isaiah foresees that the future depends on a suffering, not a victorious, servant. This servant will perform great healing signs (Isaiah 61, etc.), and rebuild the ancient spiritual ruins. And it is to this greatest of all stories that we must now turn.

Notes

1. See, for instance, John 9:1–3.
2. Mathematically, the model of damped sine curve is helpful. The ups and downs continue, but the severity of them decreases steadily.
3. Keeping a prayer diary is a useful habit.
4. St John of the Cross (1542–1591) writes much about this. A good introduction to this powerful writer is given by Sister Eileen Lyddon in *Door Through Darkness* (New City, 1994).
5. See p. 258ff and p. 336ff for more on this. There are many specialised books written about this important subject.
6. John Wesley's celebrated comment that he was so busy that he needed to pray for four hours each day springs to mind.
7. From Cardinal Wolsey's speech in William Shakespeare's *Henry VIII*, Act 3, Scene 1.
8. The work of the Steward's Trust, and the New Wine Conference, for instance. Many families are extremely grateful to these organisations for the help given to their teenagers at testing times.
9. Another good text for those interested in inner healing (see note 5 above).
10. See especially M. Dudley and G. Rowell, eds, *The Oil of Gladness* (SPCK, 1993) and Ch 8 Question 15.
11. C.S. Lewis, *Reflections on the Psalms* (Fontana, 1961), chapter 3.
12. Tobit 3. See also p. 30.
13. The writer of 2 Samuel 24 attributes this to the anger of the Lord against Israel.
14. See p. 99ff.

15. See John Bright, *A History of Israel* (SCM, 1960), p. 116 and elsewhere.
16. See W. Keller, *The Bible as History* (Hodder and Stoughton, 1956), pp. 232 ff.
17. Peter Wagner, *Territorial Spirits* (Sovereign World, 1991), pp. 129 ff.
18. See pp. 225ff.
19. See pp. 96ff and 292ff.

3

The Gospel Witness

The healing ministry of Jesus is well known, and it would be inappropriate to attempt to look at each and every Gospel story. Instead, I would like to try to establish certain key principles and important ideas. What did Jesus say about healing and deliverance? What did Jesus see as the significance of his own ministry of healing and deliverance? What were the key features of this ministry? What did Jesus teach the disciples? What did Jesus say about spiritual warfare?

The Gospel Witness

Jesus teaches about healing and deliverance

One of the most important healing stories in the Gospels, I believe, is the healing of the epileptic boy recorded in Matthew 17:14–23, Mark 9:14–29, and Luke 9:37–43. The setting is very dramatic. Jesus, accompanied by Peter, James and John, has left the other nine. They have climbed a high mountain, Jesus has engaged in deep prayer, and they have witnessed the extraordinary and wonderful event known to us as the Transfiguration. Then they descend the mountain, and like Moses after his mountain-top experience, they return to chaos!

Jesus is immediately confronted by a distraught father, a dangerously sick child, an argumentative and sceptical crowd which includes religious leaders, and a group of disillusioned disciples. Even for Jesus, what follows is quite a battle. After a violent exorcism (and we should note the frequent Gospel link between physical healing and spiritual deliverance), the sceptical onlookers think that the boy is dead; but Jesus quickly lifts him up, and

78

restores him to his grateful father. Jesus and the twelve retreat from the scene; and for once in their lives the disciples ask a sensible question! 'Why couldn't we drive it out?' (Mark 9:28; Matthew 17:19). Jesus effectively gave three answers – two directly, and one indirectly.

Three key statements about healing and deliverance

The need for a life based on prayer

According to Mark, Jesus said, 'This kind can only come out by prayer (and fasting)' (Mark 9:29). Jesus doesn't just mean that the actual healing is accomplished by prayer – that would be completely obvious even to his opponents. He means that the basis of such a ministry must be a life of prayer. The Gospels record many occasions when Jesus is to be found in prayer, sometimes for a whole night, always at key occasions in his life. St Luke (Luke 9:28) notes the time before the Transfiguration as one such occasion. The disciples needed to learn the real discipline of continuous prayer – often accompanied by fasting. The additional words 'and fasting' are not found in the best texts of Mark 9:29, but Jesus' life and teaching make it clear that fasting was, for him, a necessary spiritual discipline. If the words 'and fasting' were added by a spiritually minded second-century scribe, then they reflect the view of the sub-apostolic church that such disciplines were vital if the Church was to be effective.

The necessity of faith

According to Matthew, Jesus said, 'Because you have so little faith' (Matthew 17:20). Jesus taught much about faith. He commended it especially when he found it in unexpected situations. The woman in the crowd (Mark

5:24–34) who was determined to touch his garment, and was healed of a serious bleeding problem, was commended for her faith. He rebuked the disciples for their lack of faith (in the storm on the Sea of Galilee, Mark 4:35–41), for instance), and marvelled at the lack of faith in Nazareth which severely limited his own ministry (Mark 6:1–6).

With faith it is possible to discern God's will and to see who has the faith to be healed (see Acts 14:9 for a clear example). With faith it is possible to receive such an anointing that there is a general season of healing (see below and Luke 5:17). With faith it is possible to discern the spiritual climate, and avoid wasting one's time in unproductive places (see Luke 10:10). With faith it is possible to build up others in their faltering faith, as Jesus did with the boy's father.

Jesus asked the boy's father, 'How long has he been like this?' 'From childhood,' he answered. 'It has often thrown him into fire or water to kill him. But if you can do anything, take pity on us and help us.' 'If you can!' said Jesus. 'Every thing is possible for him who believes.' Immediately the boy's father exclaimed, 'I do believe, help me overcome my unbelief!' (Mark 9:21–24)

Here, the boy's father displays an honest level of faith. Jesus doesn't rebuke it, but accepts it, and gets on with the spiritual battle. Throughout his ministry, Jesus frequently encouraged the faith of others.[1] His rebukes were reserved for his disciples,[2] and for his local towns who witnessed great things but remained unmoved (Luke 10:13–15). Modern exponents of the healing ministry often leave their followers feeling guilty when they are not instantly and miraculously healed. Such teaching is both cruel (it adds one degree of suffering to another) and unbiblical.

Jesus lays the burden of faith on the prayer team and

not on the distraught friends and relatives of the sick person. My old friend, Fred Smith,[3] who had, I believe, a genuinely 'apostolic' ministry of healing, used to say, 'If people aren't healed, I get down on my knees and apologise to God for my lack of faith.'

The spiritual climate of the day

According to Luke, Jesus commented to the crowd: 'O unbelieving and perverse generation; how long shall I stay with you and put up with you?' (Luke 9:41, cf Matthew 17:17, and Mark 9:19). Jesus found his generation particularly unbelieving (Luke 11:29 and Luke 10:13–15). This may help to explain the rather surprising phrase 'and the power of the Lord was present for him to heal the sick' (Luke 5:17). The idea that Jesus needed 'the power of the Lord' in order to heal suggests that the prevailing unbelief, particularly present in Nazareth, Korazin and Bethsaida, could almost neutralise his healing power.

Compassion – a Jesus word

The Greek word translated 'compassion' occurs many times in the Gospels. Jesus' usage usually carries the nuance of a deep understanding of someone else's need, coupled with the willingness and ability to help.

From among many Gospel incidents,[4] a very good example is just before the feeding of the 5,000. 'When Jesus heard what had happened, he withdrew by boat privately to a solitary place. Hearing of this, the crowds followed him on foot from the towns. When Jesus landed and saw a large crowd, he had compassion on them and healed their sick,' (Matthew 14:13–14).

Despite having his solitude disturbed, Jesus had compassion on the crowd. He saw, and fulfilled, their obvious need for physical healing. He taught them. 'When Jesus landed and saw a large crowd, he had compassion on them, because they were like sheep without a shepherd. So he began teaching them many things' (Mark 6:34), doubtless showing them where they could find a shepherd. Then he fed them, meeting their practical needs. Finally, he withdrew from them to pray – not allowing them to manipulate him into becoming a king (John 6:15).

Compassion in Jesus' life and teaching

Jesus' compassion met their physical and spiritual needs, but it also included a certain firmness in dismissing the crowd and returning to solitary prayer. Interestingly, it is a word that occurs in three of his most famous parables. The king, in the parable in of the unmerciful servant (Matthew 18:27), takes pity (shows compassion – the same word in Greek). The good Samaritan (Luke 10:33) takes pity on the man who has been robbed, and the Father (Luke 15:20) has compassion for his returning son.

These three parables are at the heart of the healing ministry. The first underlines the need for us to be willing to forgive others; the second the need for us to take effective practical action to help those who have been wounded and bruised in everyday life; and the third gives us a picture of the wonder of God's compassionate love.

People can easily come into the ministry of healing and deliverance with wrong motives. All too easily we are driven either by the need to do good (so as to be accepted by others), or by desire for power (so as to be looked up to by others). Jesus shows us that the only pure motive is compassion – seeing someone else's real need and seeking God's wisdom and grace as to how to meet it.

Jesus and the people he prayed for

Jesus heals because of friends and family

Many of the people whom Jesus healed met him because of their friends or family. Some cried out to him for healing. Others, often the demonised, initiated a confrontation which invariably led to the expulsion of the demon, and the healing of the person concerned. Occasionally, Jesus initiated the healing, usually to demonstrate something to his opponents, or out of compassion to the afflicted.

We cannot draw too many conclusions from the individual Gospel stories, as along with them there is a mass of multiple healings (see below p. 88), and many others left unrecorded. 'Jesus did many other miraculous signs in the presence of his disciples, which are not recorded in this book' (John 20:30).

Friends and family of the ill people usually displayed great faith and persistence.[5] The paralytic man (Mark 2:2ff) owed everything to his courageous friends. Even allowing for the fact that the roof of the house would have been flat, and not made of any very solid material, it required remarkable courage and determination to get the man onto the roof, acquire the necessary ropes, and let the man down through the hole. I can just imagine the complaints of the sick man, as he grew more and more embarrassed by their efforts!

Jesus acknowledged their faith, and proclaimed that the man was forgiven. To demonstrate his forgiveness, Jesus told him to take up his mat and walk. The man himself had not acknowledged his need of forgiveness, nor had he displayed any faith – at least, not until he got up and walked! The faith, on this occasion, was displayed by the friends.

Jesus heals because of persistence

By contrast, blind Bartimaeus (Mark 10:46 ff) heard that Jesus was nearby and made such a racket that everyone near him tried to shut him up. Interestingly, Jesus asked him, 'What do you want me to do for you?' Bartimaeus' reply demonstrated his faith and he was healed. When people come for prayer it is good to ask them what they want the Lord to do for them – it gives them a chance to express their real needs and to demonstrate their faith.

Demons are drawn to Jesus like a magnet

Demonic encounters were usually initiated by the aggressive attitude of the demons. The healing of the Gadarene man is typical. Jesus approaches his territory (Mark 5:1ff), and from a long way off, the demon confronts Jesus, 'What do you want with me, Jesus, Son of the Most High God?'

Like moths are drawn to destruction by the light of a moth trap, so demons were magnetised towards the presence of Jesus. They simply couldn't keep quiet, exposing themselves to inevitable expulsion and destruction. The resulting conflicts were noisy, violent and unpleasant. Often the demon had enough power to resist for a short time (Mark 5:8, for instance), or to cause apparent harm to their former victim (Mark 9:26, for instance).

The striking characteristic of the encounters in the Gospels, and in Acts, is that the demons simply cannot remain concealed. Sometimes they are the cause of physical illness, and at other times of what we could call psychiatric illness. But in the Gospels, their presence is plain. Neither Jesus, nor his disciples, had to go in search

of the demonic. When they encountered the kingdom of
Satan there was a spiritual explosion, and no one was left
in any doubt as to whom was in charge. Present-day
exponents of the deliverance ministry would do well to
follow similar guide-lines (see pp. 264ff).

Jesus heals as a sign

Particularly in John's Gospel,[6] Jesus' healings are a sign to
an unbelieving world. Some of his healings, although
obviously beneficial to the sick person, demonstrated his
theological authority. For instance, the healing of the man
with the withered hand (Mark 3:1 ff) was done publicly,
on the Sabbath, to expose the ridiculous attitude of the
Pharisees on the question of Sabbath observance.

What did Jesus look for from those he healed?

Jesus looks for wholeness

As we have seen (p. 80), Jesus frequently commended the
faith of those who brought people to him, or encouraged
the faith of the individual who wanted healing. Often
Jesus emphasised spiritual wholeness, the Greek verb
σωξω is usually translated 'saved' (eg Luke 7:50), but is
also translated 'made well' (eg Luke 8:48).

Jesus was clearly looking for more than physical healing, he was expecting a real spiritual change and a radical
response. In this way, his healing encounters were no
different from his encounters with people who had other
problems.

Thus he said, 'Rise and go, your faith has made you
well,' (Luke 17:11. AV 'whole') to the Samaritan leper,
which was very similar to his final word to the sinful
woman who anointed him in the house of Simon the leper
(Luke 7:50).

Varied response of those healed by Jesus

Some of those he healed responded positively. Blind Bartimaeus, when healed, followed him; the Gadarene demoniac, when released, wanted to follow him, but obeyed when given the far more difficult task of staying behind and telling his family what had been done for him. These responses were similar to those of Zaccheus (Luke 19:8) and others who were dramatically changed by their encounters with Jesus.

Sometimes, Jesus seemed startlingly stern. After the healing of the man at the Pool of Bethesda, Jesus sought him out and made the searching comment, 'See, you are well again. Stop sinning or something worse may happen to you' (John 5:14). Similar warnings were given to the woman taken in adultery, 'Go now, and leave your life of sin' (John 8:11), and to those freed of evil spirits that the final state could be worse than the first (see Matthew 12:45).

Not all those who were healed benefited spiritually. Some seemed to carry on as though nothing had happened – the nine lepers (Luke 17:11 ff) are one obvious example. Others celebrated their healing by doing the exact opposite of what Jesus had told them, thereby hindering his wider work (eg Mark 1:45). This varied response, ranging from obedient gratitude to apparent indifference to the spiritual reality, is also experienced today (see chapter 10). The leader of the Good News Crusade, Don Double, once remarked to me, 'We have our least effective evangelism on the nights when we concentrate on healing.'

Jesus and the significance of his own ministry

Signs of the Messiah

A poignant, and important moment in Jesus' ministry
came when John the Baptist, in prison and facing death,
wonders whether he has got it all wrong. Was Jesus really
the Messiah? This sort of question troubles most of us
from time to time, and we can all take heart from Jesus'
gracious reply:

He sent them to the Lord to ask, 'Are you the one who was to
come, or should we expect someone else?' When the men came
to Jesus, they said, 'John the Baptist sent us to you to ask "Are
you the one who was to come, or should we expect someone
else?"'

At that very time Jesus cured many who had diseases, sicknesses and evil spirits and gave sight to many who were blind.
So he replied to the messengers 'Go back and report to John
what you have seen and heard. The blind receive sight, the lame
walk, those who have leprosy are cured, the deaf hear, the dead
are raised, and the good news is preached to the poor. Blessed is
the man who does not fall away on account of me.'

(Luke 7:19–23)

Note especially verse 21, not included by Matthew
(Matthew 11:2–6), showing that Jesus gave John's disciples
a practical demonstration of his fulfilment of the Isaiah
prophecies! Instead of rebuking John's apparent lack of
faith, Jesus provided the necessary evidence, and spoke
highly of his prophetic ministry. This story seems pivotal
in establishing Jesus' healing ministry as part of the
evidence of his Messianic role.

Key Old Testament texts include Isaiah 61:1–4 and
Isaiah 35:1–6. The first of these was the basis for Jesus'
famous introductory sermon at Nazareth. Here he

stunned his hearers not only with the words 'Today this
Scripture is fulfilled in your hearing' (Luke 4:21), but also
with his sharp comments that some of the key miracles in
the lives of Elijah and Elisha were performed to non-
Israelites!' Perhaps, not surprisingly, Jesus' teaching
provoked considerable anger and even led to the first
recorded attempt to kill him since his infancy.

Jesus and multiple healings

Jesus heals many

The Gospel writers quite casually record many occasions
when Jesus healed many people at the same time. Only St
John reserves his accounts of Jesus' healings to individual
cases of deep spiritual significance. It is worth reading
them all (see Matthew 4:23–24; 8:16; 9:35; 14:14, 35;
15:30; 19:2; 21;14; Mark 1:32f; 3:10–11; Luke 4:40–41;
6:17–19; 7:21 and, by implication, John 6:2).

These were clearly times when 'the power of the Lord
was with him to heal' (Luke 5:17). The incidents in
Matthew's Gospel are often in lonely places away from
the sceptical and prying eyes of Jesus' religious opponents.
They include a general tour of Galilee where preaching,
healing and deliverance are intermingled, the healing of
great crowds around the house of Peter's mother-in-law, a
general compassionate ministry to the harassed crowd
which ended with a significant call for prayer for more
labourers to be called into the harvest field, healing
before both miraculous feedings, healings in two lonely
places, and in the countryside (presumably) of Judea.
The great exception is the dramatic account of the
healing of the blind and the lame in the Temple pre-
cincts on the first Palm Sunday. Another occasion when

Jesus' healing ministry seemed designed to infuriate his opponents!

Mark and Luke don't provide many different examples. Mark has a colourful incident where Jesus teaches from a boat (Mark 3:7ff), and heals many, as the crowd, especially the sick, push forward to touch him.

Jesus heals few

A rather more unusual response occurs in Nazareth. Luke records the dramatic (hostile) response to his sermon (Luke 4:16f), while Mark and Matthew record what was, by Jesus' standard, a surprising result. Mark records, tersely:

> Jesus left there and went to his home town, accompanied by his disciples. When the Sabbath came, he began to teach in the synagogue, and many who heard him were amazed . . . 'What's this wisdom that has been given him, that he even does miracles! Isn't this the carpenter? Isn't this Mary's son and the brother of James, Joses, Judas and Simon? Aren't his sisters here with us?' And they took offence at him.
>
> Jesus said to them, 'Only in his home town, among his relatives and in his own house is a prophet without honour.' He could not do any miracles there, except lay his hands on a few sick people and heal them.
>
> (Mark 6:1–5; see also Matthew 13:53–58)

This is a very important story, from which we should listen to the widely held view (with which this author concurs!) that healing seems to be much more common when ministering in Third-World countries than in the prosperous West. At least part of the explanation would seem to be that the level of faith and expectation is often much lower in the West than in many other parts of the world.

As Jesus draws closer to Jerusalem, individual and multiple healings decline sharply. The darkening shadow of the cross considerably reduced the healing dimension of Jesus' work. This, too, is important; we can learn that while healing is a sign of the kingdom, the cross is the gateway to it. These are not of comparable importance. The lesser (healing and deliverance) must make way for the ultimate purpose of his life (the cross). The angels in heaven are doubtless pleased when anyone is healed by Jesus, but they rejoice when a sinner repents (Luke 15:10)!

Jesus and his Father's will

Another vital factor in Jesus' freedom, or otherwise, to heal is his relationship with his Father.

> Jesus gave them this answer: 'I tell you the truth, the Son can do nothing by himself, he can only do what he sees his Father doing, because whatever the Father does the Son also does. For the Father loves the Son and shows him all he does. Yes, to your amazement he will show him even greater things than these.'
>
> (John 5:19–20)

This takes us into the heart of the healing mystery. When is there a special anointing of the Spirit? What is the general will of the Father? What restricts the action of the Son? We need to be quite clear that there are no easy answers to these questions. Simplistic theologies stating that it is always the will of the Father to heal won't do. The anointing of the Spirit depends upon the sovereign will of God and cannot be turned on like a tap by praise, invocation (Come, Holy Spirit), or any other means. The actions of the Son were not consistently towards healing, but entirely dependent upon his Father's grace.

We have already referred to the healing at the Pool of Bethesda.[7] John's account makes it quite clear that just one man, out of a multitude of invalids, was healed. Ours not to reason why. Other stories, too, suggest a certain individuality in Jesus' ministry. His apparent reluctance to heal the Syrophoenician's daughter (Matthew 15:21–28) shows that he did little ministry outside the boundaries of Judah and Israel. Clearly, too, the healing of lepers, and the raising of the dead, were sufficiently rare occurrences to be noted in detail by the Gospel writers. It is notable that none of the fifteen multiple healings (see p. 88) recorded by the evangelists mentions either lepers being healed or the dead being raised.

For our own purposes, this ought to prevent us from *assuming* that it is always God's wish to heal. We will need to seek the anointing of the Spirit. Sometimes we will receive the gift of faith, and we will sense the outcome of our prayers. On other occasions, like the disciples with the epileptic boy, we may be defeated by our own prayer-lessness, our lack of faith, or the (negative) spiritual climate around us.

Sometimes it requires greater faith to trust God when nothing much seems to have happened. Jesus did just this after the bruising encounter in Nazareth. Immediately after, he sent the twelve out (Judas Iscariot included) to heal and to drive out demons (Mark 6:7ff).

Jesus and the conflict with evil spirits

Jesus and the ministry of deliverance

Mark's account of the start of Jesus' public ministry (Mark 1:21–28) begins with the deliverance of a man with an unclean spirit. The disruption to worship, the speech by the spirit displaying a mixture of knowledge and arrogance (by naming Jesus as the Holy One of God the spirit was trying to gain the ascendancy), and the physical power displayed by the spirit before it left was typical of such events in the Gospels, and not unusual in such ministry today.

Jesus' power in these situations was awesome. Nowhere is it more clearly seen than in the healing of the Gadarene demoniac.

This story (see Mark 5:1ff) gives a graphic picture of a man whose life had been completely destroyed by the destructive power of a host of evil spirits. We are given no indication, here or elsewhere, as to how the evil powers had gained access, but we are given a portrait of a man with immense power, living a terrifying and solitary life. His dramatic healing presented several problems. Theologians and animal rights people have agonised about the pigs, and the locals found the sight of the man 'clothed and in his right mind' just as alarming as his previous state. They quickly begged Jesus to leave them alone!

Clearly, evil spirits were very frightened of Jesus and wanted to remain in 'their' territory (Mark 5:10). He doesn't dispatch them to hell, and neither should we. I believe that if we are in this situation, we should reverently and firmly tell them to go to Jesus for whatever purpose he may have for them. We may hope that they are destroyed. What we must never do, and which I have heard done, is to tease them and mock them about their impending fate. 'But even the Archangel Michael, when he was disputing with the devil about the body of Moses, did not dare to bring a slanderous accusation against him, but said, "The Lord rebuke you!"' (Jude 9). The Archangel Michael didn't pronounce judgement upon the devil, and we certainly shouldn't step outside the bounds of decency when dealing with his minions.

As we have already seen in the account of the healing of the epileptic boy, Jesus regarded this sort of ministry as a major spiritual battle. Certainly the onlookers were particularly impressed by his ability to silence, and to remove, evil spirits (see for instance Mark 1:21–28). Here, and on other occasions, the spirits were sufficiently powerful to disobey Jesus – up to a point. The evil spirit here wasn't silent; in the case of the epileptic boy it came out in a frightening and violent manner; in the case of the Gaderene demoniac the multiple spirits seemed to bargain with Jesus not to be removed from their territory. He also warned them when casting out an evil spirit it might return with its friends and relatives to cause even more chaos – presumably if the cleansed person hadn't repented and turned to God (Luke 11:24–26).

Healing and deliverance linked

There are two incidents in Jesus' public ministry where healing and deliverance are intertwined.

> On a Sabbath Jesus was teaching in one of the synagogues, and a woman was there who had been crippled by a spirit for eighteen years. She was bent over and could not straighten up at all. When Jesus saw her, he called her forward and said to her, 'Woman, you are set free from your infirmity.' Then he put his hands on her, and immediately she straightened up and praised God.
>
> Indignant because Jesus had healed on the Sabbath, the synagogue ruler said to the people, 'There are six days for work. So come and be healed on those days, not on the Sabbath.'
>
> The Lord answered him, 'You hypocrites! Doesn't each one

of you on the Sabbath untie his ox or donkey from the stall
and lead it out to give it water? Then should not this woman,
a daughter of Abraham, whom Satan has kept bound for
eighteen long years, be set free on the Sabbath day from
what bound her?'

When he said this, all his opponents were humiliated, but
the people were delighted with all the wonderful things he was
doing.

(Luke 13:10–17)

What did Jesus mean by a 'spirit of infirmity'? His later
comment that the woman 'whom Satan bound for eighteen
long years' emphasises the demonic origin of the disease.
We should probably see this illness as caused by an evil
spirit, but we should be cautious. Some modern ministries
see cancer, arthritis and other serious illnesses as invariably
caused by evil spirits. The Scriptures are not so definite.

Stories like the healing of the blind man (John 9) where
the illness is attributed neither to the sin of the man, nor
the sin of his parents, and still less to Satan should warn us
against a simplistic approach. I have seen, particularly in
Zambia, dramatic physical improvements after deliverance ministry, and it is not surprising that the indwelling
of evil spirits should also cause physical suffering.

The other particularly interesting healing is recorded at
the end of Mark's dramatic first chapter.

A man with leprosy came to him and begged him on his
knees, 'If you are willing you can make me clean.'

Filled with compassion,[8] Jesus reached out his hand and
touched the man 'I am willing,' he said 'Be clean!'. Immediately the leprosy left him and he was cured. Jesus sent him
away at once with a strong warning, 'See that you don't tell
this to anyone. But go, show yourself to the priest and offer
the sacrifices that Moses commanded for your cleansing, as a
testimony to them.' Instead he went out and began to talk
freely, spreading the news. As a result, Jesus could no longer

enter a town openly, but stayed outside in lonely places. Yet the people still came to him from everywhere.

(Mark 1:40–45)

Commentators note the authoritative language of Jesus' prayer of healing. The terse words 'I will, be clean' are similar in tone to words of exorcism. Leprosy was the most feared disease in the ancient world.

Deliverance was a common part of Jesus' public ministry. We listed above (p. 88) fourteen examples of multiple healings. Six of these also include deliverance ministry, sometimes listed quite casually amid the diseases dealt with. For instance,

> Jesus went throughout Galilee, teaching in their synagogues, preaching the good news of the kingdom, and healing every disease and sickness among the people. News about him spread all over Syria, and people brought to him all who were ill with various diseases, those suffering severe pain, the demon possessed, the epileptics and the paralytics, and he healed them. (Matthew 4:23–24)

Most of the other examples of multiple healings don't exclude the possibility of exorcisms.

Some theological considerations

We now look briefly at a number of important questions raised by Jesus' ministry and the Gospel accounts. We shall consider the vexed question of 'is healing in the atonement?', consider Jesus' attitude to the origins of sickness and suffering, reflect on the theological problem of accidents and undeserved suffering, and then at the whole question of Jesus' attitude to Satan.

Healing and the atonement

Healing and Isaiah 53

Only Matthew makes the link between Jesus' healing ministry and Isaiah 53 which, for other New Testament writers, is the classic prophecy about the atonement (see especially 2 Corinthians 5:21; 1 Peter 2:24; 3:18; 1 John 2:2).

> When Jesus came into Peter's house, he saw Peter's mother-in-law lying in bed with a fever. He touched her hand and the fever left her, and she got up and began to wait on him.
>
> When evening came, many who were demon-possessed were brought to him, and he drove out the spirits with a word and healed all the sick. This was to fulfil what was spoken through the prophet Isaiah: 'He took up our infirmities and carried our diseases.'
>
> (Matthew 8:14–17)

This particular incident, recorded also by Mark and Luke, is uniquely linked by Matthew with the work of the suffering servant.

Michael Green[9] has an important and balanced comment:

> The evangelist's conclusion of this trio of healings is remarkable. He sees it as the fulfilment of Isaiah 53:4. That was, of course a messianic prophecy, but it applied in the first instance to the sinbearing which Jesus undertook for men upon the cross. There are many passages in the New Testament which show how important this chapter of Isaiah 53 was for the early Christians. It helped them to understand what Jesus achieved for them at Calvary. But here the Isaiah passage seems to be used with a secondary application. It is related not to the death of Jesus, but to his healing ministry. And it seems to say that so costly was this healing that Jesus took up our infirmities on himself, and carried our diseases.

He bore our sicknesses as well as our sins. There is no suggestion of Calvary here. There is no justification for those who
would claim that Jesus bore our sicknesses as well as our sins
upon the Cross. But Matthew does see the healing ministry of
Jesus as part of the pain and hardship which Isaiah foresaw
for the Servant of the Lord in Chapters 40–55 of his book. Of
course, sickness is related (though not, according to Scripture, directly related) to sin, and so it is not possible entirely
to dissociate the healing ministry from the vicarious suffering
in this picture of the Servant. But Matthew sees him here
coming from the mountain of revelation (Chapters 5–7) and
entering into the valley of the shadow, where sickness and
demonic forces held sway. And he was willing to carry the
burden of pain, ostracism and defilement of broken mankind,
just as he would later bear its sin. Here is a fulfilment of the
prophet's words deeper than he could ever have imagined.

We shall return to this in chapter 8, question 24, but for
the moment we note the link between Jesus' healing work
and Isaiah 53 without over-emphasising it. Jesus made a
number of prophetic utterances concerning his death, but
he always linked his death with his need to suffer, his life
as a ransom for many, and never with his healing work.

Taking this a little further, we see that Green and Cullmann[10] are showing us that, for Matthew, the healing
miracles point beyond themselves to the cross. They are
not part of the atonement, but a sign warning of the
intensity of future suffering. This will come as a surprise
to any used to the triumphalism of some approaches to
healing. But when we consider the conflicts that Jesus'
healings and exorcisms produced, we will begin to
appreciate the wisdom of this approach.

Every exorcism was costly, often involving unwanted
disclosures of who Jesus was. The healings were
exhausting, and produced fierce controversy with the

Pharisees about forgiveness, the Sabbath, and the source of his power. His disciples misunderstood them, and the news of his miracles often impeded his deeper purposes. Mark even hints that his family thought that he was out of his mind (Mark 3:21). Healing for Jesus was a costly gift.

Jesus and the origin of sickness and suffering

Many writers want to simplify this question and attribute everything directly to Satan. There is some scriptural support for this view. Peter's sermon to Cornelius' household (Acts 10:34–43) includes 'how God anointed Jesus of Nazareth with the Holy Spirit and power and how he went around doing good and healing all who were under the power of the devil, because God was with him' (v.38).

Indirectly, as the architect of the fall, Satan can be held responsible for all sickness and accident as well as direct demonic interference. But before we blindly accept this, and start seeing any illness as needing exorcism, and every person as likely to be demon-possessed (which is certainly the teaching of some), we need to step back and remember that Satan only operates within the permitted will of God. Even the fall happened because God allowed it. '*O felix culpa* [O happy fault]' says the second-century theologian St Irenaeus of Lyons. He is writing about the fall which he sees as a necessary preliminary to the greater blessings won by Jesus through the cross and resurrection.

Illness caused by sin

Sometimes Jesus attributed illness to sin; most clearly in the case of the paralytic man let down through the roof by his faithful friends (Mark 2:1–12). Jesus infuriated the religious leaders by publicly forgiving the man's sin as a *necessary* preliminary to his healing.

On one celebrated occasion, Jesus refused to assign a cause to a man's illness.

> As he went along he saw a man blind from birth. His disciples asked him, 'Rabbi, who sinned, this man or his parents, that he was born blind?' 'Neither this man nor his parents sinned,' said Jesus, 'but this happened so that the work of God might be displayed in his life.'
>
> (John 9:1–3)

This man's illness was part of the general fallen state of humankind. Jesus had a similar, and very pastorally important, view about accidents and political injustice.

Suffering caused by accidents and unjust policies

> Now there were some present at that time who told Jesus about the Galileans whose blood Pilate had mixed with their sacrifices. Jesus answered, 'Do you think that these Galileans were worse sinners than all the other Galileans because they suffered this way? I tell you, no! But unless you repent, you too will all perish. Or those eighteen who died when the tower in Siloam fell on them – do you think they were more guilty than all the others living in Jerusalem? I tell you, no! But unless you repent, you too will all perish.'
>
> (Luke 13:1–5)

The people killed by the falling tower, and those murdered by Pilate's vicious leadership, were neither especially wicked nor heroically good. They were ordinary people who happened to be in the wrong place at the wrong time.

Jesus and Satan

The prince of this world

We now consider briefly Jesus' attitude to Satan. Importantly, he acknowledges Satan's power as prince of this world. 'I will not speak with you much longer, for the prince of this world is coming. He has no hold on me' (John 14:30; see also John 12:31). And, again, the devil took him to a very high mountain and showed him all the kingdoms of the world and their splendour. 'All this I will give you,' he said, 'if you will bow down and worship me' (Matthew 4:8–9).

Although Jesus rebuked Satan and told him to go, he didn't deny his claim to be able to give him the kingdoms of this world. Satan's power is considerable, although ultimately limited by God's sovereignty.

The limits of Satan's power

Many European writers,[11] use an analogy from the Second World War. When the American, British and other allies landed successfully on the Normandy beaches in France in June 1944, victory was certain; but there was a great deal of unpleasantness to follow. In particular, the Allies had no control over Hitler's ability to launch powerful rockets on London, and possibly even to invent nuclear weapons.

One theologian says, 'The devil is bound to a line which can be lengthened even to the point that, for a while, Satan can make himself independent, and has to be fought against by God.'[12] This would explain how territorial spirits can exercise considerable power, and whole regimes can be apparently closed to the gospel. Evil cannot prevail, but we can choose evil and greatly hinder God's purposes. The citizens of Sodom (Genesis 19), and the followers of the cult of Diana in Ephesus (Acts 19), would seem to be examples of such a choice.

This may help to explain the difficulties that those ministering in the areas of healing and deliverance can face. At one level there is a prevailing lack of faith, and even cynicism, such as Jesus found in Nazareth and with the crowd surrounding the epileptic boy. At another, there are the devastating counter attacks brought by Satan against teams of intercessors in spiritual warfare and the like. Jesus, himself, faced this first when Satan infiltrated the Twelve, destroying Judas and sifting Peter and the others. He also faced it alone in the garden when he would gladly have headed north for the peace and quiet of the Galilean lakeside. 'Father, if you are willing, take this cup from me, yet not my will, but yours be done' (Luke 22:42).

Jesus and spiritual warfare

Satan's defeat at Calvary

We have already seen that Jesus recognised Satan's power, referring to him twice as the 'prince of this world' (John 12:31; 14:30). The earlier inference is particularly significant. 'Now is the time for judgment on this world; now the prince of this world will be driven out. But I, when I am lifted up from the earth, will draw all men to myself.'

After Calvary, Satan is fatally wounded. Here Satan and his armies suffered an irreversible defeat. St Paul puts it very clearly: 'And having disarmed the powers and authorities, he made a public spectacle of them, triumphing over them by the cross' (Colossians 2:15).

Demonic organisation

This text, together with others considered later, strongly suggests that Satan's forces are organised. Several times

Jesus referred to Satan as Beelzebub – 'The Lord of the Flies', or 'Lord of the House' (Matthew 10:25; 12:24,27, and parallel passages in Mark and Luke). In the parable of the sheep and the goats, Jesus refers to the 'Devil and all his angels' (Matthew 25:41). Both these texts confirm a measure of organisation in the demonic world. This is confirmed by the often neglected story of the evil spirit who returns to the cleansed house with seven more spirits (Luke 11:24–26), a story which shows the pastoral necessity of turning to Christ after any sort of deliverance ministry.

Are the spirits territorial?

Although the New Testament doesn't explicitly teach that this organisation includes territorial authority, several incidents in the Gospels, and others from Acts which we will consider in the next chapter, strongly hint at this level of organisation. We have already noted (p. 92) that the evil spirits who were infesting the Gadarene demoniac wanted to stay in their familiar area. 'And he begged Jesus again and again not to send them out of the area' (Mark 5:10). That statement suggests a strong territorial affinity for the spirits. If we add to that the locals' extraordinary spiritual blindness, there is strong evidence that the dark powers held considerable sway in the Decapolis, although their hold had been clearly loosened by this incident, or Jesus would scarcely have sent the man back to live in the region.

Jesus and Bethsaida

The healing of the blind man *outside* Bethsaida (Mark 8:22–26) is intriguing. Why did Jesus take the man away from the village? Why, on this unique occasion, did Jesus need to pray twice? Why did he tell the blind man not to return to the village? Perhaps there is a clue in Luke

10:13 where Bethsaida, among other places, is mentioned as peculiarly spiritually blind. Was Bethsaida enemy territory? Was it a place where Satan's angels held strong sway?

Neither here, nor in the Decapolis, nor in the towns which rejected the mission of the seventy-two (Luke 10:10), nor in the places that refused the mission of the twelve (Mark 6:11) does Jesus encourage a spiritual battle. His battle is with Satan, in the garden of Gethsemane, and on the cross. Here was the cup which he drank to the full.

Authority is in heaven

The famous text of Matthew 16:19 may provide a clue. If we accept the NIV margin translation, 'I will give you the keys of the kingdom of heaven; whatever you bind on earth *will have been*, and whatever you loose on earth *will have been* loosed in heaven', then we can see that the binding of Satan is achieved in heaven and confirmed on earth, rather than as the result of authoritative prayer on earth which is confirmed in heaven. If this is correct, it underlines a point made by many writers[13] that warfare prayer is only to be undertaken as a result of very clear instructions from the Lord.

Many incidents in the Old Testament support this view. We have already seen how Daniel's task (Daniel 10) was to pray and fast while the spiritual battle took place in the heavenly places. Likewise Moses prayed while the Amalekites were defeated (Exodus 17:10), and Jehosaphat's army was involved in praise and worship while the enemy destroyed each other (2 Chronicles 20:13–30).

The subtlety of Satan

However, Satan has one even deadlier weapon, sublety, which includes both concealment and disguise. The first incident in the Bible (Genesis 3:1) illustrates the subtlety of Satan, and the first conflict incident in the Gospels (Mark 1:21f) shows an evil spirit flushed into the open by the authority of Jesus' teaching. Satan infiltrates Jesus' family, encouraging them to quietly lock him up (Mark 3:20–30) and then gets the religious leaders to commit the ultimate blasphemy of accusing Jesus of healing by the devil's own power. Later Satan enters into the very heart of one of the twelve (Luke 22:3; John 13:2) and is allowed to test Peter (Luke 22:31).

Satan disguised

Elsewhere, Satan comes disguised as an angel of light (2 Corinthians 11:14), capable of working signs and wonders (2 Thessalonians 2:9) which could almost deceive the elect (Mark 13:22). These necessary warnings can cause division in today's Church where some would see *today's* 'miracles' as fulfilment of those warning prophecies.

Ultimately, the only safe test is doctrinal. (1 John 4:1–3 and John 16:14). Is Jesus glorified by the signs? Is he acknowledged as Lord?

Satan thought not to exist

In today's Church in the West, Satan has adopted a simpler ploy – he doesn't exist. Although this attitude leads to some impossible theological positions (like the 'Barnabas' bible which has a nice cartoon of Adam blaming Eve, Eve blaming the serpent, and a smug serpent saying, 'You can't blame me, modern theology says that I don't exist'), it fits the modern mind well. The demonic

powers and authorities of Scripture become the multinationals, corrupt states, world banking authorities in
modern thinking.

Suffice it to say that it suits Satan to lie concealed. We
have commented on Jesus' first public confrontation with
a demon (Mark 1:21f). What we should note here is that
the demon would have preferred concealment, but was
driven into open warfare by the power, authority and
holiness of Jesus' presence.

Many modern-day believers, this author included, have
reluctantly acknowledged the existence of evil spirits when
confronted by their unexpected presence!

Jesus and Satan – conclusion

We may conclude that while Jesus seemed to recognise the
territorial and organisational power of Satan, he didn't
regard it as of primary importance. He had come to
proclaim, and to personify, the kingdom of God. He
came 'to destroy the work of the Devil' (1 John 3:8). He
accomplished this in single combat, first in the wilderness
and then on the cross.

As we shall see in the next chapter, some territory
was captured by preaching accompanied by signs and
wonders, some by power encounters with Satan's forces.
In many cases, even in the Apostolic church, the victory
was only temporary. In some cases (Ephesus, for
instance) Satan seems to have remained in long-term
control despite a bruising encounter with the forces of
light.

Nevertheless, the ministry of healing is disliked by Satan
because it is a demonstration of the ultimate power,
victory and goodness of God. If Satan can infiltrate it
via spiritualism or New Age therapies, he is well pleased.

The ministry of deliverance goes much further, and sets people free (provided they repent and turn to Jesus) to praise and serve God in a new way. Effective prayer against territorial spirits is a real invasion of Satan's fiefdom as ruler of this world. Such prayer is like tackling a wasps' nest – it had better be effective, otherwise there will be a stinging counter attack.

Long-term victories depend upon good strategy. Jesus did much to encourage and to organise the training of his followers, and to this important matter we now turn.

Jesus and the training of his followers

Healing and training

Jesus expended considerable energy in training both the twelve and a wider group of seventy in mission.

> Then Jesus went round teaching from village to village. Calling the Twelve to him, he sent them out two by two and gave them authority over evil spirits. These were his instructions, 'Take nothing for the journey except a staff – no bread, no bag, no money in your belts. Wear sandals, but not an extra tunic. Whenever you enter a house, stay there until you leave that town. And if any place will not welcome you or listen to you, shake the dust off your feet when you leave, as a testimony against them.' They went out and preached that people should repent. They drove out many demons and anointed many sick people with oil and healed them.
>
> (Mark 6:7–13; see also Luke 10:1–24 and Matthew 10:5–16)

Healing and deliverance were the outward signs which demonstrated the coming of the kingdom of God. Matthew puts the basic message very clearly: 'As you go, preach this message, "The kingdom of heaven is near"' (Matthew 10:7). Luke records the results: 'The seventy-two returned with joy and said, "Lord, even the demons submit to us in your name."''

There is a basic continuity between these missions and the many healings recorded in Acts. There is no suggestion that these missions were unique to the time of Jesus and his Apostles. Years later Paul wrote to Timothy, 'And these things you have heard me say in the presence of many witnesses entrust to reliable men who will also be qualified to teach others' (2 Timothy 2:2). This would surely have included teaching on such important matters.

Jesus didn't confine healing to the twelve, nor did he object to those completely outside his circle working in his name. 'Master', said John, 'we saw a man driving out demons in your name and we tried to stop him, because he is not one of us.' 'Do not stop him,' Jesus said, 'for whoever is not against you is for you.' (Luke 9:49–50)

The overwhelming impression is that Jesus welcomed the ministry of healing and deliverance as an important part of his whole proclamation of the coming of the kingdom of God, that he taught a wide circle to practise it, and that he expected it to continue after his death.

The disputed conclusion of Mark's Gospel is important.

He said to them, 'Go into all the world and preach the good news to all creation. Whoever believes and is baptized will be saved, but whoever does not believe it will be condemned. And these signs will accompany those who believe. In my name they will drive out demons, they will speak in new tongues, they will pick up snakes with their hands, and when they drink deadly poison, it will not hurt them at all, they will place their hands on sick people, and they will get well.' After the Lord Jesus had spoken to them, he was taken up into heaven and he sat at the right hand of God. Then the disciples went out and preached everywhere, and the Lord worked with them and confirmed his word by the signs that accompanied it.

(Mark 16:15–20)

Few scholars accept this as part of the original text, nevertheless, the words must reflect the belief of the Church at the time that they were written. This is important. Those powerful words are either Jesus' original words to the disciples, post-resurrection, or they reflect the belief and expectation of the early Church – say, in the mid-second century. If so, they are strong evidence for both the importance and the continuity of the ministries of healing and deliverance long after the death of the Apostolic group.[14]

A summary of Jesus' teaching and practice

In conclusion, I would like to return to the incident of the epileptic boy (see p. 78). Here Jesus clearly teaches the priority of prayer, the necessity of faith, the importance of helping people grow in faith, the difficulties caused by the prevailing climate of unbelief. To this we may add that Jesus saw his own ministry of healing and deliverance as a vital sign of his being the Messiah, that he had no simplistic theology of healing based either on the atonement or the interference of Satan, and that he saw the practical teaching of his disciples, *and a wider group*, as a priority. However, there were more important matters even than healing and deliverance. To this, the Gospel witness is unequivocal.

Very early in the morning, while it was still dark, Jesus got up, left the house and went off to a solitary place where he prayed. Simon and his companions went to look for him, and when they found him, they exclaimed: 'Everyone is looking for you!' Jesus replied, 'Let us go somewhere else – to the nearby villages – so that I can preach there also. That is why I have come.' So he travelled throughout Galilee, preaching in their synagogues and driving out demons.

(Mark 1:35–39)

This significant passage puts the healing ministry in its proper perspective – important, wonderful, majestic, but not the ultimate priority. Preaching the kingdom and making disciples (Matthew 28:16–20) – these are the priorities for every Christian!

Notes

1. See, for instance, Matthew 9:22, 29; Mark 10:52, Luke 7:9, etc.
2. Mark 4:40, for instance.
3. See page 212ff.
4. See Mark 1:41; 8:22; Matthew 9:36 and 20:34; Luke 7:13, etc.
5. See Mark 7:24–30.
6. The signs in John's Gospel include John 2:11; 4:54; 6:14.
7. See page 18.
8. William Lane, *The Gospel of Mark* (Marshall, Morgan and Scott, 1974), p. 84, note 141, where he argues that 'indignation' rather than 'compassion' is the correct reading of this text. This strengthens the link with exorcism in this healing.
9. Michael Green, *Matthew for Today* (Hodder and Stoughton, 1988), p. 98. Also chapter 8, question 24.
10. Oscar Cullmann, *Christology of the New Testament* Study Edition (SCM, 1959), p. 69.

11. For instance, Oscar Cullmann, *Prayer in the New Testament* (SCM, 1995) p. 141.

12. Cullmann, *op. cit.* p. 141, and also John Woolmer, *Thinking Clearly about Prayer* (Monarch, 1997) p. 80f.

13. See Peter Wagner, *Territorial Spirits* (Sovereign World, 1991) chapters 1 and 14, and elsewhere.

14. A biography of Sadhu Sundar Singh (1889–c.1929) which I cannot now trace, refers to him at the point of death. He had been poisoned by his family because of his conversion to Christianity. He asked for Mark 16 to be read to him, fell into a deep sleep, and woke up completely well. A.J. Gordon in *Healing* (Christian Publications, 1992) p. 196, gives a similar story of a missionary who was poisoned in Sumatra. Mel Tari, *Like a Mighty Wind* (Coverdale, 1971), gives a number of examples of using this text against snakes, crocodiles and poison.

4

Healing and Deliverance in the Apostolic Church

In this chapter we look at the priorities of the Apostles – the growth of the Church which was greatly aided by accompanying signs and wonders. We observe the ministry of the leading Apostles including, especially, power encounters in Samaria, Cyprus, Philippi and Ephesus.

Healing and Deliverance in the Apostolic Church

The priorities of the Apostles

Luke's overall aim is to describe the remarkable growth of the Church in the immediate years after Jesus' death and resurrection. On almost every page, he makes it clear that the extraordinary, almost laughable, message (Acts 17:32) is enhanced and made possible to believe by the ministry of signs and wonders. We read of many accounts of healing and deliverance, as well as many other incidents involving guidance, prophecy and angelic intervention.

The pages are full of supernatural events, including many full-scale spiritual battles with dark powers – notably in Samaria (Acts 8), on Cyprus (Acts 13), in Philippi (Acts 16) and in Ephesus (Acts 19). Not surprisingly, this is all too much for some commentators who want to consign the authorship and writing of Acts as unhistorical and mid-second century. This has been refuted by many critics,[1] and the experience of the Church, not least in the latter part of the twentieth century,[2] has been to rediscover that this is exactly the sort of way that God acts when his people start expecting him to act in power!

First, we must look at the message that the Apostles preached.

The preaching of the Apostles

Peter and other Apostles testify to Jesus' power of healing and deliverance

Each of the four sermons of Peter, as reported and summarised by Luke, mentions healing and/or deliverance. On the day of Pentecost, he summarised Jesus' early ministry in these interesting words: 'Men of Israel, listen to this. Jesus of Nazareth was a man accredited by God to you by miracles, wonders and signs, which God did among you through him, as you yourselves know' (Acts 2:22).

After the healing of the lame man, Peter made it very clear both to the onlookers (Acts 3:16) and to the religious leaders (Acts 4:9–10) that the man was completely healed by the name of Jesus and through the faith that Jesus gives.

Peter's address to Cornelius' household was cut short by the Holy Spirit's intervention, but not before he had again emphasised the importance of this side of Jesus' ministry: 'You know what has happened throughout Judea, beginning in Galilee after the baptism that John preached – how God anointed Jesus of Nazareth with the Holy Spirit and power, and how he went around doing good and healing all who were under the power of the devil, because God was with him' (Acts 10:37–38)

We have rather fewer accounts of Paul's preaching. One evangelistic sermon (Acts 13:16–41) concentrates on the resurrection; a hurried sermon after the healing of the

crippled man at Lystra (Acts 14:13–17) has little time to
develop any theme other than God's goodness before it is
interrupted by the opposition; the sermon to the Ephesian
elders (Acts 20:13–17) is essentially prophetic and
pastoral; but one of his 'testimonies' addressed to the
Jerusalem crowd mentions the healing of Paul's own
temporary blindness by Ananias. (Acts 22:13)

Stephen (Acts 6 and 7) performed 'great wonders and
signs', and doubtless would have mentioned this aspect of
Jesus' ministry if he'd been given the chance. But he, too,
found his sermon cut short (Acts 7:52) as soon as he
mentioned Jesus.

I think it is safe to assume that when Luke reports that
'Philip went down to a city of Samaria and proclaimed the
Christ there' (Acts 8: 5), this included plenty of reference
to Jesus' healings and exorcisms.

We now turn, in more detail, to the work of the leading
Apostles.

The ministry of Peter

Peter follows Jesus very closely

There are far too many examples to comment on each in
detail, but it is noticeable how closely Peter follows the
methods of his master.

In Joppa there was a disciple named Tabitha (which, when
translated, is Dorcas), who was always doing good and helping the poor. About that time she became sick and died, and
her body was washed and placed in an upstairs room. Lydda
was near Joppa, so when the disciples heard that Peter was in
Lydda, they sent two men to him and urged him, 'Please
come at once!' Peter went with them, and when he arrived
he was taken upstairs to the room. All the widows stood

around him, crying and showing him the robes and other clothing that Dorcas had made while she was still with them. Peter sent them all out of the room, then he got down on his knees and prayed. Turning towards the dead woman, he said, 'Tabitha, get up.' She opened her eyes, and seeing Peter she sat up. He took her by the hand and helped her to her feet. Then he called the believers and the widows and presented her to them alive. This became known all over Joppa, and many people believed in the Lord.

(Acts 9:36–42)

Peter's authority like that of Jesus

The account is very similar to the raising of Jairus' daughter (Luke 10:49–56). Not only does Peter remove the wailing onlookers, but his authoritative words, 'Tabitha, get up', are very similar to the Aramaic words that Jesus presumably used when addressing Jairus' little girl. The Aramaic words used by Jesus were probably '*Talitha koum*', whereas Peter says, '*Tabitha koum*.' One famous text (the Western) of Mark 5:41, confused by all this, even reads '*Tabitha*' instead of '*Talitha*'.[3]

The earlier healing of Aeneas (Acts 9:32–22) is also similar in style to the Gospel healing of the paralysed man. It also demonstrates that such signs were a very important aid to apostolic evangelism. Just as Peter learnt directly from Jesus, so we should learn both from the Gospels and from those who can teach us today. This is the true apostolic succession (see 2 Timothy 2:2).

When Peter saw the lame man (Acts 3:1ff), he didn't waste any words!

Peter looked straight at him, as did John. Then Peter said, 'Look at us!' So the man gave them his attention, expecting to get something from them. Then Peter said, 'Silver or gold I do not have, but what I have I give you. In the name of Jesus

Christ of Nazareth, walk.' Taking him by the right hand he helped him up and instantly the man's feet and ankles became strong.

(Acts 3:4–7)

The authority is similar to that displayed by Jesus on many occasions, notably the healing of the paralysed man (Mark 2:1–12) and the healing of the leper (Mark 1:41–42). The gesture of helping the man to his feet is similar to Jesus' encouragement to people to believe – for instance, the healing of the blind man (Mark 8:22–26) where Jesus took the man by the hand, spat on his eyes (an 'aid' to faith in those days!), and even prayed a second time.

It is also interesting that Peter is unconcerned by the man's obvious lack of expectation of healing (let alone faith!). The faith that Peter refers to (Acts 3:16) was clearly exercised by Peter and John. His healing was an important sign which infuriated the authorities just as Jesus' healing of the blind man (John 9) had done.

Peter and deliverance

Peter was also involved in the deliverance ministry. Luke mentions this quite casually:

As a result, people brought the sick into the streets and laid them on beds and mats so that at least Peter's shadow might fall on some of them as he passed by. Crowds gathered also from the towns around Jerusalem, bringing their sick and those tormented by evil spirits, and all of them were healed.

(Acts 5:15–16)

Elsewhere there are many references to miraculous signs which obviously included both healing and deliverance (see Acts 2:43, 5:12). We shall refer later to Peter's dramatic confrontation with Simon Magus.

The Apostles pray for more more healing

We get a few windows into the actual prayer life of the Apostolic church (see Acts 1:14, 24; 2:47; 6:4; 11:27; 12:5; 13:1–3), but the Apostles' reaction to the threats of the religious leaders after the healing of the lame man is particularly instructive. Far from backing off, they pray for more power, more signs, more healing!

> 'Now, Lord, consider their threats and enable your servants to speak your word with great boldness. Stretch out your hand to heal and perform miraculous signs and wonders through the name of your holy servant Jesus.' After they prayed, the place where they were meeting was shaken. And they were all filled with the Holy Spirit and spoke the word of God boldly.
>
> (Acts 4:29–31)

As their prayers were answered, they needed more helpers! Very quickly, these were appointed.

The ministry of the seven deacons

Seven men are chosen for a mundane task but they have to be filled with the Holy Spirit!

The choosing of the seven deacons (Acts 6:1ff) is interesting. They were chosen to sort out a social problem – grumbling widows (!), but their qualifications were to be unambiguous: 'Brothers, choose seven men from among you who are known to be full of the Spirit and wisdom. We will turn this responsibility over to them' (Acts 6:3).

Stephen's appointment had an immediate effect! 'Now Stephen, a man full of God's grace and power, did great wonders and miraculous signs among the people' (Acts 6:8). We may presume that these signs included healing and deliverance, and note that such 'up-front' ministry was not confined to the twelve!

Stephen's ministry was quickly cut short, but in the dispersion that followed his death, Philip landed up in Samaria. His preaching was also accompanied by miraculous signs – certainly including healing and deliverance.

> Philip went down to a city in Samaria and proclaimed the Christ there. When the crowds heard Philip and saw the miraculous signs he did, they all paid close attention to what he said. With shrieks, evil spirits came out of many and many paralytics and cripples were healed. So there was great joy in that city.'
>
> (Acts 8:5–8)

Much joy in the city! This is one of the normal reactions to effective ministry. Much joy because of new life in Christ, much joy because of healed bodies, much joy because of deliverance from the powers of darkness. Charles Wesley's great hymn 'And can it be' (said by some to be the first hymn he wrote after his conversion), puts it well:

> Long my imprisoned spirit lay
> fast bound in sin and nature's night;
> Thine eye diffused a quickening ray –
> I woke, the dungeon flamed with light;
> my chains fell off, my heart was free.
> I rose, went forth, and followed Thee.

Power encounters

Philip's ministry in Samaria has the marks of a power encounter. What I mean by a 'power encounter' is a sharp spiritual battle, after which the spiritual climate seems to change decisively. We shall look at several other such examples in Acts, and in modern Christian experience. In some cases, the decisive incident seems to be the defeat, or even the conversion, of a key individual, in others it is a victorious encounter with demonic forces.

Samaria was a somewhat unpropitious place for Philip's ministry. It had been the centre of considerable religious rebellion in Old Testament times, culminating in its defeat by the Assyrians and repopulation with a myriad of different peoples and their gods. In the Gospels, apart from the wonderful encounter with the woman at the well (John 4), Jesus experienced rejection in the region (Luke 9:51–55), causing James and John to want to call down fire on the unfortunate village.

Whether, as a result of the Samaritan woman's teaching, Philip's preaching, or Simon Magus' partial conversion, there was a considerable victory. The opposition led by Simon crumbled, but we are left in doubt of his own spiritual position after his unfortunate attempt to purchase the power of the Holy Spirit (Acts 8:18ff). Canonical Scripture leaves the matter unclear, but both some apocryphal literature[4] and the Early Fathers feature Simon Magus opposing Peter even as far as Rome. Justin (c.AD150) surprisingly, and probably erroneously, records that he was honoured with a statue 'to Simon the holy god'. Whatever the truth of all this, his power over the people was broken, and Philip's ministry prospered, until the Holy Spirit whisked him away for a significant evangelistic encounter in the desert.

Once, when preaching in a very rural part of Zambia, I was nearing the end of a sermon on Philip's ministry in Samaria when proceedings were disrupted by a turbaned member of the Mothers' Union who fell out of her pew screaming! I stopped speaking, and with the help of others, carried her out of the church – literally kicking and screaming. The priest calmly carried on with the service. After a short time of prayer, she calmed down, and we encouraged her to name and renounce the spirits that were troubling her. Soon she seemed quite well, and we all returned to the church.

Later in the day, I had two surprises. First, she served us lunch (which reminded me of Peter's mother-in-law!), and then I discovered that she was the priest's wife. I thought back in amazement to the service, and how he had calmly continued the service as though this was what normally happened!

The ministry of Paul

The last great witness to healing and deliverance in Acts is St Paul. First, of course, he had to receive healing. Blinded by his amazing encounter with the risen Lord (Acts 9:8), the wonderfully reluctant Ananias is sent to heal him.

> Then Ananias went to the house and entered it. Placing his hands on Saul, he said, 'Brother Saul, the Lord – Jesus, who appeared to you on the road as you were coming here – has sent me so that you may see again and be filled with the Holy Spirit.' Immediately, something like scales fell from Saul's eyes, and he could see again. He got up and was baptised, and after taking some food, he regained his strength.
>
> (Acts 9:17–19)

Ananias' prayer was simple and effective. Christian history is full of unknown saints who have been led to pray for great people at critical times. That is one of the great joys of such ministry. For instance, in *Thinking Clearly about Renewal,*[5] Mark Stibbe recalls his own conversion, and how he was led to faith by a member of staff at school. This man, a great prayer warrior, has been a spiritual signpost to very many, yet remains quietly and prayerfully out of the limelight.

Paul's ministry contains many examples of healing and deliverance. It begins with the encounter with Elymas on the island of Cyprus.

Cyprus (Acts 13:4–12)

The encounter with Elymas has all the marks of another power battle. He was a sorcerer, deriving his magical powers from the devil. Probably he saw Paphos as his territory. Clearly he had considerable influence, and he was even part of the entourage of the proconsul. In a real sense, spiritual and earthly powers were interlocked.[6]

When Barnabas and Saul started to speak to the proconsul, Elymas faced a crisis. Somewhat foolishly, he tried to intervene. Paul taught him a very sharp lesson, and left the proconsul in no doubt as to where true spiritual power was to be found.

We don't know if Elymas repented, but certainly the proconsul believed, and the island of Cyprus, home of Barnabas, became a fruitful place for the gospel. Such spiritual battles can bring casualties. In this case there were serious consequences; first, John Mark returned home – possibly frightened and out of his depth in the spiritual fireworks; secondly, Paul and Barnabas had a terrible row (Acts 15:36–41) on the subject of Mark's defection. Fortunately, Barnabas stood by Mark, and the future Gospel writer was gradually restored to favour (even with Paul, see 2 Timothy 4:11) and became a key figure in the ministry of Peter in Rome.

Galatia (Acts 14:1–20)

Signs and wonders, a normal part of Paul's ministry The mission continues in Iconium where Paul's preaching is confirmed with signs and wonders – a normative experience, I would think! (Acts 14:3). This view is supported by 1 Thessalonians 1:5 – 'because our gospel came to you not simply with words, but also with power with the Holy Spirit and with deep conviction. You know how we lived among you for your sake.'

The visit to Thessalonica as recorded in Acts 17 is a fairly slow affair involving preaching, persuasion and considerable opposition. Luke makes no mention of signs and wonders – he has mentioned them so often that he probably expects his readers to regard them as normal!

Paul heals a lame man who had faith The chronological account in Acts next mentions the dramatic healing of the cripple in Lystra (Acts 14:8ff). Two things are especially noteworthy: 'He listened to Paul as he was speaking. Paul looked directly at him, saw that he had faith to be healed and called out, 'Stand up on your feet!' At that, the man jumped up and began to walk' (Acts 14:9). Paul saw the man's faith. He had listened to the preaching, and believed!

The crippled man at Lystra is healed because he had faith, the crippled man at the Gate Beautiful is healed because he is in the right place at the right time. The Acts of the Apostles doesn't give us a tidy theology of the work of the Holy Spirit! 'Thinking clearly' requires us to accept the paradox and the mystery, rather than producing neat packages wrapped up to be repeated in future generations!

It is also interesting to note the reaction of Barnabas

and Paul to the crowd's adulation: 'Men, why are you doing this? We too are only men, human like you. We are bringing you good news, telling you to turn from these worthless things to the living God, who made heaven and earth and sea and everything in them' (Acts 14:15).

'We are only men, human like you!' How different from Jesus (Luke 5:8; 17:16; John 9:38) who allows Peter and others to fall at his feet in an attitude of worship and awe.

Philippi (Acts 16)

In Philippi, Paul has a dramatic encounter with the slave girl who has a spirit of divination. We shall discover the present reality of these sort of occult powers later (see especially Chapter 8, questions 17 and 18). It is interesting that the spirit spoke the truth: 'These men are servants of the most high God.' This was also the case in the Gospel stories of deliverance (Mark 1:24 for instance), and can be the case today. What amazes me is Paul's patience! Paul allowed her to continue for many days!

A spiritual battle   The actual prayer of deliverance was a simple, clear command, delivered in the name of Jesus. The girl's power to foretell the future was removed, her owners were furious, all hell broke out and, hopefully, the girl joined the company of the believers. The result of the furore was the imprisonment of Paul and Silas. We might say that 'hell hath no fury like a demon defeated'. Despite the amazing conversion of the gaoler, Paul's ministry in Philippi was finished. The magistrates apologised for Paul's false imprisonment and punishment, but persuaded him to leave the city. Nevertheless, Paul left behind a flourishing church which, judging by his epistle to the Philippians, continued to prosper. Once again a simple display of spiritual power, this time combined with the sign of the earthquake, led to considerable spiritual results.

Athens (Acts 17:16–34)

Paul only visited Athens for a few days, while waiting for Silas and Timothy to join him after the conflicts in Berea (Acts 17:15). Luke, nevertheless, recorded his visit in great detail. Attempted evangelism took place on an intellectual level. Paul debated current philosophical issues with the Athenians, and all was quite friendly until he mentioned judgement and the resurrection.

For our purposes, it is interesting that there is no real spiritual battle, no signs and wonders, and few conversions. There is no record that Paul ever revisited Athens, nor that any church was founded there.

The spiritual opposition in Athens was more subtle and more insidious. Athens was a multicultural city, interested in religion, uninterested in faith. Intellectual pride and gentle sneering at definitive beliefs seemed to mark the Athenian attitude. This, of course, is one of the hardest spiritual climates in which to work. There were no obvious 'powers' to confront, just a subtle, vacuous dismissal of anything which was too definite – all rather reminiscent of parts of Western Europe today.

Ephesus (Acts 19)

Similar encounters took place in Ephesus (Acts 19:11ff).

God did extraordinary miracles through Paul. Handkerchiefs and aprons that had touched him were taken to the sick, and their illnesses were cured and the evil spirits left them. Some Jews who went around driving out evil spirits tried to invoke the name of the Lord Jesus over those who were demon-possessed. They would say, 'In the name of Jesus, whom

Paul preaches, I command you to come out.' Seven sons of Sceva, a Jewish chief priest, were doing this. The evil spirit answered them, 'Jesus I know and Paul I know about, but who are you?' Then the man who had the evil spirit jumped on them and overpowered them all. He gave them such a beating that they ran out of the house naked and bleeding.

(vv.11–16).

Attempted exorcisms by non-Christians   The efforts of the sons of Sceva were highly entertaining. Nevertheless it is an important story. First, it illustrates that Jewish people were willing to attempt exorcisms and recognised the need for such ministry. Secondly, they were quite willing to use the techniques of Paul, and the name of Jesus – even if not yet converted. Thirdly, it shows the power of evil spirits. The supernatural strength of the man with the evil spirit is something that many of us have encountered on occasions. I have a chair in my study that broke when an ex-Marine started to shake as he attempted to renounce his past occult involvement. Fourthly, it shows how the spirits can, on occasions, speak quite clearly and logically.[7] I remember well when Michael Green and I were praying for a Guyanan girl who was showing great signs of demonisation, a spirit suddenly spoke through her saying, 'You lot are a load of amateurs, I'm not leaving!' I'm glad to record that the evil spirit proved somewhat inaccurate in its predictions, and departed swiftly after we had prayed.

This failed exorcism, perhaps provoked by Paul's success, proved the key event in Ephesus. Once again, the true power was seen to be wielded by the Apostles' preaching and praying in the name of Jesus. The immediate result was much repentance (v.18), the celebrated bonfire (v.19), and the word of the Lord prevailing (v.20). We shall see later[8] the importance of destroying objects that have been used in any form of witchcraft. The citizens of Ephesus have set us an important precedent which we would do well to heed.

However, behind all this magic and sorcery lay a stranger, more sinister force. The goddess Artemis, not the harmless huntress of Roman mythology but the ancient mother goddess of Asia Minor whose temple was one of the seven wonders of the ancient world, was a formidable opponent. Her cult, presided over by many eunuchs and three grades of priestesses was, according to one writer,[9] 'of unsurpassed cosmic power'. She was called 'Saviour', 'Lord', and 'Queen of the Cosmos', and she possessed an authority and power superior to astrological fate. Small wonder that her cult drove many to magic and sorcery, and employed others in making silver shrines.

This encounter did much to establish a church with a powerful spiritual base. It is no coincidence that Paul wrote a great deal about spiritual powers in his epistle to the Ephesians. Nevertheless, the power of Artemis was not broken, only bruised. The subsequent riot, led by the silversmiths, again forced Paul to retreat, and by the time the Revelation of St John was written, the church's light was waning (Revelation 2:1-7). Later, of course, it was extinguished as the province of Asia turned to Islam.

Troas (Acts 20:1-12)

Paul's next major recorded miracle was at Troas where the unfortunate Eutychus fell asleep while Paul 'talked on and on'. There is a certain similarity with Elijah's raising of the widow's son (1 Kings 17:17ff). In each case, the great men were associated with a tragic death

– Elijah by his presence with the family, and Paul by his lengthy preaching. In each case God heard their prayer with a singular miracle.

Malta (Acts 28:1–10)

It is sometimes remarked 'that there is much less healing in the latter part of the Acts'. That is perfectly true, but if you look at the circumstances, the remaining chapters contain little except Paul's arrest, trials and dangerous sea voyages. However, there is considerable miraculous work by the Holy Spirit (see Acts 20:22f; 21:4–6, 10–12; 26:9; 27:10, 23–26, 34) and a final burst of healing activity on the island of Malta.

> There was an estate nearby that belonged to Publius, the chief official of the island. He welcomed us to his home and for three days entertained us hospitably. His father was sick in bed, suffering from fever and dysentery. Paul went in to see him and, after prayer, placed his hands on him and healed him. When this happened, the rest of the sick on the island came and were cured. They honoured us in many ways and when we were ready to sail, they furnished us with the supplies we needed.
>
> (Acts 28:7–10)

I once attended a particularly sceptical diocesan healing conference where the speaker made the point about the lack of healing in the latter part of Acts.[10] I challenged him in a later discussion group and quoted the story of Paul in Malta. 'Ah,' he said, with a slightly sickly smile, 'But what does verse 10 say?' I replied, 'They honoured us in many ways and when we were ready to sail, they furnished us with the supplies we needed.' 'And who is meant by "us"?' 'Paul, Luke and his companions,' I said. 'Exactly,' and the smile grew as he stood up to deliver the coup de grace. 'Luke healed them with his herbal remedies!' 'I think the herbal remedies washed overboard in the storm at sea,' I replied. Our speaker left the discussion group without uttering another word.

As so often, Paul's ministry in Malta turned on one event. When the viper came out of the fire and attached itself to his hand (Acts 28:3), the islanders saw this as a simple act of natural justice. When Paul was unharmed, they decided that he was a god. After that, it was quite natural for healings to take place. Doubtless this visit, and the signs that accompanied it, prepared the soil for the gospel to take root in Malta.

Rome (Ats 28:11–end)

Paul had already written to the Roman church. His theological tour de force drew towards its conclusion with some powerful words on a familiar theme.

> Therefore I glory in Christ Jesus in my service to God. I will not venture to speak of anything except what Christ has accomplished through me in leading the Gentiles to obey God by what I have said and done – by the power of signs and miracles, through the power of the Spirit. So from Jerusalem all the way around to Illyricum, I have fully proclaimed the gospel of Christ.
>
> (Romans 15:17–19)

By contrast, the Acts of the Apostles ends with Paul's perplexing encounter with the Jewish leaders in Rome. Paul, somewhat bewildered it seems, quoted (like Jesus in the parable of the sower) Isaiah's prophecy (Isaiah 6:9–10) about spiritual blindness.

As so often, Paul turned his attention to the Gentiles, and preached the kingdom of God 'boldly and without hindrance'. We may find Luke's ending somewhat abrupt, but he has accomplished his task of showing how the gospel, invariably accompanied by signs and wonders, has been preached 'in all Judea and Samaria, and to the ends of the earth' (Acts 1:8).

The deaths of Paul and Peter[11] brought the Church into a very different era, but as we shall see in Chapter 6, it used the same methods, and experienced similar miracles, through the next few centuries.

Conclusion

We might say that the Acts of the Apostles records a long series of power encounters. In Jerusalem, after the initial honeymoon when the Apostles were popular and revered, everything changed following the healing of the lame man. Peter and the Apostles boldly extended their ministry, drawing others, like Stephen, into leadership.

Stephen's martyrdom, as so often happens, merely unleashed a more effective and diverse ministry. The gospel spread into Samaria, under Philip, and into surrounding territory, under Peter. The Gentile harvest began with the conversion of Cornelius, while the most significant consequence was the effect of Stephen's death on Saul of Tarsus (Acts 8:1).

Paul's ministry included notable power encounters in Cyprus, Philippi and Ephesus. Many other places which he visited were also touched by miracles and healings. Athens and perhaps Rome seem to have been the only significant cities where the gospel was preached in a largely intellectual way.

Luke concentrates on the preaching and ministry of the apostolic leaders. There are, however, hints that others were involved. Paul's restoration from near death in Acts 14: 20 must have been accompanied by much prayer from his recent converts. The ministry in Malta led to the whole group being honoured (Acts 28:10) which again suggests that they were all involved in the prayer for the sick on the island.

We now turn from the high drama of Acts to the more theoretical pages of the epistles of Paul and others.

Notes

1. See F.F. Bruce, *The Book of the Acts* (Marshall, Morgan and Scott, 1954), p. 17ff.
2. See chapter 7, for instance.
3. See F.F. Bruce, *op. cit.*, p. 212, note 66.
4. See F.F. Bruce, *op. cit.*, p. 178, notes 23–27.
5. Mark Stibbe, *Thinking Clearly about Renewal* (Monarch, 1998), p. 25.
6. See Peter Wagner, *Warfare Prayer* (Monarch, 1992), p. 69
7. See also p. 33.
8. See p. 345, and Wagner, *op. cit.* chapter 4 throughout.
9. See Wagner, *op. cit.*, p. 97ff.
10. See Acts 18:1–18. Paul ministers in Corinth. No miracles are recorded there (one of the very few cities in Acts where no miracles are written down). However, 2 Corinthians 12:12 makes it plain that the Corinthian church saw plenty of signs and wonders. The church grew there.
11. The death of the leading Apostles caused considerable problems for the Early Church. I Clement, written in AD 96, says that 'sinful jealousy' caused both their deaths (see Section 5 of his letter).

    There is strong archeological evidence to support Peter's martyrdom in Rome. See especially John Walsh, *The Bones of St Peter* (Victor Gollanz, 1983), and Dr Guaducci, *St Pierre Retrouvé*, 1974, for fascinating accounts of this. This is important evidence corroborating the historical spread of the gospel to Rome in the mid first century.

5

Healing and Deliverance in the New Testament Letters

In this chapter, we see that the writers of the New Testament letters expected and experienced a supernatural gospel. We examine Paul's teaching on signs and wonders, his experience of illness, his important understanding of the frailty of the body and the prospect of death. We look at Paul's understanding of the principalities and powers – probably as they affect secular government.

We look briefly at the non-Pauline writings, noting especially the important instructions of the Epistle of James concerning healing.

Healing and Deliverance in
the New Testament Letters

When we turn to the Epistles, we can easily be surprised by the lack of teaching about healing and deliverance – matters which were so prominent, as we have just seen, in the Gospels and Acts.

We need to remember that most of the Epistles were written *earlier* than the Gospels and Acts. Healing and exorcism were part and parcel of the experience of the new churches. The famous comment of Papias (c. AD 60–130) is important. Writing about the Gospels, he comments: 'Mark, having become interpreter of St Peter, set down accurately, though not in order, everything he remembered of the words and actions of the Lord.' In other words, Mark wrote his Gospel based mainly on the preaching of Peter in Rome. What did Peter preach about? It must have been mainly the parables and sayings of Jesus, combined with a considerable sprinkling of healing and deliverance stories. If that is so, it is scarcely surprising that Peter, and by implication, Paul and John, see little need to refer to them in their letters. Their letters are concerned with practical problems in Christian

134

living, right doctrine in the light of the cross and resurrection – the 'signs and wonders' can be left to the spoken word and the testimony of the living experience of the believers!

What is clear is that Paul, together with Peter, John, James, Jude and the writers of Hebrews and Revelation, expected and experienced a supernatural gospel. Like one modern writer, they expected 'the supernatural to be natural'.[1] Although there are few references to healing, and none to deliverance, there are many references to the activity of Satan and to aspects of spiritual warfare. Although they don't directly answer the questions to which we would like an answer (see chapter 8), they give us plenty of clues from which to build our theology.

For convenience, we shall turn first to St Paul, and then look at the rest of the New Testament.

The writings of Paul

The lack of many direct references to healing in Paul's epistles still comes as quite a surprise. 'To another faith by the same Spirit, to another gifts of healing by that one Spirit' (1 Corinthians 12:9), is one of just two clear references.

Many commentators regard the miraculous powers (v.10) and the gift of distinguishing between spirits (v.10) as referring to exorcism and related ministries. Paul also includes healing in his list of ministries within the Church. He seems to have expected healing to be part of the ongoing life of the Church.

'And in the church God has appointed first of all apostles, second prophets, third teachers, then workers of miracles, also those having gifts of healing, those able to help others, those with gifts of administration, and those speaking in different kinds of tongues. Are all apostles? Are all prophets? Are all teachers? Do all work miracles? Do all have gifts of healing? Do all speak in tongues? Do all interpret?'

(1 Corinthians 12:28–30)

Paul's teaching on signs and wonders

Paul clearly expects healing to be manifold in the Church, and to be exercised by those who have been given evidence of having received the gift. Elsewhere there are a number of references to signs and miracles which, judging by similar passages in Acts, would undoubtedly include healing and deliverance. In this context, we should note Romans 15:13, and especially Romans 15:19 – 'by the power of signs and miracles, through the power of the Spirit. So from Jerusalem all the way around to Illyricum, I have fully proclaimed the gospel of Christ.'

'Fully' preaching the gospel of Christ could well mean a preaching ministry distinguished by signs and miracles as in Acts 14:3. Anyway, it is clear that Paul is expecting the Roman church to exercise the gifts of the Spirit (Romans 12:3–8) even if the list given, with the notable exception of prophecy, would strike us more as natural gifts being endued with a supernatural quality in contrast to the much more miraculous nature of the list in 1 Corinthians 12. 'My message and my preaching were not with wise and persuasive words, but with a demonstration of the Spirit's power' (1 Corinthians 2:4). Paul's opening salvo to the difficult Corinthian church is clearly designed to place the miraculous workings of the Holy Spirit firmly on his agenda as well as theirs. Later he reminds them of the miracles they have experienced: 'The things that mark an apostle – signs, wonders and miracles

– were done among you with great perseverance' (2 Corinthians 12:12).

Paul longs for the Galatians to remember their
supernatural experiences

The whole tenor of Galatians is the supernatural nature of the gospel. It contains some of Paul's most impassioned words.

> You foolish Galatians! Who has bewitched you? Before your very eyes Jesus Christ was clearly portrayed as crucified. I would like to learn just one thing from you. Did you receive the Spirit by observing the law, or by believing what you heard? Are you so foolish? After beginning with the Spirit, are you now trying to attain your goal by human effort? Have you suffered so much for nothing – if it really was for nothing? Does God give you his Spirit and work miracles among you because you observe the law, or because you believe what you heard?'
>
> (Galatians 3:1–5)

The Galatian church had experienced miracles at the time of its founding, and clearly Paul is wanting this to continue – with or without his personal presence. There is no suggestion that the miracles were needed to establish the Christian presence, and now are no longer necessary. The basis of Paul's heartfelt writing is that the Galatians should not revert to a sterile synthesis of law and grace, but rather be led by the Spirit and return to the original gospel of conversions, signs and wonders that he and Barnabas had presented to them.

The letter to the Ephesians contains many references to spiritual warfare (especially Ephesians 6:10–20, and also Ephesians 1:21f; 2:2, and 3:10), and the great prayer of Ephesians 3:14–21 includes: 'Now to him who is able to

do immeasurably more than all we ask or imagine, according to his power that is at work within us' (Ephesians
3:20). It is certainly encouraging them to expect signs
and wonders (how different that verse sounds when
intoned at the end of some impeccably worthy, but dull
sermon!).

*Paul's Epistles demonstrate a considerable openness
to the signs and wonders that accompanied the
giving of the Holy Spirit*

Philippians has one of the great passages on the ultimate
victory of Christ (Philippians 1:21f). Colossians has much
that is of use in spiritual warfare (see below) without
touching the issues of healing and deliverance.

The letters to the Thessalonians have an important
reference to the power that accompanied Paul's preaching (1 Thessalonians 1:5), a clear acceptance of the
importance of prophecy and being open to the Spirit
(1 Thessalonians 5:19– 20). The second letter warns very
clearly about counterfeit signs (2 Thessalonians 2:9),
echoing Jesus' teaching in the Sermon on the Mount
(Matthew 7:22), and the spiritual confusion of the end
times (Matthew 24:24; Mark 13:22). These solemn words
remind us that the evidence of discipleship required is fruit
(Matthew 7:20; Galatians 5:20ff, etc.) not miraculous
powers. Satan is very subtle and will either try and make
the preaching ineffective by discouraging the signs that
should accompany it (Acts 2:43; 14:3; Mark 16:17), or by
causing far worse confusion by counterfeiting them.

Healing accompanied by false means such as spiritism,[2]
will do great harm to the kingdom, while faithful preaching which doesn't expect signs and wonders may be greatly
blessed in other ways.

The pastoral epistles don't have any direct references to

our subject, but three texts are important. 'Do not neglect your gift, which was given you through a prophetic message when the body of elders laid hands on you' (1 Timothy 4:14). 'For God did not give us a spirit of timidity, but a spirit of power, of love and of self-discipline' (2 Timothy 1:7). 'And the things you have heard me say in the presence of many witnesses entrust to reliable men who will also be qualified to teach others' (2 Timothy 2:2).

Paul commends the training of others

The first shows that spiritual gifts were given in response to the prayers of church leaders – and not just the Apostles. The second is a prayer for a lovely triangle of spiritual virtues – power, love, self-control. With all three, the Spirit is really free to move in someone's life; with any of the three missing, there is a dangerous lack of balance. The third is a crucial task for the continuation of ministry. Just as Jesus trained the seventy, as well as the twelve, so here Paul teaches a true apostolic succession. With the teaching we would expect a continuation of the signs and wonders that authenticated apostolic preaching. If the Apostles needed this confirmation, how much more do their less gifted successors!

What is interesting, and important for our clear thinking, is the number of references to illness in Paul's writings.

St Paul and illness

Paul's illness a blessing to the Galatians   There are five texts which refer to illness in the Epistles. Two concern Paul (Galatians 4:12- 16 and 2 Corinthians 11), and three of his friends Epaphroditus (Philippians 2:25–30),

Timothy (1 Timothy 5:23) and Trophimus (2 Timothy 4:20). There is also a positive reference to medicine where Paul refers to Luke as 'the beloved physician' (Colossians 4:14). Of these, the most interesting, and least commented on, is the Galatian text. Here Paul says that his illness brought great blessing to the Galatians. Because of it, he was able to reach them and bring them under the sound of the gospel. The Greek phrase ασθενιαν της σαρκος is open to several translations, but nearly all commentators, except those whose theological views do not allow for the possibility of an illness bringing blessing, accept that here the correct meaning of the word is physical illness. The text suggests that the illness was serious, and hints that it may have been an unpleasant eye condition: 'What happened to all your joy? I can testify that, if you could have done so, you would have torn out your eyes and given them to me' (Galatians 4:15).

What is important is that Paul recognises that once again his physical weakness, and the frustration of his plans (cf. Romans 1:13) were used by God for his purposes. Nowhere does he support the view that 'illness is my cross', equally he doesn't support the view that 'good health is always God's intention'.

In 2 Corinthians 12, Paul gives us a great insight into his own spiritual life. Not only does he tell us of his amazing revelation (vv.1–4), but he also writes at length about the 'thorn in my flesh' (v.7) which was not removed despite pleading prayer.

Paul's celebrated thorn The incident of Paul's thorn has been much discussed. Michael Green says the majority of commentators see this as a physical ailment. Some, mainly of a Pentecostal persuasion, are unwilling to see this as a physical problem. For some, the thorn must be a purely spiritual attack, otherwise the whole theology of God's willingness to heal is fatally wounded.

One book that I read years ago even came up with the masterly statement that if Paul had more faith it would have been removed – which, of course, directly conflicts with 2 Corinthians 12:9.

From time to time, people use Paul's thorn as a reason not to seek healing. In the light of 2 Corinthians 12:7 – 'To keep me from becoming conceited because of these surpassingly great revelations, there was given me a thorn in my flesh, a messenger of Satan, to torment me' – this seems either rather spiritually arrogant or somewhat foolish. Can anyone else realistically claim to have had this level of revelation?

Illness of Epaphroditus, Timothy and Trophimus
Epaphroditus' serious illness is difficult to comment on. We don't know enough of the circumstances. Obviously, Paul and others prayed for him, whether they laid hands upon him and whether his recovery was natural or supernatural we cannot know. At all events, the incident serves to remind us that Christians are not, and were not, even in those halcyon days of the Early Church, immune from life-threatening illness. Timothy, who seems to have been a rather frail young man, is given practical advice not to drink too much of the local water. This can serve as a simple reminder that we need to take all obvious precautions to avoid illness, and not to expect divine immunity from the natural problems that surround us!

Trophimus' illness was one of the inconveniences that Paul had to face during his final imprisonment, at least he was supported by Luke, whose herbal remedies were perhaps of help. (see p. 128).

A mysterious text   Finally, in this section, we must consider one of Paul's most perplexing statements: 'Now I
rejoice in what was suffered for you and I fill up in my
flesh what is still lacking in regard to Christ's afflictions
for the sake of his body, which is the church' (Colossians
1:24).

What does Paul mean? We can be certain that he didn't
mean that the atonement (the affect of Christ's death) was
in any way incomplete!

But could he be referring to the sufferings of himself
and others, especially in the ministry of healing and deliverance? We have already seen (see p. 97) that the healing
ministry of Jesus was very costly, and in a real sense
foreshadowed the greater suffering of Calvary. Paul's
own experiences, particularly in Philippi (Acts 16) where
his ministry was painfully curtailed after the exorcism of
the slave girl, and also in Lystra where the healing of the
lame man led to complete misunderstanding and then to a
narrow escape from death (v.20) suggests to me that the
disciples gathered in prayer around Paul, and that he was
then completely restored in health after a very unpleasant
experience.

The theology is that the risen Christ, in Paul, suffers –
just as the risen Christ on the Damascus road (Acts 9: 4)
says, 'Saul, Saul, why do you persecute *me*?' (my italics).
As Christ suffers within the wounded healer, so the
prophecy of the suffering servant (see p. 96f) is further
fulfilled.

Earthly frailty and the heavenly vision

Therefore we do not lose heart. Though outwardly we are
wasting away, yet inwardly we are being renewed day by day.
For our light and momentary troubles are achieving for us an
eternal glory that far outweighs them all. So we fix our eyes

not on what is seen, but on what is unseen. For what is seen is temporary, but what is unseen is eternal.

Now we know that if the earthly tent we live in is destroyed, we have a building from God, an eternal house in heaven, not built by human hands. Meanwhile we groan, longing to be clothed with our heavenly dwelling, because when we are clothed, we will not be found naked. For while we are in this tent, we groan and are burdened, because we do not wish to be unclothed, but to be clothed with our heavenly dwelling, so that what is mortal may be swallowed up by life. Now it is God who has made us for this very purpose, and has given us the Spirit as a deposit, guaranteeing what is to come.'

(2 Corinthians 4:16–5:5)

Paul's great hope   Nowhere does Paul encourage the view that 'death is the ultimate healing' – he has a much more positive view! Death is to be looked forward to, to be embraced with courage and joy. It is the best state. After death, we are fully with Christ – the trials, fears and tribulations of this world are thrust away.

Paul writes on this theme elsewhere – notably in Philippians 1:20–26 and 2 Timothy 4:6–8. He is not presumptuous, realising that he, himself, and other leaders could fail to finish the race. 'No, I beat my body and make it my slave so that after I have preached to others, I myself will not be disqualified for the prize' (1 Corinthians 9:27).

Nevertheless, his life and writing are full of his living hope. Despite warning prophetic words, he is determined to go to Jerusalem.

After we had been there a number of days, a prophet named Agabus came down from Judea. Coming over to us, he took Paul's belt, tied his own hands and feet with it and said, 'The Holy Spirit says "In this way the Jews of Jerusalem will bind the owner of this belt and will hand him over to the Gentiles."' When we heard this, we and the people there pleaded with Paul not to go up to Jerusalem. Then Paul answered, 'Why are you weeping and breaking my heart? I am ready not only to be bound, but also to die in Jerusalem for the name of the Lord Jesus.' When he would not be dissuaded, we gave up and said, 'The Lord's will be done.'

(Acts 21:10–14)

Paul knew that the mystery of his life and his death were in the Lord's hands. He was fully able to trust the Lord who had called him so dramatically.

Paul's understanding of our human frailty   It is often said that Christians should die in ripe old age, falling to the ground with minimal suffering like a ripe apple. This sort of theology causes great difficulty to those who suffer from long and debilitating illnesses like some cancers, multiple sclerosis, and motor neurone disease. Paul's teaching about the 'earthly tent wearing out' (2 Corinthians 5:1) should help us to avoid such insensitivity which can cause great grief, especially to the relatives of God's people undergoing much suffering.

Just as Jesus (see chapter 3, p. 99) has a robust theology of accident, so has Paul of illness and death. The important thing is that ultimately we are in God's hands.

The Lord who says, 'I bring prosperity and create disaster' (Isaiah 45:7) also says, 'Even to your old age and grey hairs I am he, I am he who will sustain you . . . and I will rescue you' (Isaiah 46:4). We have a glorious future, and a wonderful present, provided that we will learn 'to live by faith and not by sight' (2 Corinthians 5:7). We may not understand the mysteries of illness, we may fear the pains of death, but we can be supremely confident 'that he who began a good work in you will carry it on to completion until the day of Christ Jesus' (Philippians 1:6).

If healing doesn't feature over much in Paul's writings, we now turn to spiritual warfare which certainly does!

Deliverance and spiritual warfare in the epistles

Main texts on spiritual warfare   While there are no simple texts on deliverance (how to recognise, or how to deal with the problem), there is much on spiritual warfare. Paul mentions Satan on a number of occasions: Romans 16:20; 1 Corinthians 5:5; 7:5; 2 Corinthians 2:11; 11:3; 12:7; 1 Thessalonians 2:18; 2 Thessalonians 2:9; 1 Timothy 1:20; 5:15).

Of these, perhaps the key text for our purposes is 'in order that Satan might not outwit us. For we are not unaware of his schemes' (2 Corinthians 2:11). This shows that Paul saw his ministry as being engaged in a major spiritual battle with the power of Satan and his minions. Of course, the ultimate defeat of Satan and his powers was assured by the cross. 'And having disarmed the powers and authorities, he made a public spectacle of them, triumphing over them by the cross' (Colossians 2:15).

But the battle continues. It continues in the heavenly places, which is the main theme of the final book of the Bible, and it continues in individual lives. The ministry of deliverance that Paul accomplished for the slave girl in Philippi (Acts 16: 18) and in Ephesus (Acts 19: 11–20), undoubtedly continued in the New Testament Church. Certainly the problem of Satan and his messengers hadn't disappeared, and neither had the means of overcoming it.

Peter on spiritual warfare The powers and authorities may have been disarmed by the victory at Calvary, but they continued to need to be defeated in each individual person in whom they had obtained a serious foothold. Peter has an important word on this theme: 'Be self-controlled and alert. Your enemy the devil prowls around like a roaring lion looking for someone to devour. Resist him, standing firm in the faith, because you know that your brothers throughout the world are undergoing the same kind of sufferings' (1 Peter 5:8–10).

Peter knew that the evil powers needed to be resisted, he also had experience of dealing with them (Acts 5:15–16). He would have expected this work to continue until the final surrender of Satan and his troops.

To return to Paul, he recognises Satan sometimes as an angel of light (2 Corinthians 11: 14), he is not ignorant of his devices, and curiously he sometimes hands sinners over to him – apparently for their ultimate spiritual good. This probably means that they were excluded from the Christian community until they showed the fruits of repentance. 'Hand this man over to Satan, so that the sinful nature may be destroyed and his spirit saved on the day of the Lord' (1 Corinthians 5:5). 'Among them are Hymenaeus and Alexander, whom I have handed over to Satan to be taught not to blaspheme' (1 Timothy 1:20).

Whatever else we may conclude from these two pastoral incidents, there is no suggestion of any sort of prayer of deliverance in either case.

Paul on the problems of the flesh The New Testament (see Romans 7, Galatians 5:16–26, and many other places) gives a high profile to the problem that all Christians face – the flesh, that part of our nature that remains in persistent rebellion against the Spirit. 'I know that nothing good lives in me, that is, in my sinful nature. For I have the desire to do what is good, but I cannot carry it out' (Romans 7:18).

Here the great Apostle is writing, as nearly all agree, about his state as a mature Christian believer, and he highlights the battle. He would like to live in the freedom of Romans 8:

> Because those who are led by the Spirit of God are sons of God. For you did not receive a spirit that makes you a slave again to fear, but you received the Spirit of sonship. And by him we cry, 'Abba, Father'. The Spirit himself testifies with our spirit that we are God's children. Now if we are children, then we are heirs – heirs of God and co-heirs with Christ, if indeed we share in his suffering in order that we may also share in his glory. I consider that our present sufferings are not worth comparing with the glory that will be revealed in us.'
>
> (Romans 8:14–17)

But he is frequently burdened by the flesh (Romans 7), and physical ailments. However, that doesn't mean that he needs prayer for deliverance! I say this because some writers give the impression (while often proclaiming that they don't mean this!) that it is normal for Christians to be demonised. For example: '"Where, Lord?" they asked. He replied, "Where there is a dead body, there the vultures will gather"' (Luke 17:37).

One well-known speaker sees the vultures as evil spirits gathering around the carcasses of the spiritually dead. Thus, after conversion, as well as facing the problem of the flesh, it is normal to need deliverance – a process which in such circles often goes on and on and never seems to finish. This is not only erroneous, it is very dangerous, leading vulnerable Christians to be dependent on spiritual gurus and also leading people to suppose that their bad temper, impatience or dubious sexual thoughts can be exorcised – whereas the New Testament would expect them to be dealt with by repentance, self-control and the growing harvest of the Holy Spirit.

St Paul and spiritual warfare

The spiritual powers behind secular authorities   One of the key New Testament words is εξουσια (power). It can refer to secular power, spiritual power or to power in the heavenly places. A very important text is Romans 13:1 – 'Everyone must submit himself to the governing authorities, for there is no authority except that which God has established. The authorities that exist have been established by God.'

Here we would naturally think that Paul is referring to secular power, and the text causes some difficulty, not least when contrasted with the writer of Revelation's view of secular authority (Revelation 13, especially), and Paul's own rather negative view of the secular judiciary (1 Corinthians 6:1–6). Cullmann[3] notes that in this passage, as in Ephesians 3:10 and Colossians 1:16, Paul uses the plural, εξουσιαι. He argues that this plural usage definitely refers to angelic powers that stand behind the state government. These powers are, like Satan (Revelation 20:2), bound, but allowed a considerable measure of independence.

His thesis, and it is really important for an understanding of spiritual warfare, solves the apparent contradiction between Romans 13 and Revelation 13. He acknowledges that the 'powers' behind human governments may, or may not be, demonic. These angelic beings, *created by God*, are ultimately subject to their creator, but have considerable moral freedom in this age. This becomes particularly deadly when rulers, like Hitler, or perhaps Stalin,[4] turn to occult sources for guidance.

The tension between the present and the future, between the 'already fulfilled and the not yet completed', is key to understanding the New Testament not least in the whole area of practical prayer for healing and deliverance.

Even if we don't accept this analysis (and it certainly makes good sense to me, and more importantly, unifies parts of the New Testament where there is apparent division), we cannot deny that Paul is deeply concerned with the problem of the spiritual powers and authorities.

Numerous references (some already cited) include Romans 8:38; Colossians 1:16 and 2:15; Ephesians 1:21; 2:2; 3:10 and 6:12; also 1 Corinthians 2:8 and Titus 3:1 which have the same double meaning (secular and spiritual) which we have already argued for in Romans 13:1. Another vital text is 2 Corinthians 10:3–5:

> For though we live in the world, we do not wage war as the world does. The weapons we fight with are not the weapons of the world. On the contrary, they have divine power to demolish strongholds. We demolish arguments and every pretension that sets itself up against the knowledge of God, and we take captive every thought to make it obedient to Christ.

This is the closest Paul comes to teaching us to take the offensive in the spiritual battle. The only real weapon that we have is prayer, covered by the blood of Christ (the evil powers hate mention of the blood of Christ. It reminds them of their worst strategic mistake, and they have no defence against it), and using the sword of the Spirit (the Bible).

Paul and the true sign of an Apostle   It is notable that in the following chapters Paul sees his greatest enemies as false apostles, his thorn in the flesh, and Satan masquerading as an Angel of Light. He boasts (2 Corinthians 11:30) mainly of his weakness, touching on his deepest spiritual revelation (2 Corinthians 12:3–4), only to return to the theme of weakness. He claims his authority because of 'the things that mark an apostle – signs, wonders and miracles'. The genuineness of them (2 Corinthians 12:12), as opposed to Satan's false signs, is established only because he belongs to Christ (2 Corinthians 10:7), has the truth of Christ (2 Corinthians 11:10), and is a servant of Christ (2 Corinthians 11:23). Christ's power rests on him (2 Corinthians 12:9), that is why he is content to be weak when others want to be strong.

As well as producing false signs, the evil powers produce false doctrine and ethical practice. For example, Paul sees (1 Timothy 4:1) that deceiving spirits and demons will attempt to destroy the doctrinal purity of the Church. Many of the African bishops at the 1998 Lambeth conference[5] clearly felt the same of their liberal Western counterparts, especially when discussing sexual ethics – which, incidentally, was one of the main applications made by Paul in 1 Timothy 4!

Before we sum up this important part of Paul's teaching, we should note that liberal theology which tends to see secular powers such as the World Bank, multinationals, and employers of child labour as demonic, and evangelical-charismatic theology which sees the demonic forces as exercising direct control in these areas, and over particularly horrific governments, reach the same sort of practical conclusion from very different standpoints.

I find that the comment of Origen, though more properly part of the next chapter, particularly helpful.

According to God's laws, no daemon[6] has been allotted control of earthly things. But through their own wickedness, perhaps, they divided among themselves those regions where is not to be found any knowledge of God or the life lived after His will, or where there are many alien to God. Perhaps, on the other hand, as worthy to govern and to punish the wicked, they were appointed by the Logos who administers the universe to rule those who have subjected themselves to evil and not to God.

Origen could really be summing up Paul! There are strong spiritual powers, with territorial authority, but their control depends on the spiritual state of the different regions. This accords well with modern experience (see p. 229ff) where missionaries meet real spiritual power in places untouched by the gospel.

For our purposes, it is sufficient to see that Paul is quite clear there is a major spiritual battle going on beyond our normal vision. This accords well with the teaching of Jesus, the broad canvas of the Old Testament, and the experience of discerning evangelists in today's world. We are not likely to get far in the areas of healing and deliverance if we choose to ignore it. Paul's call to us (Ephesians 6:10f), is to 'be strong in the Lord and in his mighty power', and 'to pray in the Spirit on all occasions'. He does not call us to take the offensive unless, like him, we are confronted by the likes of Elymas, the slave girl in Philippi, or the effects of the spiritual powers of Diana of the Ephesians (see again 2 Corinthians 10:3–5).

We now turn, briefly, to the other New Testament writers.

The non-Pauline writings

The Epistle to the Hebrews shows that the writer's hearers first received a gospel which included the usual signs. 'How shall we escape if we ignore such a great salvation? This salvation, which was first announced by the Lord, was confirmed to us by those who heard him. God also testified to it by signs, wonders and various miracles and gifts of the Holy Spirit distributed according to his will' (Hebrews 2:3–4).

Hebrews 12:12–13, 'Therefore, strengthen your feeble arms and weak knees! "Make level paths for your feet", so that the lame may not be disabled, but rather healed', seems to associate healing with a holy, disciplined, forgiven life, and Hebrews 13:8, 'Jesus Christ is the same yesterday and today and for ever', has often been used to justify the continuation of such gifts in the life of the Church. If Jesus is the same 'today' and 'for ever' as he was 'yesterday' in his lifetime, then we may expect his healing power to be present among us.

A vital text for the Christian healing ministry

James, in his letter, gives us a crucial text on healing:

Is any one of you in trouble? He should pray. Is anyone happy? Let him sing songs of praise. Is any one of you sick? He should call the elders of the church to pray over him and anoint him with oil in the name of the Lord. And the prayer offered in faith will make the sick person well, the

Lord will raise him up. If he has sinned, he will be forgiven. Therefore, confess your sins to each other and pray for each other, so that you may be healed. The prayer of a righteous man is powerful and effective.

(James 5:13–16)

The instructions are very clear. If you are ill, seek help from the leaders of the church, let them pray and await developments. We shall discuss the important question of the need for confession of sin later (see Chapter 8, Question 4). It is true that this instruction is unique, but so is Matthew 28:16–20 in regard to evangelism. Nowhere does Paul exhort others to go out and share the word in the way that he and the other apostles have done, but that hasn't deterred the more faithful members of the Church from obeying Jesus' great commission. Likewise, the lack of other explicit instructions shouldn't deter us from seeking healing prayer *whenever* the need arises.

The prayers of the saints

In this broad sweep through Scripture, we should also note Revelation 5:8. 'And when he had taken it, the four living creatures and the twenty-four elders fell down before the Lamb. Each one had a harp and they were holding golden bowls full of incense, which are the prayers of the saints.'

What does St John mean? The saints here may, perhaps, include the righteous dead. If that is so, then to ask the saints to pray for us may not be as untheological as the Reformed tradition would have us believe. It probably isn't necessary, it may not be desirable, but just as Jesus often did very strange things to help the faith of those whom he healed, so such prayer, if permissible, might be encouraged to help the prayers of those who are too modest to think that their own efforts can accomplish much.[7]

The book of Revelation has many references to spiritual warfare, some of which can be taken dangerously out of context. In particular 'the number of the Beast' (Revelation 13:18) has led some churches to see credit cards, etc., as the work of the devil. What is clear from this strange book is that the battle is essentially spiritual. The persecution of the Church, as in AD 90 under Domitian, when Revelation was probably written, is the work of the 'powers' – that is, secular authorities ruled, or were at the very least empowered, by demonic forces.

We should not forget that Revelation has a wonderful vision of heaven – crystal-clear water, trees for the healing of the nations, a celestial city with broad streets, and worship and prayer for the saints to engage in.

We get a foretaste of this when we see people healed, or set free from the dark powers; we need this vision to sustain us on what can be a bruising earthly pilgrimage. In concluding this chapter, we must ask one last theological question.

Did the Apostles expect the ministry of healing and deliverance to continue?

If it wasn't for the fact that many distinguished Christians,[8] and some denominations, take the view that the gifts of the Spirit, and especially healing, ceased at the end of the apostolic age, it would scarcely be necessary to mention it.

Who can exercise these ministries?

In reply, at this stage, we note that Jesus trained a much wider band than the Twelve to heal and to exorcise (Luke 10:1–24), that he didn't object to those outside the band exercising this ministry. '"Teacher," said John, "we saw a man driving out demons in your name and we told him to stop, because he was not one of us." "Do not stop him," Jesus said, "No-one who does a miracle in my name can in the next moment say anything bad about me"' (Mark 9:38–39).

Paul saw the gift of healing as given to many who were not Apostles (1 Corinthians 12:9–12:28), and that although gifts like prophecy will pass away (1 Corinthians 13:8), it will be when perfection comes. Furthermore, James expected the elders of the Church to pray for, and to anoint, the sick (James 5:13–16).

It is difficult to see why such gifts should suddenly cease. Part of their purpose was to confirm the truth of the word preached (Acts 14:3). If that was true in the golden age of Peter and Paul, how much more necessary would it be in later years! As we shall see in the next chapter, many of the brightest exponents of the Christian faith experienced, and welcomed, this ministry. If they were all in error (and if the efficacy of such healings is allowed, then by what power did they heal?), then we have serious spiritual problems in the lives of such spiritual giants as Augustine of Hippo and Martin Luther.

It seems to this writer that an unprejudiced reading of the Scripture should lead us to the conclusion that, despite all the problems, and all the potential misuse of power, that Christ expected his disciples not only to fulfil the great commission (Matthew 28:16–20), but to spread his word accompanied by signs and wonders.

Notes

1. Attributed to Jackie Pullinger, author of *Chasing the Dragon*, and renowned for her work among drug addicts in Hong Kong.
2. See chapter 8, questions 17 and 18.
3. Peter Wagner, *Territorial Spirits* (Sovereign World, 1991), especially the last chapter contributed by Oscar Cullmann.
4. See Michael Green, *I believe in Satan's Downfall* (Hodder and Stoughton, 1981), pp. 164–166.
5. A meeting of Anglican bishops held every ten years. Most recently in 1998.
6. Origen, *Contra Celsus*, translated by H. Chadwick (Cambridge University Press, 1965), p. 476. 'Daemon' means a more than earthly power which can be benevolent or hostile.
7. See, for instance, my discussion of the ministry of Brother André and Curé d'Ars in chapter 6, p. 186ff, and 7, p. 215ff.
8. See Benjamin Warfield, *Counterfeit Miracles* (Banner of Truth, 1972), for a classic statement, following Calvin, of the Reformed position on this subject.

6

The Witness of the Church (AD 100–1900)

In this chapter we see how healing and deliverance; practised by many Christians, not just well-known leaders, helped evangelise the Roman Empire. We look at the early history of the British church through the eyes of a great historian, and we see how some of the Protestant leaders, after the Reformation, still expected and prayed for healing.

The Witness of the Church (AD 100–1900)

The life and witness of the Church through two millennia has been somewhat erratic. Periods of great growth, often under intense persecution, have been intermingled with times of darkness, stagnation, complacency. At times the Church has looked for political power, at others it has sided with the poor and the oppressed. There have been periods of division and controversy. Recently, despite the obvious weakness of Western Christendom, there have been welcome signs of growing unity, evangelism, and many reported signs and wonders.

Throughout the centuries, the work of healing and deliverance has carried on, at times burning with an almost apostolic brightness, sometimes nearly extinguished. In this chapter we shall look at some of the best-known examples, pointing the way to others via the notes. We shall look at the Early Fathers, the witness of Bede, the post-Reformation period, and a Catholic saint. We shall leave the expansive healing ministry of the twentieth century for a separate chapter.

The Early Fathers (c.100–500)

Our first witness, Quadratus, writing c.125, knew people healed by Jesus. He provides independent evidence of the healing power of Jesus, and its long-term effect.

> But the works of our Saviour were always present, for they were true, those who were cured, those who rose from the dead, who not merely appeared as cured and risen, but were constantly present, not only while the Saviour was living, but even for some time after he had gone, so that some of them survived even to our own time.[1]

The witness of Justin (c.100–165)

Our next witness, Justin Martyr, has a number of reported comments which suggests that the deliverance ministry was common in the Early Church. This is because demons were associated with pagan gods, and especially with food sacrificed to them (1 Corinthians 8 & 10:14–22). Exorcism, perhaps even more than healing, asserted the Lordship of Christ in a multi-faith world.

> For numberless demoniacs throughout the whole world and in your city, many of our Christian men, exorcising them in the name of Jesus Christ, who was crucified under Pontius Pilate, have healed, and do heal, rendering helpless and driving the possessing devils out of the men, though they could not be cured by all the other exorcists and those who used incantations and drugs.[2]

The often-repeated assertion that such demons will not yield to prayers in the name of others is important – exorcism is a powerful witness in the Early Church evangelism. Justin also shows that the ministry of healing and deliverance was exercised by many Christians, not just the famous leaders.

Iranaeus of Lyons (c.130-200)

Irenaeus of Lyons is another early witness. He was a distinguished theologian, pastor, and possibly a martyr. Iranaeus makes a strong distinction between Christian miracles and signs performed by occult means (see 2 Thessalonians 2:9).[3]

> In the course of a long discussion on this subject, he says, 'Those who are in truth Christ's disciples, receiving grace from him, do in his name perform miracles . . . Some do really and truly cast out demons, with the result that those who have been cleansed from evil spirits frequently believe in Christ and join themselves to the Church. Others still, heal the sick by laying their hands upon them, and they are made whole . . . it is not possible to name the number of the gifts which the Church throughout the world has received from God, in the name of Jesus Christ, who was crucified under Pontius Pilate, and which she exercises day by day for the benefit of the Gentiles . . . Nor does she perform anything by means of angelic invocations, or by incantations, or by any other wicked or curious art; but by directing her prayers to the Lord, who made all things, in a pure, sincere and straightforward spirit, and calling on the name of our Lord Jesus Christ, she has been accustomed to work miracles for the advantage of mankind.' In contrast to the partial or temporary cures effected by Gnostics and pagan magicians, the cures effected by this reliance on the name of the Lord Jesus Christ are, he claims, both permanent and complete.

Tertullian (160–220)

Tertullian, writing at the end of the second century, gives the impression that such occurrences were still common. He challenges his readers:

Hitherto it has been merely a question of words. Now for a test case, now for a proof that 'gods' and 'demons' are simply different names for the same thing. Let someone be brought before your judgment seats who is plainly demon possessed. Bidden to speak by any Christian whatsoever, that spirit will confess he is a demon, just as frankly as elsewhere he has falsely asserted he is a god.[4]

He also writes:

For the clerk of one of them who was liable to be thrown upon the ground by an evil spirit was set free from his affliction, as was also the relative of another, and the little boy of a third. And how many men of rank, to say nothing of common people, have been delivered from devils and healed of disease.[5]

I find Tertullian's first quoted comment particularly significant. He believes, like Justin, that any Christian could challenge the demons – it was not just a ministry for the especially gifted.

Minucius Felix, writing perhaps at the beginning of the third century, gives a graphic description of demons tearing people's bodies, 'driven out by words of exorcism and the fire of prayer'. They left their victims 'reluctantly, in misery, they quail and quake'.[6] All this is certainly in agreement with the Gospels (see Mark 1:26 for instance).

Clement of Alexandria (c.150–215)

Clement of Alexandria gives simple and dignified instructions for visiting the sick. He also gives the impression that this ministry was to be undertaken by the body of Christ and not some spiritual élite. 'Let them, therefore, with fasting and prayer, make their intercessions, and not with the well arranged and fitly ordered words of learning, but as men who have received the gift of healing confidently, to the glory of God.'[7] Fasting was clearly important in the Early Church.

Origen (c.185–254)

Origen is another towering witness to the power of exorcism and healing in the name of Jesus. He makes much of this in his celebrated work *Contra Celsus*.

> So far, indeed, are we from serving daemons, that by prayers and formulas from the holy scriptures we even drive them out of human souls and from places where they have established themselves, and sometimes even from animals. For frequently the daemons effect some device for the injury of these as well.[8]

> If the Pythian priestess is out of her senses and has not control of her faculties when she prophesies, what sort of spirit must we think it which poured darkness upon her mind and rational thinking? Its character must be like that of the race of daemons which many Christians drive out of people who suffer from them, without any curious magical art or sorcerer's device, but with prayer alone and very simple adjurations and formulas such as the simplest person could use. For generally speaking, it is the uneducated people who do this kind of work. The power in the word of Christ shows the worthlessness and weakness of the daemons, for it is not necessary to have a wise man who is competent in the rational proof of the faith in order that they should be defeated and yield to expulsion from the soul and body of a man.[9]

He, too, also makes the point that this work can be done by the simplest of believers! He writes in similar terms of healing.

Some display evidence of having received some miraculous power because of this faith (in Jesus), shown in the people they cure, upon those who need healing they use no other invocation than that of the supreme God and of the name of Jesus, together with the history about him. By these also we have seen many delivered from serious ailments, and from natural distractions and madness, and countless other diseases, which neither men nor daemons had cured.[10]

Healing was very simple, performed in the name of Jesus, by gifted believers.

Many other writers in this era repeat the same theology. Green[11] mentions Tatian, Cyprian and the Apostolic Constitutions. Hippolytus, in the apostolic tradition,[12] makes the point that if someone in the laity seeking ordination has already 'received a gift of healing by a revelation', it is unnecessary to lay hands upon him! Clearly, such gifts were sufficiently common towards the end of the second century for advance guide-lines to be laid down.

Apostolic Constitutions

The whole witness of these early years is summed up in the Apostolic Constitutions.[13]

These gifts were first bestowed upon us, the apostles, when we were about to preach the Gospel to every creature, and afterwards it was necessarily provided to those who had now come to faith through our agency, not for the advantage of those who perform them, but for the conviction of unbelievers, that those whom the word did not persuade, the power of signs might put to shame.

The primary purpose of these signs was, as ever, to advance the cause of the kingdom, and to help evangelism.

Origen on territorial spirits

Origen[14] also concedes that there are places where the daemons (p. 151) exercise considerable spiritual power, especially 'supposed holy places' where curious spells were used when they were originally set up. Most importantly, as we have also seen in the last chapter, Origen also saw the real possibility of daemons controlling whole regions of the universe to rule 'those who have subjected themselves to evil.'

Gregory the Wonderworker (c.213–270)

This is extraordinarily interesting. Cullmann, writing in the twentieth century, takes a similar view of the possibility of whole regions being under demonic control. One of Origen's most famous pupils certainly took this very seriously. Gregory the Wonderworker effectively evangelises a whole area by first leaving a demon in a heathen temple stripped of his power. (See p. 229 for a similar twentieth century story.) This leads to the conversion of the temple warden, who becomes Gregory's first convert and eventual successor as bishop. Later, Gregory performed an exorcism on a youth with the memorable words, 'Not I is it that commands you, but Christ who flung you with the swine into the sea: Quit this youth!' As the demon heard the name of the divine majesty, he cried out loudly saying, 'Alas for me, for Jesus! Alas for me, on account of his disciple.' At the end of all this, in a region where there had been only a handful of Christians, there were only a few left unconverted.[15] Once again, the most effective evangelism was preceded by spiritual warfare which released *both buildings and people* from demonic control.

This familiar link between spiritual warfare and successful evangelism was repeated many times in the annals of the Early Church.[16]

We now turn to two even more remarkable witnesses.

St Martin of Tours (336–397)

St Martin had the benefit of a contemporary biographer, Sulpicius Severus (363–420). Sulpicius was a successful lawyer, but after the death of his wife, he retired into solitude as a monk, and was greatly influenced by St Martin.

Biography of St Martin by Sulpicius Severus

The comment of *The Oxford Dictionary of the Christian Church* is interesting.[17]

> The most famous of his extant writings are his 'Chronicle' (finished c.403) and the 'Life of St Martin', written during the lifetime of the saint, but published only some time after his death. The former, written in elegant and easy Latin, is a summary of sacred history from the creation of the world to AD 400, intended as a textbook for educated Christian readers. It shows remarkable critical sense and is an important source especially for the history of Priscillianism. The 'Life of St Martin', on the other hand, which is inspired by deep devotion to its hero, suffers from credulousness and inordinate prevalence of the miraculous element. It became at once extremely popular and a much imitated model of mediaeval hagiography.

The sceptical comment on the 'Life of St Martin' seems to reflect rather more on the theological prejudices of the unnamed writer than on the truthfulness of Sulpicius. If he showed such good critical sense in one writing, why dismiss the other?

Rex Gardner[18] is rather more perceptive. His comments

on St Martin's wide influence, and the trick by which he was consecrated Bishop of Tours, speak volumes for his reputation – not least in the area of healing.

> The leprosy settlement of Kumi lies deep in the bush, and is not unlike many others in East and West Africa. However, we were surprised and intrigued to find that its mud-and-thatch church was dedicated to St Martin of Tours. Why should a twentieth century group of Ugandan Christians have as their patron saint a monk-bishop who lived in fourth century Gaul?
>
> The choice was made by the patients who no doubt identified themselves with the poor man destitute of clothing whose pleas for help were disregarded by other bystanders, but who was befriended by Martin, then a young cavalryman in the Roman army. He divided his cloak in two, gave one half to the man and wrapped the remaining half round himself. That night he had a vision of Christ arrayed in the part of the cloak he had given to the beggar, and heard him announce to the angels, 'Martin, who is still a catechumen, clothed me in this robe.'

Leaving the army he became a monk and acquired a reputation as a healer, a holy man whose prayers carried weight in the court of heaven. His election as a bishop was achieved by a hoax. His reluctance was well known, so a citizen of Tours was sent with a story about his wife being very ill. When Martin arrived in Tours, a mob crowded around him and insisted on his immediate consecration!

It is good, too, to have first-hand details of some of the famous miracles.[19]

> Moreover, the gift of accomplishing cures was so largely possessed by Martin, that scarcely any sick person came to him for assistance without being at once restored to health.

This will clearly appear from the following example. A certain girl at Treves was so completely prostrated by a terrible paralysis that for a long time she had been quite unable to make use of her body for any purpose, and being, as it were, already dead, only the smallest breath of life seemed still to remain in her. Her afflicted relatives were standing by, expecting nothing but her death, when it was suddenly announced that Martin had come to that city. When the father of the girl found that such was the case, he ran to make a request on behalf of his all but lifeless child. It happened that Martin had already entered the church. There, while the people were looking on, and in the presence of many other bishops, the old man, uttering a cry of grief, embraced the saint's knees and said, 'My daughter is dying of a miserable kind of infirmity; and what is more dreadful than death itself, she is now alive only in the spirit, her flesh being already dead before the time. I beseech thee to go to her and give her thy blessing; for I believe that through you she will be restored to health.' Martin, troubled by such an address, was bewildered and shrank back, saying that this was a matter not in his own hands; that the old man was mistaken in the judgment he had formed; and that he was not worthy to be the instrument through whom the Lord should make a display of his power. The father, in tears, persevered in still more earnestly pressing the case, and entreated Martin to visit the dying girl. At last, constrained by the bishops standing by to go as requested, he went down to the home of the girl. An immense crowd was waiting at the doors to see what the servant of the Lord would do. And first, betaking himself to his familiar arms in affairs of that kind, he cast himself down on the ground and prayed. Then gazing earnestly upon the ailing girl, he requests that oil should be given him. After he had received and blessed this, he poured the powerful sacred liquid into the mouth of the girl, and immediately her voice returned to her. Then gradually, through contact with him, her limbs began, one by one, to recover life till, at last, in the presence of the people, she arose with firm steps.

It is interesting that St Martin poured the healing oil in the girl's mouth! His ministry was widespread. Even as an old man, he evangelised the Gauls, mainly through exorcisms and healing. We can be grateful to Sulpicius for his lengthy biography. There is nothing in it (contra *The Oxford Dictionary of the Christian Church*!) which has not been experienced in most other centuries.

Elsewhere things were getting a little more formal. Apostolic Constitutions[20] (c.350) gives instruction as follows: 'Do thou now sanctify this water and this oil through Christ in the name of him that offered, or of her that offered, and give to these things a power of producing health and driving away diseases, of putting to flight demons and of dispersing every snare through Christ our hope.'

While earlier, St Macarius is recorded as effecting a cure by persistent anointing.[21]

> But at the time that we were there with St Macarius, there was brought to him from Thessalonica a noble and wealthy virgin who during many years had been suffering from paralysis. And when she had been presented to him, and had been thrown down before the cell of the blessed man, he, being moved with compassion for her, with his own hands anointed her during twenty days with holy oil, pouring out prayers for her to the Lord, and so sent her back, cured, to her own city.

Oil was an important 'sign' of the Spirit's activity and power. The Early Church remembered that Jesus sent his disciples out to anoint with oil (Mark 6:13ff), and the specific instruction of James (James 5:13f).

Now we must turn to the greatest mind of the Early Church.

St Augustine of Hippo (354–430)

In his early writings,[22] Augustine wrote that Christians are not to look for the continuation of the healing gift. He assumed that such gifts were no longer needed or available. Then his views changed! His scepticism gave way to belief in the continuing presence of Christ's healing power; and he himself became reluctantly involved

> . . . once I realised how many miracles were occurring in our own day . . . and also how wrong it would be to allow the memory of these marvels of divine power to perish from among our people. It is only two years ago that the keeping of records was begun here in Hippo, and already, at this writing, we have nearly seventy attested miracles.[23]

He gives details of many of these. One of the most exciting is the case of Innocatius, a devout Christian and a leading citizen of Carthage. He was suffering from painful ulcers, and had had several unsuccessful operations for their removal. An eminent surgeon declared that there was no hope except for another operation. But the church had other ideas. Augustine gives a detailed account as follows.[24]

> We then went to pray; and while we were kneeling and prostrating ourselves, as on other occasions, Innocatius also prostrated himself, as if someone had forcibly thrust him down, and began to pray in what manner, with what earnestness, with what emotion, with what a flood of tears, with what agitation of his whole body. I might almost say with what suspension of his respiration by his groans and sobs, who shall attempt to describe? Whether the rest of the party were so little affected as to be able to pray, I knew

not. For my part I could not. This, alone, inwardly and briefly, I said: 'Lord, what prayers of thine own children wilt thou ever grant if thou grant not these? For nothing seemed more possible but that he should die praying. We arose, and after the benediction by the bishop, left him, but not till he had brought them to be with him in the morning, nor till they had exhorted him to calmness. The dreaded day arrived, and the servants of God attended as they had promised. The medical men made their appearance, all things required for such an occasion are got ready, and, amidst the terror and suspense of all present, the dreadful instruments are brought out. In the meantime, while those of the bystanders whose authority was the greatest, endeavoured to support the courage of the patient by words of comfort, he is placed in a convenient position for the operation, the dressings are opened, the seat of the disease is exposed, the surgeon inspects it, and tries to find the part to be operated upon with his instrument in his hand. He first looks for it, then examines by the touch; in a word, he makes every possible trial, and finds the place perfectly healed. The gladness, the praise and thanksgiving to a compassionate and all powerful God which, with mingled joy and tears, now burst from the lips of all present, cannot be told by me. The scene may more easily be imagined than described.'

This lovely story has all the hallmarks of genuine testimony; note especially the prayers, the pleading of St Augustine, the doubts and uncertainties, and the spontaneous joy at the successful conclusion. Medical practitioners today sometimes have similar surprises (see p. 322).

His biographer, Posidius,[25] was a close friend. He records that when Augustine was dying he was visited by a sick friend who asked for the laying on of hands. Augustine, at first, refused on the grounds that he didn't have a personal gift of healing. But the man persisted, and said that he had had a vision, and been told in a dream,

'Go to Bishop Augustine and get him to lay his hands on him, and he will recover.' Augustine responded by doing just that, and the man was healed.

Augustine himself wrote, 'I have been concerned that such accounts should be published because I saw that signs of divine power like those of older days were frequently occurring in modern times.[26]

Michael Green makes a far more cautious comment in the first edition of his *Evangelism in the Early Church*:[27]

Where medical knowledge is so advanced as it is in the West, where 2,000 years of Christian evidences, not to mention the sacred Scriptures, abound to authenticate Jesus' Messiahship, the conditions would appear to be lacking in which we might have a right to expect miracles in the New Testament sense, though we cannot exclude the possibility. However, in missionary areas, where there is only a tiny church in a vast pagan stronghold, where there is a shortage of medical means, where there may be no translations of the Scriptures available, or where the people are as yet illiterate where, furthermore, there are definite spiritual lessons to be reinforced by it – there, on the fringes of the gospel outreach, we have a situation in which we may expect to see God at work in miraculous ways today. That he does so is attested by all the missionary societies working in primitive areas.

After Green's experiences of healing and deliverance (see especially chapter 1 of this book), it is good to know that he, like Augustine, has had to revise his theology in the light of experience! Perhaps this shouldn't surprise us. Christians tend to be modest and cautious, and it is much safer to leave such ministry in the distant age of the Apostles.

A summary of the witness of the Early Fathers

The Early Fathers give an impressive witness to the continuation of the ministry of healing and deliverance long after the days of the Apostles. Indeed, the very strong impression is that many of them saw healing and deliverance as a quite normal part of the Church's witness, and something which ordinary Christians could expect to be involved in.

However, after the dramatic conversion of the Emperor Constantine (c.312), the Church suddenly became respectable, and powerful. The miraculous faded somewhat, and Augustine and Martin are two of the few witnesses to this sort of continued expectation and experience. Ramsay Macmullen[28] concludes his book with a devastating comment about the end of the fourth century:

> Silencing, burning, and destruction, were all forms of theological demonstration; and when the lesson was over, monks and bishops, generals and emperors, have driven the enemy from the field of our vision.

This is in sharp contrast to his eloquent testimony to the importance that healing and deliverance played in spreading the gospel both in the first three centuries of Christendom and thereafter on the missionary frontiers.

Thomas Aquinas (1225–1274) and Pope Gregory X (1210–1276)

Scarcely surprisingly, the Church entered a dark age. Centuries later, Pope Gregory said to the great theologian, Thomas Aquinas, 'The Church can no longer say, "Silver and gold have I none."' Aquinas replied, 'No, nor can she say any longer, "In the name of Jesus of Nazareth rise up and walk."' Riches and respectability had all but extinguished the need for faith and dependence upon God. But in the intervening centuries, the miracles had continued, largely due to the influence of the very spiritual Celtic church.

The witness of Bede

The most famous historian of the early British church was the Venerable Bede (670–735), a holy man who lived his life in various monasteries from the age of seven. His writings were much used on the continent, and give us a real light into the preceding centuries.

Bede was interested in the famous Celtic saints, descendants of St Patrick in Ireland, who evangelised the north of England with a ministry accompanied by many signs and wonders. He was also interested in the evangelism which began in southern England under the Roman missionary Augustine, the first archbishop of Canterbury.

Augustine, too, experienced signs and wonders. So much so that the godly and wise Pope Gregory I (540–604) warned Augustine of the dangers of an authority based on miracles, quoting effectively from the sermon on the mount (Matthew 7:22), and the mission of the seventy (Luke 10:1ff).[29] It seems likely that this caution towards the miraculous, though thoroughly biblical, reflects a change of attitude and expectation in the official Church after the conversion of Constantine.

Bede's writing continues to report a significant number of miracles. The wood of a cross set up by King Oswald (605–642) caused numerous miracles, and others took place at the spot where the godly king was killed,[30] and at his tomb.

This creates quite a theological problem – surely this is just rank superstition and needs to be rejected? Fortunately, or unfortunately, depending on your point of view there is biblical precedent. 'Once while some Israelites were burying a man, suddenly they saw a band of raiders, so they threw the man's body into Elisha's tomb. When the body touched Elisha's bones, the man came to life and stood up on his feet' (2 Kings 13:21). See similarly Acts 5:12–16 and Acts 19:11–12.

Bede also emphasises that Oswald was a great man of prayer, and very generous to the poor. He encouraged the leading missionaries of the day, acting as interpreter for the great Irish missionary Aidan when he preached to the leading members of the king's court.

Miracles in the early Celtic church

Michael Mitton,[31] writing about the Celtic church, emphasises their belief in the miraculous, especially healing. There were many miracles associated with John of Beverley, a contemporary of Bede, one of the most famous of which I have summarised.[32]

In a village, not far away from the oratory near Hexham, where John often stayed for Lent, there lived a youth who was completely dumb, and who also had a problem of being unable to grow hair on his head. John got the lad to visit him, made the sign of the cross on his tongue, and made him say '*gae*', the word for assent and agreement. The boy was able to respond, and gradually learnt the alphabet, and then words, and then sentences. He began to talk a great deal. John sent him to a doctor to be cured of his scabby head. Soon he had a beautiful head of hair, and refusing a place in the bishop's household, went home talking much and rejoicing greatly.

Bede says the record was given by the most reverent and truthful Berhthun, once his deacon and now abbot of Beverley.

Bede[33] also writes about spiritual warfare. He writes about Cedd (c.650) building a monastery in a place of ill repute which he had cleansed by prayer and fasting throughout Lent. Thus the famous monastic site of Lastingham came into being.

Similarly, he records how Cuthbert chose a deserted, barren place where he wished to build a hermitage. First he drove out the evil spirits, then started to cultivate the land, and prayed for water to be provided. Through prayer, the soil previously barren, proved fruitful, and his hermitage became a place of pilgrimage. Eventually he was summoned to become a bishop. He did his uttermost to refuse, but was compelled to come and respond to the call. His life was full of miracles, and after his death they continued at his tomb.

Bede and spiritual warfare

Bede records a number of battles with fire,[34] giving examples of Canterbury and Bamburgh being saved from fire by the prayers of Mellitus, Bishop of London (c.610) and Aidan, Bishop of Lindisfarne (c.645). We will find greater difficulty in accepting his account of how Satan interrupted Cuthbert's evangelism of Melrose, attacking the village with sheets of false fire. Michael Mitton[35] comments that such events are not unknown on the mission field in recent years.

In other places,[36] Bede seems to feel that the local gods were pretty powerless; his record of King Edwin's conversion (627) included the destruction of the heathen altars by Coifi, their chief priest, who apparently decided that the old religion had 'no virtue nor profit in it'. This contrast, spiritual warfare in one place and powerless idols in another, is quite scriptural – compare 1 Corinthians 8:4, 'and an idol is nothing at all', with the many biblical passages on spiritual warfare quoted in chapters 2–6.

Healing after the Reformation

The Reformers reacted strongly against healing as preached in the Catholic Church, opposing such practices as asking the saints to intercede, praying at the tombs of holy men, or worse still, touching their relics. Centuries earlier, Chaucer[37] had had caustic words about 'pigges' bones' in his Prologue to *The Canterbury Tales*. In the Catholic Church, the expectation for miraculous healing also seems to have lessened, although as we shall see, there were notable exceptions.

Calvin, in particular, was strongly opposed saying that 'Satan perverts the things which otherwise would be the works of God and misemploys miracles to obscure God's glory'.[38] He believed[39] that healing following anointing belonged to the miraculous gifts that accompanied the first preaching of the Church, thus he condemned the Roman practice of blessing oil and anointing 'half-dead carcasses' – this was not what was meant by the practice described by James. Such anointing, Calvin commented, was 'a mere hypocritical stage play'.[40]

Luther had a rather different view. The Lutheran historian Seckendorf [41] reports him as saying, 'How often has it happened and still does, that devils have been driven out in the name of Christ, and also by calling on his name in prayer, that the sick have been healed'. Various miracles are recorded. The healing of his Reformation colleague Philip Melanchthon is particularly significant:

> His eyes were set, his consciousness was almost gone, his speech had failed, and also his hearing, his face had fallen, he knew no one, and had ceased to take either solids or liquids. At this spectacle Luther is filled with the utmost consternation, and turning to his fellow travellers says: 'Blessed Lord, how has the devil spoiled me of this instrument!' Then turning away towards the window he called most devoutly on God.

Luther then prays:

> He beseeches God to forbear, saying that he has struck work in order to urge upon him in supplication, with all the promises he can repeat from scripture that he must hear and answer now if he would ever have the petitioner trust in him again.

This daring prayer has echoes of Elijah's prayer (1 Kings 17:26) where he says, 'O Lord my God have you brought tragedy also upon this widow I am staying with, by causing her son to die?'

> After this, taking the hand of Philip, and well knowing what was the anxiety of his heart and conscience, he said, 'Be of good courage, Philip, thou shalt not die. Though God wanted not good reason to slay thee, yet he willeth not the death of a sinner, but that he may be converted and live. Wherefore, give not place to the spirit of grief, nor become the slayer of thyself, but trust in the Lord who is able to kill and to make alive.' While he uttered these things Philip began, as it were, to revive and to breathe, and gradually recovering his strength, is at last restored to health.

Melanchthon, himself, was in no doubt as to the miraculous nature of his healing, and neither was Luther. 'I should have been a dead man had I not been recalled from death itself by the coming of Luther.'

Luther speaks in the same manner writing to friends: 'Philip is very well after such an illness, for it was greater than I had supposed. I found him dead, but, by an evident miracle of God, he lives.'

Again, referring to his attendance at the Diet, he says, 'Toil and labour have been lost, and money spent to no purpose, nevertheless, though I have succeeded in nothing, yet I fetched back Philip out of Hades, and intend to bring him now, rescued from the grave, home again with joy, etc.' Sentiments with which the Early Church Fathers would have agreed. Healing could be part of the Reformed tradition; but for the most part, especially under Calvin's heavy hand, it was discouraged.

Healing in Scotland after the Reformation

We might well have expected that the Scottish Kirk (Church) would echo Calvin's negative view of the healing ministry. To a great extent they did, but nevertheless there are many extraordinary events recorded. John Knox was one of the famous leaders of the Scottish Reformation. He is famous for the phrase (about the queens of England and Scotland), 'The monstrous regiment of women'! John Knox's son-in-law was one John Welch. Young's *Life of John Welch* contains dramatic prophecies, the gift of knowledge, and a most extraordinary time of prayer for the son of his wife's cousin, Lord Ochiltree. This took place c.1600.[42]

The patient, the son of Lord Ochiltree, Mrs Welch's cousin, who had come to stay with them in France, fell sick of a grievous sickness, and after he had long wasted with it, closed his eyes and expired as dying men do. So to the apprehension and the sense of all spectators he was no more than a carcase, and was therefore taken out of his bed and laid on a pallet on the floor, that his body might be the more conveniently dressed, as dead bodies used to be. This was to Mr Welch a great grief, and therefore he staid with the young man's body full three hours lamenting over him with great tenderness. After twelve hours friends brought in a coffin, whereinto they desired the corpse to be put, as the custom is. But Mr Welch desired that, for the satisfaction of his affections, they would forbear the youth for a time, which they granted, and returned not till twenty-four hours after his death were expired.

Then they returned, desiring with great importunity the corpse might be coffined, that it might be speedily buried, the weather being extremely hot, yet he persisted in his request earnestly begging them to excuse him once more, so they left the youth upon his pallet for full thirty-six hours. But even after that, though he was urged, not only with great earnestness, but displeasure, they were constrained to forbear for twelve hours more. After forty-eight hours were past Mr Welch was still where he was, and then his friends received he believed the young man was not really dead, but under some apoplectic fit, and therefore proposed to him, for his satisfaction that trial should be made upon his body by doctors and surgeons, if possible any spark of life might be found in him, and with this he was content. So the physicians are set to work, who pinched him with pinchers in the fleshly parts of his body, and twisted a bow-string about his head with great force, but no sign of life appeared in him, so the physicians pronounce him stark dead, and then there was no more delay to be desired.

Yet Mr Welch begged them once more, that they would but step into the next room for an hour or two, and leave

him with the dead youth, and this they granted. Then Mr
Welch fell down on the pallet and cried to the Lord with all
his might for the last time, till at length the dead youth
opened his eyes, and cried out to Mr Welch, whom he
distinctly knew, 'O Sir, I am all whole but my head and
my legs' and these were the places they had sore hurt with
their pinching. He became an eminent noble in Ireland,
Lord Castlesteuart.

Gardner[43] also records many other miracles of healing,
prophecy, words of knowledge from the often persecuted
Scottish church in the next centuries. Later church histor-
ians, following Calvin, distanced themselves from these
sort of matters. One describes the prayers over the future
Lord Castlesteuart as 'not very edifying', and 'a handle
for casting reproach on serious religion'.

Healing in non-conformist circles in England

Richard Baxter preaches on and experiences healing

In England, one of the great Puritan leaders, Richard
Baxter (1615–1691), who is famous for his pastoral care
(recounted in *The Reformed Pastor*), records a healing that
he received. He was very worried by a small hard tumour
that he feared was cancerous. For several months he tried
to dissolve it by medicine, then one Sunday morning he
was to preach on 'eminent providences'.

In obedience to my conscience, I said: 'How many times have
I known the prayer of faith to save the sick when all physicians have given them up for dead. It has been my own case
more than once or twice, or ten times, when means have all
failed, and the highest art of reason has sentenced me hopeless, yet have I been relieved by the prevalence of prevailing
prayer.'

When I went to church that morning I had my tumour as before (for I frequently saw it in the glasse, and felt it constantly). As soon as I had done preaching, I felt it was gone, and hastening to the glasse, I saw that there was not the least vestigium or cicatrix, or mark wherever it had been: nor did I at all discover what had become of it. I am sure I neither swallowed it nor spit it out, and it was unlikely to dissolve by any natural cause, that had been hard like bone a quarter of a year, notwithstanding dissolving gargarismes. I thought it fit to mention this, because it was done just as I spoke the words here written.[44]

Baxter clearly believed that God had healed his tumour as a result of his testimony, but of greater interest is his, almost casual, reference to effective healing prayer both for himself and for others.

Healing among the Moravians and the Wesleyans

Count Zinzendorf (1700–1760)

Count Zinzendorf, one of the leaders of the Moravians, had a considerable influence on John Wesley and others. Indeed, as Wesley's journal tells us, it was the courage of the Moravians during a storm on a sea crossing to America that made him begin to realise that he wasn't truly a Christian believer. As well as displaying great courage, the Moravians also believed in healing.

To believe against hope is the root of the gift of miracles; and I owe this testimony to our beloved Church, that apostolic powers are there manifested. We have had undeniable proofs thereof in the unequivocal discovery of things, persons, and circumstances, which could not humanly have been discovered, in the healing of maladies in themselves incurable, such as cancers, consumptions, when the patient was in the agonies of death, etc. all by means of prayer, or of a single word.[45]

John Wesley (1703–1791)

John Wesley, himself, prayed for his own healing, and often presented natural herbs, or nettles, for the healing of others. In his diary,[46] he recalls many remarkable events and the one recorded below is very similar to a biblical exorcism.

At eleven I preached at Bearfield to about three thousand, on the spirit of nature, of bondage and of adoption. Returning in the evening, I was exceedingly pressed to go back to a young woman in Kingswood. (The fact I nakedly relate and leave every man to his own judgment of it.) I went.

She was nineteen or twenty years old, but, it seems, could not write or read. I found her on the bed, two or three persons holding her. It was a terrible sight, anguish, horror, and despair above all description appeared in her pale face. The thousand distortions of her whole body showed how the dogs of hell were gnawing her heart. The shrieks intermixed were scarcely to be endured. But her stony eyes could not weep. She screamed out, as soon as words could find their way, 'I am damned, damned; lost forever! Six days ago you might have helped me. But it is past, I am the devil's now. I have given myself to him. His I am. Him I must serve. With him I must go to hell. I will be his. I will serve him. I will go with him to hell. I cannot be saved. I will not be saved. I must, I will, I will be damned!' She then began praying to the devil. We began: *Arm of the Lord, awake, awake!*

She immediately sank down as asleep, but as soon as we left off, broke out again with inexpressible vehemence. 'Stony hearts, break! I am a warning to you. Break, break, poor stony hearts! Will you not break? What can be done more for stony hearts? I am damned that you may be saved. Now break, now break, poor stony hearts! You need not be damned, though I must.' She then fixed her eyes on the corner of the ceiling and said: 'There he is: ay. There he is! Come just now. Take me away. You said you would dash my brains out: come, do it quickly. I am yours. I will be yours. Come just now. Take me away.'

We interrupted her by calling again upon God, on which she sank down as before, and another young woman began to roar out as loud as she had done. My brother now came in, it being about nine o'clock. We continued in prayer till past eleven, when God in a moment spoke peace into the soul, first of the first tormented, and then of the other. And they both joined in singing praise to Him who had 'stilled the enemy and the avenger'.

To all of this, we could add evidences from the life of George Fox, the early Baptists, and more testimonies from Methodists. As the Church spread out into the mission field, such occurrences became more common, and A.J. Gordon (see note 2 of this chapter) and others wrote powerfully of their experiences in the nineteenth century. Space precludes more than one example.

The ministry of a sober German theologian

J.C. Blumhardt (1805–1880)

Blumhardt was a very well-read Lutheran pastor who is spoken of with approval by no less an authority than Karl Barth. Ultimately he founded a famous Kurhaus (healing centre) at which he ministered for nearly thirty years.

He was greatly influenced by a sharp conflict with Satan which lasted for two whole years. He describes how a lady called Gottliebin Dittus had come into contact with witchcraft through an aunt.[47]

> The demons played a growing role in her life until in desperation she turned to Blumhardt for help. For two years, beginning in December 1841, they struggled with her problem. During this difficult period, Blumhardt developed the practice of praying for Gottliebin repeatedly.
>
> Trying to cope with the angst of not being able to achieve complete victory, he sought the counsel of Professor Wilhelm Stern, who reminded him of Mark 9:29. Some of the manuscript evidence for this passage contains a reference to fasting as well as prayer, and that prompted Blumhardt to give more attention to fasting. The climax was reached about 2 a.m. on December 28, 1843. Blumhardt was praying for Gottliebin when he perceived that her sister Katharina had also come under demonic influence. He had turned to pray for her when suddenly she shrieked, 'Jesus is victor! Jesus is victor!' and fell silent. Blumhardt recorded that her screams were so loud that half the village was able to hear them. At that instant both women experienced complete freedom.

This dramatic healing affected his whole cosmology. Despite the adversarial nature of the exorcism, Blumhardt's healing work was quiet. He didn't hold services, preferring to counsel and pray for people individually. The residents at the Kurhaus came for as long as necessary, Blumhardt ate with them and was available to make appointments for prayer. One prominent professor of medicine, from Tubingen, was impressed by the many accounts of healings that he read in letters sent to Blumhardt by grateful people. His gentle, quick, residential ministry is an interesting forerunner for some of the places in England that we shall consider in the next chapter.

It is interesting how similar this account is to both the biblical material, and to twentieth-century experiences recorded in later chapters. Opponents of the deliverance ministry invariably say that it is a cultural problem. I cannot accept this. Wherever there is occult practice, demons will be met. They will be released by *similar* prayer whether by the Apostles in the first century, the Early Fathers in the second to fourth centuries, John Wesley in the seventeenth, century, Blumhardt in the nineteenth century, or the very many practitioners in totally different cultures in the twentieth century. Of course, our modern psychiatric insights explain many conditions that would have been previously labelled demonic, but that doesn't alter the reality that many people, even today, are freed from all ills by straightforward believing prayer in the name of Jesus.

Healing in the Catholic Church

Finally, we turn to the witness of the Catholic Church. The canonisation process for St Vincent de Paul (1580–1660), not known as a miracle worker, but rather for his great charitable works among the poor, includes four healings – the sudden cure of Claude Campion for blindness; the instantaneous restoration of speech and strength to Mary l'Huillier, dumb from her birth, and unable to move her limbs; the instantaneous cure of Sister Guerin of a malignant ulcer on her leg; and the sudden cure of Alexandre-Philippe le Grand of a long-standing paralysis.

The ministry of the Curé d'Ars

In the nineteenth century, Jean Vianney, popularly
known as the Curé d'Ars (1786–1859), had a remarkable
reputation as a spiritual counsellor. Many testimonies of
healings survive.[48] We may find it strange, and even
objectionable, that despite great faith, he always sent
his people off to pray that St Philomena, an obscure
martyr of the Early Church, should intercede for them.
I believe we should attribute this to his spiritual modesty,
shared by St Augustine of Hippo and others, and understand that Revelation 5:8 which speaks of the intercession of the saints may be interpreted as allowing that
they would intercede for those of us still on our earthly
pilgrimage (see p. 153). 'St John Vianney was a great
supporter of St Philomena, to whom he attributed all
of the many miracles which happened at Ars. He said
himself that "I feel very much inclined to forbid St
Philomena to work miracles on behalf of the body: she
must cure souls before all else."' This is an interesting
comment, which shows clearly where his spiritual priorities lay.

Nevertheless miracles did happen very frequently, and the
following is just one of many well-documented examples.
On Ash Wednesday 1857, a child of eight suffering from a
hip disease was brought, by his mother, to Ars. After seeing
the Curé, he told the child to walk to the altar of St
Philomena.

> With much difficulty, and held by the hand, the child man-
> aged to reach the altar of the holy martyr. He knelt down of
> his own accord, remaining in that attitude for nearly three
> quarters of an hour, without any apparent fatigue, directing
> his eyes in turn to the recumbent statue of St Philomena, and

to a small prayer book which his mother had given to him. As for the poor woman, she was bathed in tears and quite unable to pray, for she seemed hardly to realise where she was. At length the child stood up unaided and said, 'I am hungry,' and he began to walk about. His mother seized his hand, but he escaped, and ran in his stockinged feet to the doorway. He was eager to go outside, but unfortunately it was raining. 'Now you see, mother,' he cried, 'you should have brought my sabots.' (He had asked for them to be brought before they started out.) Taking him in her arms, the mother took him to a shop where sabots were sold. The child was so delighted when he found himself so shod, that he began to jump and leap about, and the rain having now ceased, he remained in the street, playing with some children of his own age.

Although Ars was used to miracles, this one caused a great stir in the village.

A summary of this chapter

Augustine of Hippo declared that miracles may emanate 'either from seducing spirits, or God himself'.[49] Some Protestant writers following Calvin have been quite clear. Here is Warfield on a healing at Lourdes (Pierre de Rudder's suppurating wound which healed instantly).

We are willing to believe it happened just as it is said to have happened. We are content to know that, in no case, was it a miracle . . . Even though we should stand, dumb before the wonders of Lourdes, and should be utterly incapable of suggesting a natural causation for them we know right well that they are not of God. The whole complex of circumstances of which they are part; their origin in occurrences the best that can be said of which is that they are silly; their intimate connection with a cult derogatory to the rights of God who

alone is to be called upon in our distresses, stamp them, prior
to all examination of the mode of their occurrences as not
from God . . . that God is one, and that He alone is to be
served with religious veneration, is no doubt an old revelation. It is nevertheless a true revelation. And he who takes it
as such can never believe that miracles are wrought at
Lourdes . . . 'The whole place,' says Benson, 'is alive with
Mary.' That is the reason why we are sure that the marvels
are not the direct acts of God.[50]

This takes us firmly into the controversy that Jesus had
with the Pharisees in Mark 3:22–30.

We may, for theological reasons (eg guilt by association,
as with Warfield above, who says the place is 'alive with
Mary' therefore it cannot be of God), dismiss some of the
cases cited above; but there is too much first-hand evidence to be neutral. It will be a curious theology which
regards Augustine of Hippo, Luther and the Curé d'Ars as
performing the works of the devil. Perhaps the only safe
test is the one offered by Jesus himself speaking of the
Holy Spirit: 'He will bring glory to me, by taking what is
mine and making it known to you' (John 16:14).

Do the healing and deliverances recorded in this
chapter bring glory to Jesus? Did they lead to conversions,
and to more effective discipleship? One thing is certain,
they may have been sporadic enough for many people to
be able to ignore the issue, but when we reach the twentieth century, whether in the staid circles of the Anglican
Church, or the revivalist atmosphere of Pentecostalism,
the charismatic movement which has crossed all major
church boundaries, or the revived biblical approach of
parts of the Catholic Church, there is sufficient activity
for everyone to be aware of what is going on.

Like St Augustine, we will need to make our own judgement. Each side will quote Scripture – for instance, Jesus

prophesied an increase in false miracles at the end times (Mark 13:22). But the belief of this writer, greatly reinforced by the reading done for this chapter, is that there has been a steady stream of such events throughout the history of the Church, especially in the first three centuries, and that such things have nearly always brought glory to God, and increased the faith of believers.

Ramsay MacMullen in a summary of his overall thesis writes that 'the conversion of the Roman Empire to Christianity was based on miracles, on a head-on challenge to non-Christians to a test of power, and on a contemptuous dismissal of *merely rational paths towards true knowledge of the divine.*'[51]

He quotes that redoubtable champion of orthodoxy, Athanasius, writing c.350 of his contemporary St Anthony converting people with demonstrations of healing and exorcism. Athanasius himself comments, 'We convince because people *first* trust in what they can actually see and *then* in reasoned argument.'

All of which is very similar to the experiences of Paul and Barnabas in Iconium, who spoke boldly for the Lord 'who confirmed the message of his grace by enabling them to do miraculous signs and wonders' (Acts 14:3).

That was the way forward for the Apostolic Church, that was the way which, by and large, changed the Roman Empire; that was the way which has been substantially recovered in the twentieth century. To that we now turn in the next chapter.

Notes

1. Cited by R.A.N. Kydd in *Healing through the Centuries* (Hendrickson, 1998), p. 20 quoting Eusebius, *Ecclesiastical History 3* (Loeb Classical Library, 1.309).

2. A.J. Gordon, *The Three Great Classics on Divine Healing* (Christian Publications 1992), p. 156. Quoting Justin Martyr, *Apologie II*, chapter 6. Gordon himself testifies to a powerful healing ministry in nineteenth-century America. He also cites many examples from the mission field. He was quite a pioneer in the field, helping to prepare the way for the growth of healing in the twentieth century.

3. Michael Green, *Evangelism in the Early Church* (Hodder and Stoughton, 1970), p. 190. Iranaeus Adv Haer 2:32.

4. Michael Green, *op. cit.*, p. 191, quoting Tertullian, Apol. 23.

5. A.J. Gordon, *op. cit.*, p. 156, quoting Tertullian, *Ad Scapula IV*, 4.

6. R.A.N. Kydd, *op. cit.*, p. 23, quoting Minicius Felix, *Ocatavius 27:5*, LCL 399.

7. A.J. Gordon, *op. cit.*, p. 157, quoting Clement of Alexandria, *Epistle C*, XII.

8. Origen, *Contra Celsus*, translated by H. Chadwick (Cambridge University Press, 1965), p. 450. Origen appears to use the word 'daemons' here in the normal New Testament sense of a demon. See chapter 5, note 6 for different usage.

9. *Ibid.*, p. 397.

10. *Ibid.*, p. 142.

11. Michael Green, *op. cit.*, p. 192.

12. R.A.N. Kydd *op. cit.*, p. 28.

13. Michael Green, *op. cit.*, p. 192, quoting Apostolic Constitutions, c.AD 375.

14. H. Chadwick, *op. cit.*, p. 476.

15. Ramsay Macmullen, *Christianising the Roman Empire AD 100–400* (Yale, 1984), pp. 59ff.

16. *Ibid.*, pp. 61, 146 (note 2) writing about the reported

conversions of Goths Saracens and Gauls mainly through exorcism, often performed by Christian captives.

17. F.L. Cross, *The Oxford Dictionary of the Christian Church* (Oxford University Press, 1958), p. 1303.
18. R. Gardner, *A Doctor investigates Healing Miracles* (DLT, 1986), p. 67.
19. Sulpicius Severus, *Life of St Martin of Tours*.
20. M. Dudley and G. Rowell, *The Oil of Gladness* (SPCK, 1993), p. 86, quoting Apostolic Constitutions 8, 29.
21. *Ibid.*, p. 85, quoting *Palladius Historia Lausinca 18, 11*.
22. M. Kelsey, *Healing and Christianity: in ancient thought and modern times* (SCM, 1973).
23. Augustine, *City of God* Book 22, chapters 8–10. Translated by H.Bettenson (Penguin, 1984).
24. *Ibid.*, 22:8.
25. Possidius, *Life of St Augustine* in F.H. Hoare, *The Western Fathers* (Sheed and Ward, 1954), p. 231.
26. Augustine, *op. cit.*, p. 1043.
27. Michael Green, *op. cit.*, p. 175.
28. Ramsay Macmullen, *op. cit.*, p. 119.
29. Bede, *The Ecclesiastical History of the English People* World Classics (OUP, 1994), p. 58.
30. *Ibid.*, p. 124ff.
31. M. Mitton, *Restoring the Woven Cord* (DLT, 1995).
32. Bede *op. cit.*, p. 237ff.
33. *Ibid.*, p. 223ff.
34. *Ibid.*, p. 82 and p. 135.
35. M. Mitton, *op. cit.*, p. 149. Also J. Woolmer *Thinking Clearly about Prayer* (Monarch, 1997), p. 124, for a nineteenth-century example of deliverance from fire on the mission field.
36. Bede, *op. cit.*, p. 95f.

37. Geoffrey Chaucer (1340–1400), *The Canterbury Tales*, Prologue, line 700. Chaucer is contemptuous of the Pardoner's relics which would earn him more money in a day than his hero, the Poor Parson, would earn in months.
38. J. Calvin, *Defence of Wickliffe* p. 115. He is commenting on 2 Thessalonians 2:9.
39. J. Calvin, *Opera Selecta* V pp. 452–455, cited by Dudley and Rowell, *op. cit.*, p. 138.
40. J. Calvin, *Institutes*, iv 19, 18, cited by Dudley and Rowell, *op. cit.*, p. 138.41.
41. Seckendorf, *History of Lutheranism* B III p. 133. A.J. Gordon, *op. cit.*, p. 177ff.
42. R. Gardner *op. cit.*, p. 84ff. In the original text 'chirugeon' is used for 'surgeon'.
43. *Ibid.*, p. 85ff.
44. *Ibid.*, p. 89ff, cited from R. Baxter, *The Saints' Everlasting Rest*, II, vv. 1–5.
45. A.J. Gordon, *op. cit.*, p. 161, quoting Bost, *History of the United Brethren*, p. 111. Many other healing miracles are recounted. Zinzendorf is reported as viewing even the healing of a serious illness as a simple matter.
46. *The Journal of John Wesley*, Tuesday 23 October, 1739 (Moody Press), p. 81f. Also, on Monday 17 March, 1746, he records an incident where, after the sudden illness of himself, and the severe lameness of his horse, he thought, 'Cannot God heal either man or beast by any means with, or without any?', and he and his horse were instantly healed.
47. R.A.N. Kydd, *op. cit.*, p. 41. See also A.J. Gordon, *op. cit.*, p. 220, for further accounts of this remarkable man's ministry.

48. See, for instance, the biography by one of his successors Abbé Truchu.
49. Quoted by R. Gardner, *op. cit.*, p. 55.
50. B.B. Warfield, *Counterfeit Miracles* (Banner of Truth, 1972), p. 118–121.
51. Ramsay Macmullen, *op. cit.*, p. 112. This important book, written by a secular historian, strongly argues that the evangelism of the Roman Empire was substantially due to signs and wonders, and power encounters with 'inferior' local deities.

7

Signs of the Kingdom in
the Twentieth-Century Church

In this chapter, we consider the rediscovery and growth of the healing ministry in many parts of the Christian Church. We remember some of the pioneers in the Church of England, in Pentecostalism with its uncompromising theology of the 'full gospel', in the Catholic Church – including the spread of healing into local churches. We observe some of the unifying effects of the charismatic movement, and the powerful ministry of healing, deliverance and spiritual warfare in many churches in Third-World countries. We observe that there is much to learn from each of these strands of healing, despite their varying theologies, expectations, and practices.

Signs of the Kingdom in the Twentieth-Century Church

A remarkable century

In England, and Western Europe, there has been a sharp decline in church attendance, in vocations to full-time work in the churches, and in the general influence of the Church. Yet, beneath the surface, there has been a groundswell of renewal, a rediscovery of lay ministry (go into a small French village and you will find lay people leading the worship, giving a talk, and administering Holy Communion with the reserved sacrament), a burgeoning of the healing ministry, and a new openness to the Holy Spirit.

In America there is very high church attendance, many of the same signs of lay ministry, and yet a disturbingly high rate of crime, divorce and social deprivation. The church has had the ear of successive presidents. In 1998, President Clinton, in deep trouble because of his unfaithfulness to his wife, turned publicly to Christians for help in seeking to repent.

*Contrasting spiritual results in different parts of
the world*

In Eastern Europe and China, the Church has coura-
geously faced persecution and has experienced growth.
Attempts have been made, especially in Albania, to extinguish it, yet it has played an honourable part in helping to
free many countries from communism. In China, especially in some provinces, Christians remain a growing
thorn in an officially atheistic state. Persecution is seldom
far away.

In other parts of the world, the Church has seen
extraordinary revivals. Who in the nineteenth century
would have prophesied the incredible Christian growth
in South Korea and parts of South-East Asia? There
have been revivals in East Africa, tarnished by the awful
blood-letting in Rwanda. In Zambia, the Anglican
Church played an amazing part in a peaceful transition
of power in 1991; in South Africa, prayer played a
singular part in the defeat of apartheid.[1] Recently, in
Argentina, after the humiliation of the Falklands War,
there has been a great breakthrough in spiritual warfare
and evangelism.

Healing and deliverance in many different churches

We shall now look at healing and deliverance in five
different parts of Christendom – the Anglican Church,
the Pentecostal Church, the Catholic Church, within the
charismatic movement, and in the Third World. Inevitably such an overview is highly selective and somewhat
superficial, but one inescapable fact stands out –
whereas for most of the first nineteen centuries such
ministry was uncommon (the main exception being the
first few centuries), now it is widespread, practised

quietly in many ordinary churches, in many different countries.

It is also an area of genuine ecumenical co-operation. Christians of different traditions seem to find it relatively easy to pray together for the sick. Perhaps healing prayer can offer a real healing hope to the fractured body of Christ.

At the turn of the twentieth century, the Holy Spirit stirred several pioneers in the Anglican Church, and also in the newly burgeoning Pentecostal movement. Later on, particularly with the arrival of the charismatic movement, many Roman Catholics got involved, and healing was quickly supplemented with prayers for deliverance (sometimes too many), prayer for inner healing, and a deep concern for the healing of society. Some church groups, notably Acorn led by the Anglican bishop Morris Maddocks, explored the interface between medicine and healing. Prayer for healing, although offered very differently in different church groups, and with a variety of underlying theologies, has itself been a source of healing and unity – it is easier, for instance, for Christians of different denominations to unite to pray for healing than to share many other forms of worship.

In this chapter, we shall give fewer actual examples as the many primary sources are easily available and space is limited. Healing and deliverance are signs of the kingdom. Evangelism and social action are others – arguably more important – but not the subject of this book.

Healing and deliverance in the Church of England

The twentieth-century story begins with individuals. Names like James Moore Hickson, Dorothy Kerin,

George Bennett, Agnes Sandford, Jim Glennon and Morris Maddocks stand out, but it ends with churches, up and down the English countryside and in other Anglican provinces, holding services and praying for the sick in a way quite unthinkable a few generations earlier.

The ministry of an early pioneer

Some of the foundations were laid in 1882, when the fourteen-year-old James Moore Hickson laid his hands on a small cousin suffering from acute neuralgia. This simple act,[2] in obedience to the inner prompting of the Spirit, led to a worldwide ministry, the founding of the Divine Healing Mission (originally called The Society of Emmanuel). Jack Winslow,[3] founder of Lee Abbey, another much blessed place for retreats and conferences, records a visit of Moore Hickson to India:

It was in 1917, I think, that Mr Hickson on one of his world tours came to Ahmednagar in Western India, where I was then working. For about a week he held daily services at which he gave clear testimony to the healing power of Christ and invited any who so desired to come forward and receive the laying-on of hands with prayer for their healing. Large numbers of people, mostly Christians and Hindus flocked to the church from Ahmednagar itself and from the surrounding villages. There was no time or opportunity for any adequate preparation of those who came, and hundreds must have gone away disappointed. Nonetheless we witnessed some remarkable happenings. A Hindu gold merchant, totally blind, received his sight and offered up a gold ring in thanksgiving. An Indian Christian teacher, completely paralysed, was carried into the church by her friends and, after receiving the laying-on of hands with prayer, was able to get up and walk back a mile to her home, praising God. Among those to whom I was able to give some preparation, two were particularly benefited – a lame man who was able to throw away his crutch and an old Christian, nearly blind, who came to me after the service with great joy, pointing to things in the distance which he could now see. It was all a new and wonderful experience. We felt as if we were back in the days of the Apostles.

The significance of this ministry for the beleaguered Christian ministry in India must have been dramatic, comparable to the experiences of the evangelist J. John recorded eighty years later (see p. 227).

Moore Hickson's work continued for many years. Morris Maddocks[4] notes that his visit to Ireland in 1930 was still being talked about in 1977! He travelled all over the world and his books have testimonies, and grateful letters from bishops from every part of the British Empire and beyond.

The Rev. Howard Cobb was dying of sleeping sickness in the 1920s. His church was filled with parishioners for silent prayer. James Moore Hickson gave him the laying-on of hands, he recovered and moved to Crowhurst, which became the headquarters of the Divine Healing Mission.

George Bennett, an Anglican leader

One great warden of Crowhurst was George Bennett who wrote many books on healing, and travelled tirelessly preaching the good news. I remember hearing him speak, and seeing him pray, at St Michael's in the Northgate, Oxford, just before his death in 1978. Obviously tired, he radiated a quiet love and power – his words and his presence had their own healing quality.

In *The Heart of Healing*[5] he writes movingly of his beginning in the healing ministry. Not allowed to visit a parishioner probably dying of pneumonia, he walked away questioning his beliefs in Christ's healing power, his resurrection, and in his presence today. Suddenly he received great peace, and the certainty that he must return to the house of his sick parishioner. He describes what happened.

I shall always remember his room. The curtains were drawn and it came back to me that, despite my dark mood, it was still a bright summer day. I suppose they were drawn to ease the pressure of light on his eyes. But the greatest thing about that room – the breathtaking thing – was that it was full of the power of the living Christ.

As I crossed the room to kneel at the man's bedside, a naïvely simple thought came into my mind: the Power is here, all about us, and all He wants is someone to pull down the switch. The sick man was lying on his back, leaning slightly against the pillows, and I felt I ought to be touching him. As I did so, he raised his hand under the coverlet and I took it in mine. After a moment I spoke a prayer, the kind of prayer that any child could say. I asked our blessed Lord to fill him with divine power, to drive away the illness and to heal him. I was not there long and as I got up to leave him, he turned his face towards me and, with a smile, he said 'Thank you, George, I will be all right now. Tell my wife, won't you?' She was still standing in the hall where I had left her. 'He will be all right now,' I said to her as I went out.

And, wonderfully, so it turned out to be! In a few hours her husband was sitting up in bed. In a few days he was out and about again. The illness dispersed. No crisis ever came. In the years that followed we became great friends. I shall always treasure the beautifully engraved silver napkin ring he gave me when I left that parish. Even more shall I remember with gratitude the look he gave me following his recovery. We looked into each other's eyes as if we had shared the certain knowledge that Christ is indeed alive yesterday, today and forever, and wanting to work through his Church as ever he did of old.

George Bennett's quiet, dignified ministry brought Christian healing to many, mainly Anglican, churches which would otherwise have probably never been involved. He would have rejoiced to see the time (in the late 1990s) when healing is a normal part of many churches' prayer and ministry.

Meanwhile, God was opening up other channels for his healing grace to flow. The Guild of Health, founded by Percy Dearmer, scholar and musician; the Guild of St Raphael, and the healing centre at Burrswood were all important strands in this new work.

The healing of Dorothy Kerin is well known.[6] After an angelic vision in February 1912, she was raised from her bed, hungry and perfectly well. She spent many years in quiet preparation for the ministry that lay ahead. There was a gracious quietness about her ministry. Burrswood, which she founded, has become an important centre for healing. It is important, too, for the careful co-operation between medicine and prayer which characterises its approach.

Bishop Maddocks and Acorn

Elsewhere, God was raising up other warriors in this great prayer ministry. Morris Maddocks experienced answers to prayer in his early ministry, especially when Vicar of St Martin's, Scarborough. In 1972 he was appointed Bishop of Selby, but became convinced his true calling was in the healing ministry. In 1983, he resigned his office, and became the honorary adviser of the Archbishops of Canterbury and York in health and healing. He founded the Acorn Christian Healing Fellowship, and did much to unify the differing strands of the healing ministry as Chairman of the Church's Council for Health and Healing.

For a while he lived in Salisbury, and chaired the Healing Group in Bath and Wells. His time there led to biennial healing services in Wells Cathedral, alternating with theological lectures, and the appointment for a while of a full-time healing adviser. Healing services and prayer for healing have a natural place in many churches in the diocese. Much of what happens is very quiet and unspectacular, yet every prayer encounter is a valuable sign of God's living presence in many ordinary parish churches.

A quieter approach to healing

Bishop Morris Maddocks' influence has been particularly significant. His gentle yet authoritative leading is widely respected. He comfortably bridges the gap between the quiet, dignified ministry of many in the Anglo-Catholic tradition – practising silent laying-on of hands at the Eucharist, and anointing with holy oil only after careful preparation, and the more exuberant, more expectant charismatic Anglican way. It is more difficult to write about the quiet sacramental approach which, by its very nature and practice, usually asks fewer questions and doesn't look for, or publish, particular results. I remember one bishop, of the Anglo-Catholic tradition, telling me of his surprise when his prayers seemed to initiate a physical healing. 'I don't feel worthy to pray for people in such a way', was his incredibly modest comment. Such an attitude is very attractive, although sometimes it can lead to a formalism which seems to lack any real expectation of God's willingness to heal.

Healing in other parts of the Anglican Church

If God had been mightily at work in the Church of England, there were similar things happening in the other parts of the Anglican Communion. Space doesn't permit discussion of the healing ministry of the Episcopalian Denis Bennett in Seattle, America. Nor the wonderful episcopate of Bill Burnett in Grahamstown and Cape Town, South Africa, which included many healings – notably priests from alcoholism – and brought renewal to the Anglican Church, thus preparing the way for the leadership of Desmond Tutu and the Anglican Church's confrontation with the apartheid regime. Jim Glennon, working mainly in Sydney Cathedral, established a remarkable ministry which influenced many in the Australian church.

Healing in Singapore

To give just one example. Ban It Chiu was Bishop of Singapore in 1973. His whole episcopate, and his diocese, were greatly influenced by a totally unexpected encounter with Christian healing. He writes: [7]

'Walk, walk, in the name of Jesus – walk!' the evangelist said confidently to the man standing in front of him, and I saw a man stagger towards me in the chancel without crutches. He had not walked for a number of years, as a result of injuries inflicted on him when he was in a Japanese prisoner-of-war camp. I wanted to stretch out my hands to catch him, but he steadied himself and walked towards me awkwardly; *but he was walking*. People began to praise God all around him. Some applauded as I walked alongside him from the chancel down the side aisle of the Cathedral before I left him to make his own unaided way accompanied by his wife and the friends who had brought him to the service, back up the main aisle to his seat in the front pews.

This was only one of the many dramatic events which took place during a five-week period in June and July 1973 when services of 'Prayers for Healing' were held in some of our Anglican Churches in Singapore, but especially at St Andrew's Cathedral itself.

The services attracted big crowds even though there was no publicity. The Cathedral was crammed with 'all sorts and conditions of people' including those who came in wheelchairs and with crutches. It seemed that the majority were not Christians. The Cathedral had never in our experience seen such happenings. Some of our members were pleased that they were ministered to at last. Others were offended. The main controversy, however, centred round the 'healings'. It is true that in proportion to those who came for healing, the number who claimed to be healed was not very high, but they were sufficient to bring the crowds. Among the perplexing questions asked were 'Can these claims of healing be substantiated, or are they illusions or even frauds?' 'Were they of God even if they were done in the Name of Jesus?' 'What about those who were not healed?'

Later, he describes his own renewing experience of the Holy Spirit, and his meetings with other like-minded Anglican leaders. His leadership of the Diocese of Singapore started a period of renewal, which continues to this day, and has led to teams from Singapore travelling throughout the Far East, and to England, bringing a powerful ministry of healing and hope.

I have frequently seen Bishop Chiu at work and at prayer. His prayers greatly helped a daughter suffering from severe shoulder pains which were preventing her enjoying playing the 'cello. On another occasion, he discerned the deep pain of a relative still suffering from a broken marriage. He prayed with great sensitivity which helped her to recover from an unpleasant physical problem, as well as from the deep hurts of the past.

It is noteworthy that where the ministry of healing has received episcopal backing, it has been far more effective within the Anglican Church. Episcopacy is the Anglican way of leadership; and, for good or ill, bishops can greatly encourage, or hold back, ministry in healing and related areas.

Another very important influence on the Anglican Church, especially in Africa, has been SOMA (Sharing of Ministries Abroad). SOMA is overtly charismatic, bringing teaching about the gifts of the Spirit to many church leaders, and has been greatly blessed by God. Many African Anglican churches have a curiously old-fashioned liturgy and worship based on prayer book Anglicanism. All of this takes place with great fervour and expectation – often just needing a little teaching about the Holy Spirit to bring great changes. This can contrast unfavourably with the more exciting, Spirit-led worship of the Pentecostal and indigenous churches.

Healing and deliverance have been an important part of SOMA's teaching. Bishop Bernard of North Zambia promised God that if he was ever made a bishop he would invite a SOMA team to his diocese. When elected bishop in 1989, he quickly fulfilled his promise. Some of the consequences are recorded in chapter 1 (p. 28, & 38f), and at the end of this chapter (p. 227f). A few years later he stood in the Old Deanery at Wells (head-quarters of the linked English diocese with Zambia) and said, 'The SOMA visit transformed my diocese!' Similarly, Mrs Beth Kalaba, leader of the Mothers' Union in

North Zambia, testified that their discovery of the effectiveness of prayer for healing and deliverance had transformed the MU and reversed a drift away to other churches. Some English listeners found this quite difficult to accept!

Healing and the Pentecostal Church

The twentieth century has seen the birth, and incredible spread, of the Pentecostal churches. They have spearheaded revival in many parts of the world. From their distinctive theology, with its emphasis on the baptism of the Holy Spirit, there has emerged both the charismatic movement, which has transformed so many people within all the traditional denominations, and the house church movement, a burgeoning strand of independent churches loosely woven together and bringing effective ministry in England, South Africa and many other countries. In America, one of the most effective offshoots has been seen in the Vineyard churches founded by John Wimber.

Healing and deliverance have been an important strand of the 'full gospel'. Theologically, the healing ministry has been very different from the quieter approach of the Anglicans. Healing is often seen as a 'right', and connected with the atonement (see chapter 8, question 24 for a full appraisal of this). Words of knowledge are frequently used. A typical scenario is a gifted preacher standing at the front with a long list of ailments that will be healed if only people come forward for prayer. Sometimes the healings take place in the pews. I have been present when the Lord moves in this way and it is quite remarkable (see chapter 8, end of question 4).

A number of individuals have pioneered this work, especially Smith Wigglesworth[8] in England, Oral Roberts[9] in America, David Wilkerson[10] in America, and Jackie Pullinger[11] in Hong Kong. Later in this chapter we shall see how the Pentecostal flame has spread into many Third-World countries.

The ministry of Smith Wigglesworth

Smith Wiggleworth's independent healing ministry is well documented.[12] After experiences of the Holy Spirit in revival meetings in a Wesleyan Methodist chapel at the age of eight, at an Anglican confirmation service at the age of nine, and in the Salvation Army as a teenager, he began to pray for the sick himself. He heard of a Christian woman who was dying, and went to pray for her, with a half-pint bottle of oil in his pocket.

> I pulled the cork out of the bottle, and went over to the dying woman. I was a novice at this time and did not know any better, so I poured all the contents over Mrs Clark's body in the name of Jesus! I was standing at the top of the bed and looking towards the foot, and suddenly the Lord Jesus appeared. I had my eyes open gazing at Him. There He was at the foot of the bed. He gave me one of those gentle smiles. . . . After a few minutes He vanished, but something happened that day that changed my whole life. Mrs Clark was raised up and filled with life for many years.

He and his wife agreed never to use medicine, and he had an uncompromising theology of healing.[13]

> There is healing through the blood of Christ and deliverance for every captive. God never intended His children to live in misery because of some affliction that comes directly from the devil. A perfect atonement was made at Calvary. I believe that

> Jesus bore my sins, and I am free from them all. I am justified from all things if I dare to believe. He Himself took our infirmities and bore our sickness; and if I dare believe, I can be healed.

He put this into practice! As a young man, he was 'dying' of appendicitis. They called a doctor, not for treatment, but to avoid a coroner's inquest(!). The doctor saw he was too weak for an operation, and said he would call back later. When he did so shortly afterwards, Wigglesworth was out at work! Two friends had laid hands on him, and prayed, and he felt so well that he got up and resumed his employment as a plumber.

In 1907 he heard of the Pentecostal experiences at All Saints, Wearmouth, near Sunderland. He went searching for the gift of tongues. He was disappointed not to receive the gift, but the vicar's wife said, 'It's not tongues you need, but the baptism!' She laid hands upon him and he later said,[14]

> The fire fell . . . I was there with God alone. He bathed me in power . . . I was given a vision in which I saw the Lord Jesus Christ. I beheld the empty Cross, and I saw Him exalted . . . I could speak no longer in English, but I began to praise Him in other tongues as the Spirit of God gave me utterance. I knew then, although I might have received anointings previously, that now I had received the real Baptism in the Holy Spirit as they received on the day of Pentecost.

This led to a world-wide ministry of healing, accompanied by a breath-taking certainty that God would heal.

Pentecostal expectations

This theological certainty has been expressed by many other writers. Kenneth Hagin,[15] for instance, writes:

Through natural human truth a person realises that he is sick, that he has pain or disease. But God's Word reveals that 'He Himself took our infirmities, and bore our sicknesses' (Matthew 18: 17), and that by His stripes we are healed (1 Peter 2: 24). Isn't God's Word just as true when you have sickness and are suffering as it is when you are well? By believing what your physical senses tell you, you would say 'I don't have healing. I am sick.' But by believing the truth of God's Word you can say, 'I am healed. By His stripes I have healing.'

Colin Urquhart,[16] former Anglican priest, similarly challenges us with his sharp logic.

Here we see the Son speaking the words His Father gives Him to speak, and doing the works He saw His Father doing. Loving, Caring, Healing, Restoring. Meeting with the leper at the point of his need. Jesus didn't preach to him. He healed him! You need not doubt that God, your loving Father, desires to heal you. Either you have to say, 'God wants me to have this sickness', or you have to believe 'God does not want me to have this sickness'. If you think He wants you to have it then you have no right to go to a doctor or to try to lessen the pain, or even to pray about it. To do any of these things would be to go against what you say is God's will for you. This seems clearly ridiculous! He is certainly not a loving Father who wants to 'give good things' to His children if you think His best purpose for you is sickness and pain. So what is the alternative? He wants to heal!

Given these premises Urquhart goes on with sound advice:

In which case you have every right to pray; to ask, believing His promise; to seek the good offices of the medical profession. To believe God not only wants to alleviate the pain, but to remove the disease, whether it is physical, mental or emotional; and to give you the healing you seek in the way he chooses.

For the moment, we merely state the classic Pentecostal position: we shall consider its merits in a later chapter. (See chapter 8, question 24, and chapter 11).

Examples from the Pentecostal churches

Another powerful witness for the classic Pentecostal tradition is David Wilkerson, founder of Teen Challenge and author of *The Cross and the Switchblade*. This book had a profound influence on me, and many others. The story is well known, his main thesis was that through the baptism of the Holy Spirit, and especially speaking in tongues, drug addicts could be healed, often without withdrawal symptoms. Many, notably Nicky Cruz, author of *Run Baby Run*, became Christians. His ministry, which began as a result of spending an extra hour a day praying, and then took him to a New York murder trial, has become world wide.

Graham Pulkingham, Anglican charismatic leader in Houston, USA, testifies to the power of his prayers for him 'on the streets of New York'. For me, and many others, it was Wilkerson's simple thesis that God wanted a far more personal relationship, with much more direct guidance, and many more miracles, that was so impressive and personally helpful.

More recently the ministry of Jackie Pullinger among the notorious drug addicts of Hong Kong's Walled City has had similar results, and has been recognised as socially beneficial by the Hong Kong government. She even got an honourable mention on the BBC *9 o'clock News*!

Both these ministries are overtly Pentecostal with a deep expectation of healing and deliverance and a reliance

on the gift of tongues. Both have led many complete outsiders to find Christ, and must be considered as some of
the outstanding examples of evangelism in the twentieth
century.

The least well known of the men with significant public
ministries of healing is my old friend Fred Smith, who
died a few years ago, after a long and distinguished ministry. He was deliberately anonymous – 'only with a name
like Fred Smith could God use me in such a way' he used
to say jokingly. Gardner[17] twice refers to his ministry
without even knowing his name. His remarkable story is
well told[18] in his brief autobiography. I've seen the power
of his prayers, and his compassion with the dying, and his
perplexity at the death of a beloved grand-daughter.[19] I
remember seeing a man, yellow with cancer, going up for
prayer at Oxford Town Hall in the late 1970s. He left
radiant, obviously healed, and I followed him up and
met him months later still very well and rejoicing in his
new-found health and faith.

Example from Fred Smith's ministry

In his book, Smith tells of the healing of Dinah Hills. She
had been ill for seven years, her career as a dressmaker
ruined by a broken wrist that wouldn't heal. She couldn't
dress herself, and her husband took early retirement to
help her.

She saw an advertisement in a local paper 'Jesus heals
today'. After ten specialists she was ready to try God.

Fred, as usual, preached an evangelistic sermon *before*
praying for the sick. Dinah, and her husband Roy,
responded and then sought prayer. Fred writes: [20]

When it came to praying for the sick I had to go out of the
hall to pray for Dinah. She had trouble breathing and had left

the hall, but asked if I would come out to pray for her. I remember seeing her sitting waiting for me, with a jacket flung over her shoulders for warmth, because she could not bear putting her arm into the sleeve. Her arm was so shrunken and small it looked like a child's arm. I knew there was a queue of people waiting for me inside the hall, so I did not have time to ask many questions. I laid my hands on her head, and prayed for God to heal her arm and take away the pain. As with so many others, Dinah was overwhelmed with the power of the Holy Spirit and lay on the ground looking so peaceful she was almost glowing.

The next Sunday Dinah and Roy came to our church service. Dinah told me that the pain had gone as soon as I prayed for her, and for the next three days she had sat waiting for it to come back. After more than seven years, it was hard to believe the pain had finally gone (her breathing problem was also healed). They were both so excited, and so grateful for what God had done. Dinah's arm still looked wasted and child-like, so after the service that Sunday evening I prayed for her again. This time I commanded the muscles to fill out, and repair what was damaged. There were no signs that evening that anything was happening, but we believed that God would complete the healing He had begun.

Within two weeks Dinah's arm was fully restored. It was the same size and shape as the other, with only a six-inch scar from one of the operations to remind her of what had been She went back to her own doctor and showed it to him. 'Well, whatever happened is a miracle, and if it is good enough for you it is good enough for me!' he exclaimed. Some time later I met one of Dinah's specialists at dinner at her home. He too had no explanation, and agreed that it could only be a miracle.

Dinah and Roy lived in a small village not far from Oxford, and they were well known in the area. They wanted to tell everyone about what had happened to them, and they asked me if I would take a service in the local village hall. They put leaflets about the service through every door, and told everyone they could. When I arrived at the hall there was nowhere to park my car. There were three hundred people there that evening, and over eighty of them accepted Christ as their Saviour. I was invited to return the following week, and another sixty-eight people became Christians on that occasion.

That story is typical of Fred's ministry. He always saw healing as a gateway to evangelism. He rejoiced in the sign of healing, but saw his main ministry as evangelism.

His call to ministry began quite dramatically. He was quietly leaving an Oxford Pentecostal church, rejoicing in his new-found faith, when a man spoke to him: [21]

'I saw you come out of that church didn't I?' he asked. 'That's right,' I replied. 'Well it says on the notice board that the sick are prayed for after each service. I have been coming for six weeks, and nobody has prayed for me, and I am in deep and desperate trouble.' So I apologised on behalf of the pastor and congregation. 'If you come back tonight I will make sure that someone prays with you.'

That was not going to satisfy him. 'I can't go on any longer,' he said. 'The pain is too bad.' He told me he was going to commit suicide. I offered to ring the Samaritan emergency line, or get him some help, but he would not have any of that. 'Why don't you pray for me?' he said. 'Well, I'm not a priest or minister or anything like that,' I said. 'Don't you know how to pray? Then you pray for me to be healed.'

We were standing on one of the main streets in Oxford. I did not know what to do, but the man was desperate; perhaps I had better pray for him. After all, I had watched Ken Matthew and others pray for the sick. All they did was ask God to heal the person. I could ask that too. I took the man into a shop doorway so that we were out of the noise of the passing traffic. I had watched and listened when Ken Matthew prayed for people to be healed, so I thought I had better do what I had seen him do. I asked God to anoint my hands, to use them as instruments of His healing power. When I laid my hands on the man he jerked a few inches in the air. It rather frightened me. 'What's the matter?' I asked urgently. 'Thank you, thank you; the pain has completely gone' he replied.

Like many others, one experience of God's power was the gateway to a completely new ministry.

Fred was a great big man, a former police sergeant, but he was also a very humble one. He could easily have become famous. Radio Oxford, the Oxford Journal, and other newspapers regularly reported his ministry, yet he was careful to stand back give the glory to God.

Our family have much reason to be grateful for his friendship and his prayers. My wife, Jane, suffered a great deal from serious back problems before and after the birth of our eldest child. About eighteen months after Rachel's birth, and still uncertain as to whether we should attempt to have further children, Fred came to talk in our house to the St Aldate's healing team. Naturally, we ended with a time of prayer. He prayed for Jane, and said, 'You won't have any more serious back problems.' His words have held true for twenty years, and we have rejoiced in the safe births of Susie, Tim and Katy.

Healing in the Catholic Church

I feel considerable difficulty in writing this short section. Here, as in other areas, I am acutely aware that a little knowledge is a dangerous thing. I am also aware that some readers, particularly of an Evangelical outlook, may find this section particularly difficult.

Many Protestants have read with pleasure the writings

of Francis Macnutt (see p. 221). Indeed, the first serious book on healing that I read was *Healing*.

I would like to begin with three other, perhaps more characteristically Catholic ministries.

Brother André in Quebec

Brother André (1845–1937) ministered in Quebec. There is much written about him.[22] Apparently, there are over 4,000 first-hand accounts of healing with which he is associated! He was powerfully attracted to St Joseph, and meditated greatly on the passion of Our Lord. He was a man of deep prayer, often praying through the night. He, himself, was often in poor health. Yet despite a typically Catholic view on the potential benefits of suffering, he prayed for the healing of others.

Here is an example of his ministry.[23]

> Rudolphe Fournier is a case study. In 1911, while still a young boy, Fournier contracted a disease in his right knee. He does not identify it, but he does report that a physician said it was terminal. On hearing this, Fournier's father went to the oratory to see Brother André, who instructed him to pray and gave him a medal of St Joseph and some oil. There was no improvement, so Fournier's father went back again. When he walked into Brother André's room, he was met with a smile and the words 'Go and have faith.' Returning home, the older Fournier discovered that his son had been healed at exactly the time when Brother André spoke to him.

We may find references to a medal of St Joseph and to oil (from one of the lamps burning at the statue) rather trying. But is it any more bizarre than Jesus' spittle, Peter's shadow, or Paul's handkerchief proving efficacious?

André believed that all miracles 'came through God and

through the personal care and prayer of St Joseph'. Sometimes André received what would nowadays be called the gift of knowledge.

> There were many eyewitnesses of the following signal wonder. A great contingent of American visitors had thronged round the doors of the office all morning. At dinner time, the Brother returned to the rectory. He was already mounting the steps under the eyes of hundreds of pilgrims, when a man went up the steps to stop him and to show him through the open doors of an ambulance that had forced its way amid the tumultuous crowd, a man lying on a stretcher. 'Untie him and let him walk,' said the Brother simply, and went on into the house without further ado. The sick man got up and walked barefoot through the madly enthusiastic crowd.

Note that Brother André didn't wait to see what happened! Like some of Our Lord's 'absent' healings, there was no need to see what God had done. It is obvious, in this case, if the man was strapped to a bed that his condition was very serious. It is equally obvious that he was healed.

Brother André's own weaknesses helped him to empathise with those who were not healed (and, of course, there were many) and to understand in a positive way their experience of pain. This sensitivity to those who are not healed is a quality sometimes lacking in the wider Church.

Medjugorje

A couple of friends, one Catholic and one Anglican, have spoken to me, with awe, about the presence of the Lord in a group of small villages in what was until recently the war-torn republic of Bosnia-Herzegovina.

Briege McKenna,[24] a Catholic nun called by God to a powerful healing ministry, writes how in May 1981, in

Rome, she prayed with Father Tomislav Vlasic, a priest from Medjugorje. He was quite discouraged, his church was experiencing hard times, and the then communist government of Yugoslavia was unsympathetic.

Sister McKenna saw a picture of a white church with twin steeples. Father was sitting in the main celebrant's chair in the sanctuary of the church and streams of living water were flowing from the altar. Many people were coming and cupping the water in their hands to drink. Shortly afterwards six young people, who in 1981 were teenagers, started receiving visions of Mary. Despite being sought out by thousands of callers, they have remained humble and not sought to exploit their experiences either spiritually or financially.

Ronald Kydd in his helpful book *Healing through the Centuries*[25] has written extensively about Medjugorje. He records this statement from the *Medjugorje Messenger* of July 1991.

> My children, how many times have I invited you here in Medjugorje to prayer and I will invite you again because I desire you to open your hearts to my Son and allow Him to come in and fill you with peace and love. Allow Him, let Him enter! Help Him by your prayers in order that you might be able to spread peace and love to others, because that is now most necessary for you in this time of battle with Satan.

Experiences in Medjugorje Here, as on other occasions, the message is calling people back to repentance, back to Jesus, and in no way is it promoting additional devotions to Mary. A number of well-documented healings have occurred. Kydd cites examples which include a girl from Scotland who was paralysed for five years after a car accident. She travelled to Medjugorje in 1990, and returned the following year to give thanks. She brought X-rays and a medical certificate confirming that she would probably never walk again, or if she did, it would be with great pain. She also now had a medical certificate indicating that she was completely well.

He also comments on the change of emphasis at Medjugorje. Those involved in the visions used to assist in the prayers, and to bring comfort and advice to individual sufferers. Now prayer for the sick follows the evening Eucharist and is done without any physical contact. The emphasis is consciously away from human channels and totally focussed on Jesus. In the summer, this takes place in the open air, with lengthy times of prayer. Mary is seen quite clearly as intercessor, not as healer. One priest holds up a crucifix to emphasise that any healing flows from the cross of Christ.

If the test of such ministry is whether it glorifies Christ, then it is difficult to be critical. However, there has been considerable opposition from the local diocese, and a negative reaction, in 1988, and again in 1999 from the Vatican.

Local Catholic ministry

A more normal Catholic ministry is provided by Monsignor Michael Buckley. At one of the Bath and Wells Diocesan Healing Lectures, he gave us an hour of breath-taking stories interspersed with Irish humour and some theological commentary. His books are well known and widely read. *Do Not Be Afraid*[26] is a marvellous read. It is deeply biblical, very practical and unsensational. One of his stories begins with an evangelical introduction: 'Let me tell you a story of when religion gave way to faith and trust in God.'

He writes movingly of his attempt through prayer to bring healing to many who have deep past hurts, present fears, and often an inability to love either themselves or God. He also writes of many failures and partial successes, as well as of people who have become sufficiently healed to be able to pray for others. The ministry is gentle, patient, and aims to bring glory to God – physical healing which takes place is almost incidental to everything else.

I have talked and prayed with many local Catholics. We have had joint services of healing. We have engaged in 'spiritual warfare', praying in the prison and around sites of alleged witchcraft. What is so apparent is their love and reverence for the Bible. There is a quiet dignity in their healing services. An unattractive modern building is transformed by candlelight. Healing, prayer, anointing and confession go hand in hand. Everything is very quiet, very peaceful, very open to the still, small voice of God.

This is ecumenical co-operation at its best. Mutual prayer, and the sharing of biblically based services, brings deep unity and fellowship. It does much to build a bridge between different groups.

We move from Medjugorje and Michael Buckley to the well-known ministry of Francis Macnutt, which takes us on our journey into consideration of the charismatic movement.

The charismatic movement and healing and deliverance

Since the late 1960s, the mainline churches have been open to the Pentecostal experience known as the baptism of the Holy Spirit. There has been much less emphasis on speaking in tongues rather than on the other gifts of the Spirit, especially those connected with healing and deliverance. The former Roman Catholic priest, Francis Macnutt, who married and left the Catholic Church, but has now returned to that fold, is perhaps the most respected theological writer on the whole subject.

Ministry of Francis Macnutt

Macnutt's writing is rooted in the Bible. His classic book *Healing* takes as its third chapter the title 'Jesus saves'. He is at pains to point out[27] that the biblical passage on anointing in James 5 had been completely misused by the Catholic Church. Anointing the sick became Extreme Unction, a sacrament for the dying. Macnutt writes approvingly of the ministries of Agnes Sandford, David Wilkerson and other Protestant leaders involved in healing.

He writes biblically about faith, producing a classic diagram.[28] (See chapter 8, question 7.)

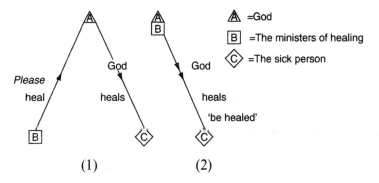

1. Illustrates the normal prayer of intercession, by the believer, to God, on behalf of the sick person.
2. Illustrates the gift of faith, where the prayer becomes a command, similar to that of Jesus in Mark 1:41 and elsewhere.

Macnutt illustrates clearly four basic kinds of healing, including prayer for repentance, prayer for inner healing (see chapter 8, question 9), prayer for physical healing, and prayer for deliverance. Unlike some of the Pentecostals cited earlier, he values medicine and encourages co-operation with doctors. He writes eloquently of the reasons why people are not healed (see chapter 8, question 3), and modestly records very few personal testimonies of healing.

Francis and Judith Macnutt have done much to promote Christian unity, which has always been a feature of the charismatic movement at its best.

The Vineyard churches

Ministry of John Wimber (1933–1998)   The ministry of John Wimber, founder of the Vineyard churches, in the USA and now world wide, is well known in England, first because of his association with David Watson (see chapter 1, p. 19), and especially in attempts to bring healing to David when he was first stricken with cancer. More recently, he has had much to do with Holy Trinity Brompton and St Andrew's, Chorleywood, two centres of charismatic Anglicanism. He wrote an influential book called *Power Healing* with a strong emphasis on effective evangelism needing to be accompanied by signs and wonders. He has an impressive group of social issues. His churches gave over $100,000 to the poor in 1989, as well as many meals. He also writes that healing includes 'breaking the hold of poverty and oppressive social structures'.[29] He encourages the teaching of others to pray for the sick, and has a theology of healing which is non-dogmatic and open to the mystery of God's sovereignty.

Like others, he seemed genuinely surprised that David Watson wasn't healed. In 1996 I heard him give some amazing studies on Ephesians at the New Wine Conference on the Shepton Mallet showground. Obviously unwell (he died early in 1998), he talked about illness in his family, his experience of healing, and the mystery involved. His whole approach was deeply impressive – humble, questioning, and yet full of faith. He, himself, suffered both from cancer and a stroke, yet he remained good humoured, optimistic, and caring for others.

He has helped bridge the gap between Anglicans, at least those of a charismatic outlook, and the independent churches of which the Vineyard group are fast becoming one of the largest.

The Toronto Airport Vineyard Church has had an extraordinary period of ministry. For a while, the leadership was not under the authority of the mainstream Vineyard Church, but this has been changed again. Whatever we feel about the 'Toronto blessing', there are amazing testimonies of healing – not least the recent experiences in Bath and elsewhere of teeth being filled with gold. Two of my children, one a medical student, witnessed this happening!

Healing has always been a main feature of churches touched by the charismatic movement. A renewed interest in deliverance has proved more controversial, especially when most illnesses are attributed to evil spirits (following Luke 13: 11), and things like spirits of anger are discerned. Although it is often denied, the effect of this sort of theology is to make it seem normal for a Christian to be demonised, whereas the Bible would seem to teach that demonisation is unusual for anyone, and very rare for Christians. Confusing the sins of the flesh (Galatians 5: 19–23) with evil spirits causes much chaos and sometimes leaves vulnerable people dependent on exorcists whose attempts at deliverance seldom seem to be completed.

We shall look at this in more detail in chapter 8, question 23).

We now turn to the witness of the Third World.

Healing and deliverance in the Third World

This century has seen some remarkable revivals, notably in Rwanda in the 1950s, in Indonesia in the 1960s, in China at the end of the century, and certainly in South Korea and Argentina. These countries have usually been under oppressive leadership which is both hostile to the gospel and to the poor.

Recently, spiritual warfare, with a specific attempt to discover and confront any ruling spirits has been a distinctive feature of such ministries. Power encounters (see chapter 4) have led to may decisive breakthroughs.

Mel Tari and the Indonesian revival

Among many documented examples, Mel Tari writing about the Indonesian revival is particularly interesting. He writes engagingly of his mistakes, and includes a story of how the Lord stopped him preaching until he had learnt to serve his brother and sister – they had been working in the heat of Indonesia, while he had been living it up in America.

He tells of a particularly dangerous village near the capital city of Timor.[30] Many people who went there were poisoned. He, and a team of six, went and ate their fill. Then they preached. Everyone was amazed. Their food had been laced with a powerful poison which usually kills in a few minutes. The local witchdoctor was converted.

Elsewhere, he speaks of the raising of the dead (and of their failure on an earlier occasion through disobedience), the miraculous crossing of a flooded river, and the turning of water into wine for Communion services. Dr Karl Koch, in his books on the Indonesian revival, tells similar stories. The reader is faced with a familiar dilemma – either the witness is a liar, or something very wonderful happened. The problem is somewhat heightened by the evidence being contemporary. We can dismiss the Venerable Bede, or Sulpicius Severus (see last chapter) as fanciful story-tellers of long ago. It is rather harder when evidence is so contemporary.

Spiritual warfare in Argentina

Meanwhile, in Argentina, recovering from the national disgrace of the Falklands War with Great Britain in 1989, remarkable evangelism is reported, preceded by spiritual warfare, and accompanied by many signs. Wagner[31] asks the question, 'What is the evangelist Carlos Annacondia doing that others aren't?' He writes as follows:

'I believe it is warfare prayer.' My friend Edgardo Silvoso agrees. Edgardo Silvoso says that Annacondia and the other prominent Argentine evangelists 'incorporate into their evangelistic work a new emphasis on spiritual warfare – the challenging of the principalities and powers, and the proclamation of the gospel not only to the people but to the spiritual jailers who held the people captive.' Prayer is the chief variable, according to Silvoso. 'Evangelists begin to pray over cities before proclaiming the gospel there. Only after they sense that spiritual powers over the region have been bound will they begin to preach.'

A permanent fixture of Annacondia's crusades is what has to be one of the most sophisticated and massive deliverance ministries anywhere. Under the direction of Pablo Bottari, a wise, mature and gifted servant of God, literally thousands of individuals are delivered from demons each of the thirty-nine to fifty consecutive nights of a crusade. The 150-foot deliverance tent, erected behind the open-air speaker's platform, is in operation from 8pm to 4am each night. Annacondia calls it the 'spiritual intensive care unit'. Scores of teams whom Bottari has trained in deliverance prayer do the actual hands-on ministry. I have never observed a crusade evangelist who is as publicly aggressive in confronting evil spirits as Annacondia. With a high-volume, high-energy, prolonged challenge, he actually taunts the spirits until they manifest in one way or another. To the uninitiated, the scenario in the vacant city lot where he holds his crusades might appear to be total confusion. But to the skilled, experienced members of Annacondia's thirty-one crusade ministry teams, it is just another evening of front-line warfare prayer in which the power of Jesus Christ over the demonic forces is displayed for all to see.

And the power of the meetings is awesome. Many miraculous healings occur. For example, so many dental miracles occur – teeth filled, new teeth and defective bridges replaced by whole teeth – that only those who have had more than two teeth filled are allowed to take the time to give a public testimony. On one occasion a dwarf was reported to grow over fifteen inches taller.

Unsuspecting pedestrians passing by the crusade meetings have been known to fall down under the power of the Holy Spirit. In the city of Santiago del Estero, a local priest decided to oppose the crusade by invading the area with a religious procession. When they arrived, the four strong men carrying the statue of the priest's favourite virgin all fell to the ground under the power of the Spirit and the statue shattered into a thousand pieces. Two of the men spent the night in the hospital and the other two in Annacondia's deliverance tent!

This is warfare prayer in action. Spirit-directed prayer opens the way for the blessings of the Kingdom of God to come upon the earth with healings, deliverances, salvation, holiness, compassion for the poor and oppressed, and the fruit of the Spirit. Above all, God is glorified, worshipped and praised.

This is truly apostolic preaching with signs and wonders following. Wagner believes Annacondia to be the most effective evangelist in the world today.

J. John in India

The British evangelist J. John, records a remarkable visit to India. May 1996 *Renewal* magazine records: 'Over 200,000 Christians gathered from all over Southern India to hear J. John, director of the Philo Trust and one of the UK's leading evangelists, address an annual retreat at the Divine Healing Centre in Chalakudy.'

J. John and his team witnessed many miracles during the meeting: 'I caught a glimpse of what it may have been like during the time of Christ,' he said on his return. 'Thousands of people were hungry to hear the gospel and many came to Christian faith. As the gospel was preached, many experienced miraculous physical healing. I felt deeply humbled by the whole experience, and moved by the simple, yet staggering faith of those attending.'

This experience has led J. John to long for healing to occur wherever he preaches. He hopes for more signs to accompany the preaching of the word.

Sharing the Ministries Abroad in Zambia

In a very limited way, my own experience of the Third World has been to expect, and to see, far more healing and deliverance than in England. Here is the testimony of Peter Hancock, who accompanied me on our first memorable SOMA trip to Zambia. This is from a letter written by him in 1991.

When I was in Fuwela in Central Zambia, there was a small 'hospital' there – very poorly fitted out and with no supplies of medicine, apart from a few things like paracetamol.

A lady was sent down from Ndola with severe stomach pains from which she had suffered for some time. She would not take any of the few pills on hand, because she maintained that the spirits would not allow her to do so. I was asked to pray with her by the hospital. I went over with the three other members of the team, including the Ven. Tobias Kaoma, a Zambian archdeacon (see chapter 1, p. 38ff) who was with me.

We went into a side room, away from the ward, and there I questioned the lady about her insistence that she was possessed by these spirits of which she spoke. She said that she had received them from her husband and, as we had been told, that they forbade her to take any medicine for her stomach pains. I had had experience of evil spirits and their possession of people in previous visits to Central Africa, so with Fr Tobias as interpreter, we began the deliverance. I spoke to the spirits in the name of Jesus, and in the power of his shed blood on Calvary, and discovered their names. There were three main ones, and each was cast out separately in the name of Jesus, and by his cross and blood. Since they each had subsidiary spirits, there were twenty-four all told. The woman was set free from them all, and prayed that the Holy Spirit would fill her empty spaces, after we had made sure that she knew Jesus as Saviour and Lord. On the following day we saw her walking about the village completely freed, and healed of her pains.

In the same visit, Tobias was ministering in deliverance in the church. He had a young woman rolling about on the floor, and making a great deal of noise. But he was sitting quietly and apparently unconcerned on a small table just watching her. I know Tobias's high reputation in Zambia for his ministry of deliverance (which really began when Peter and I visited Chipili in 1990) and I remember thinking, 'He knows something that I don't!' So I asked him why he was

just sitting there. He told me that the spirits were great
show-offs and liked to make a great deal of fuss so as to
draw attention to themselves, and so, when they had had
their 'go', he would then minister and cast them out in
Jesus' name. He never seemed to get flustered, or shout at
them.

These last three testimonies show different approaches,
each blessed by God.

Annacondia prepares the ground with intensive spiritual warfare which continues on an individual level
throughout his crusades. J. John stepped into a situation
already steeped in prayer. He preached the word – and
signs followed. Peter Hancock and Tobias Kaoma dealt
with the spirits as they revealed themselves and saw considerable fruit.

Probably most of us feel more comfortable with the last
two approaches, and yet both contemporary experience
and Scripture (see chapter 4) suggest that Annacondia's
approach needs to be taken very seriously.

Spiritual Warfare in Asia

Spiritual warfare in Thailand   World Christian Magazine[32]
tells of a couple in Thailand who saw no fruit for years
until they decided to set aside one day a week to go into
the woods and engage the territorial spirits in prayer.

In the same country,[33] a film team were showing the
Campus Crusade *Jesus* film in a rural village. They had
planned on staying in the village that night and returning home the next day. They were told they would be
sleeping in the local Buddhist temple. What they were
not told was that this particular temple was known for
miles around as a chief dwelling place of demons. Others
who had tried to sleep there had been run out before

morning. Some reportedly had been found dead the next day.

Shortly after the team had gone to sleep, Eshleman reports, 'They were awakened all at once by the immaterial presence of a hideous beast. There in the corner of the room appeared the most frightful image they had ever seen. Fear struck them all like an icy fist.' The startled team decided to put into practice what they had seen Jesus do in their own film. They prayed together and boldly cast the demon out of the temple in the name of Jesus. Nothing else was necessary, and they slept peacefully the rest of the night.

In the early morning, the villagers came to carry off the team's equipment they were sure had been left behind when the Christians were run off or killed by the demons. When they found them sound asleep 'they were confronted with the undeniable fact that God is more powerful than any other force'.

In this case, the power encounter was instituted by the spiritual opposition (cf. Elymas, Acts 13). The result was the same – a notable spiritual victory followed by effective evangelism.

Pastor Yonggi Cho, leader of the amazing church in South Korea, tells how his whole ministry began with the casting out of a demon from a woman who had been paralysed for seven years. The victory only came after months of prayer and fasting. Michael Green told me that Yonggi Cho had told him that his church was built on the site of an old pagan temple. Before building began, a massive service of exorcism took place – and the spiritual results are there for anyone with eyes to see.

Watchman Nee[34] tells of how a power encounter with the local deity, Ta Wang, on an offshore island of China led to the collapse of its power and the evangelisation of the island.

Obviously, I could give many other examples. Instead, we should note that just as an individual's ministry is often released by one deep experience (Fred Smith in Oxford, Bishop Ban It Chiu in Singapore, for instance), similarly remarkable breakthroughs occur after a 'power encounter' which changes the whole spiritual climate.

'Come, Holy Spirit'

There is, however, another highly significant approach to healing that has surfaced in the last few years. Some leaders in the healing ministry such as Peter Lawrence, Vicar of Canford Magna, and writer of many books, and those involved in the movement of the Holy Spirit known as the Toronto blessing, have seen God work in power after invoking the Holy Spirit with the simple invitation 'Come, Holy Spirit', and waiting to see what happens.

It is really outside the scope of this book to discuss the Toronto blessing which has helped many, and proved controversial and difficult for others. But when last in Zambia in 1994, I witnessed the power of this approach. The Rev. Randolph Vickers and his wife, Dorothy, leaders of the Northumberland Healing Centre, were part of my team. When they ministered in this way, we had far less trouble with evil spirits. People were frequently very simply released, as opposed to the sort of scenes I have described in chapter 1. Healing, too, seemed more frequent.

I remember in one township, anointing a man with oil who was apparently totally deaf in one ear. He was completely healed, and his local priest wrote to say that he was now singing in the church choir. That was just one of many healings that took place quietly and simply after first praying for the Holy Spirit to come, and waiting for his power to manifest itself among the congregation.

Twentieth-century conclusions

Can we sum up our brief tour through a wide variety of healing experiences in the twentieth century?

Learn from the men and women of faith, even if you cannot totally support their theology. Read about, and admire, Morris Maddocks and George Bennett in the Anglican tradition, Brother André and Francis Macnutt in the Catholic tradition, Fred Smith and Smith Wigglesworth in the Pentecostal tradition.

In our brief tour of the twentieth-century ministry of healing and deliverance, we have seen how, from modest beginnings, the ministries have developed and become vital in evangelism and church growth in many parts of the world. All healing strands can learn from one another. No one has a monopoly of the truth, there is a profound and deep mystery which no human mind can fully fathom. We may admire the fervent faith of the Pentecostals, the sacramental approach of the Catholics, the gentle, compassionate approach of many Anglicans. We can learn from the example of the leaders of all traditions, and above all, pray for the fire of the Third-World experience to descend on our sleepy, comfortable, half-empty churches. We would do well to avoid a rigid position from which we can't escape! If men of the stature of Augustine of Hippo in the ancient world, and Michael Green in the twentieth century have had to revise their theological positions, it would be wise for us to be open to God's 'wind of change'.

Finally, we should study carefully the teaching on spiritual warfare; not getting involved without clear leading from the Lord, but realising that it is an effective and vital approach in many parts of the world.

Notes

1. Michael Cassidy, *A Witness for Ever* (Hodder and Stoughton, 1995), throughout.
2. James Moore Hickson, *Heal the Sick* (Methuen, 1924), p. 6.
3. Jack Winslow, *Modern Miracles* (Hodder and Stoughton, 1968), p. 18.
4. Morris Maddocks, *The Christian Healing Ministry* (SPCK, 1981), p. 101.
5. George Bennett, *The Heart of Healing* (Arthur James, 1971), p. 16f.
6. John Woolmer, *Thinking Clearly about Prayer* (Monarch, 1997), and in many other books.
7. Michael Harper, editor, *Bishop's Move* (Hodder and Stoughton, 1978), chapter 6.
8. S.H. Frodsham, *Smith Wigglesworth: a portrait of faith* (Assemblies of God, 1949).
9. Ronald Kydd, *Healing Through the Centuries* (Henrickson, 1998), p. 202f.
10. David Wilkerson *The Cross and the Switchblade* (Lakeland, 1994).
11. Jackie Pullinger, *Chasing the Dragon* (Hodder and Stoughton, 1980).
12. S.H. Frodsham, *op. cit.*, for instance.
13. R. Kydd, *op. cit.*, p. 206.

234 HEALING AND DELIVERANCE

14. R. Gardner, *A Doctor Investigates Healing Miracles* (Darton, Longman and Todd, 1986), p. 100.
15. K.E. Hagin, *Redeemed: from poverty, sickness, and death* (Tulsa,, 1975).
16. Colin Urquhart, *Anything You Ask* (Hodder and Stoughton, 1978).
17. R. Gardner, *op. cit.*, pp. 79,158.
18. Fred Smith, *God's Gift of Healing* (New Wine Press, 1986).
19. John Woolmer, *op. cit.*, p. 78f.
20. Fred Smith, *op. cit.*, p. 78f.
21. *Ibid.*, p. 47.
22. R. Kydd, *op. cit.*, p. 83f. Includes a considerable biography translated by Real Boudreau.
23. R. Kydd, *op. cit.*, p. 83ff, quoting original sources by Rudolphe Fournier and Henri-Paul Bergeran.
24 Briege McKenna, *Miracles do happen* (St Martins Paperbacks 1987).
25. Kydd op cit. p. 102ff.
26. Michael Buckley, *Do not be Afraid* (DLT, 1995), p. 175ff.
27. Francis Macnutt, *Healing* (Ave Maria Press, 1974), p. 276ff.
28. *Ibid.*, p. 129ff.
29. John Wimber, *Power Healing* (Hodder and Stoughton, 1986), p. 38.
30. Mel Tari, *Like a Mighty Wind* (Coverdale, 1971), p. 42.
31. Peter Wagner, *Warfare Prayer* (Monarch, 1992), p. 26ff.
32. Peter Wagner, *Territorial Spirits* (Sovereign World, 1991), p. 47.
33. Peter Wagner, *Warfare Prayer* (Monarch, 1992), p. 76ff.

34. Watchman Nee, *Sit, Walk, Stand* (Kingsway, 1957), p. 57ff. This is one of the most remarkable stories of spiritual warfare leading to effective evangelism. I have recorded it in *Thinking Clearly about Prayer*, p. 123f.

8

Questions Often Asked

This chapter deals with many questions which, in the author's experience, are frequently asked at Christian meetings, seminars and conferences. One major question 'How do I get my church seriously involved in prayer for healing?' is left to the end of chapter 10, where it fits more naturally.

1) Why this emphasis on individual healing – aren't other things much more important?
2) Isn't my illness too small to bother God with?
3) What are the main reasons why people aren't healed?
4) How important is confession before prayer for healing?
5) How do I know if I have a gift of healing?
6) How important is fasting, for those involved in prayer for healing and deliverance?
7) What other gifts of the Spirit are important in healing and deliverance?
8) Can we pray for someone to be healed of homosexuality, or other sexual matters?
9) What is meant by the healing of the memories – is it scriptural?
10) What is meant by the healing of the family tree – is it scriptural?
11) What are the marks of those needing deliverance?

12) How do we pray for deliverance?
13) Can prayer for healing and/or deliverance do harm?
14) Can I pray for people who don't know that they are being prayed for?
15) When and how should anointing be used?
16) What about alternative approaches to healing such as homoeopathy?
17) When is healing spiritually dangerous?
18) What is wrong with spiritualism?
19) Why do some people fall over when prayed for – and does it matter?
20) Is there a time to stop praying for people for healing – especially when they are dying?
21) What about the relationship of the healing ministry and the medical profession?
22) Is sickness caused by the devil?
23) Can a Christian be demonised?
24) Is healing included in the benefits of the atonement?

Questions Often Asked

Anyone who gives talks on healing and deliverance soon discovers that there are certain basic questions which frequently recur. This chapter is an endeavour to answer some of them – theologically and experientially.

1) Why this emphasis on individual healing – aren't other things much more important?

Healing is important because it is part of the good news of the gospel. If people are healed, whether of something quite small like a migraine, or something life threatening, they have a story to tell. Even if they are not brought to faith by the experience (and many even in Jesus' time seemed to receive their healing and go on their way unmoved spiritually [Luke 17:11f]), they will tell others of their experience, and the name of Jesus will be uplifted.

Healing is important, too, for those who do the praying. We discover our spiritual poverty and something of God's riches. At times we are perplexed and anxious, like St Paul, for those for whom we pray (2 Corinthians 11:28), at times we are uplifted and full of joy like the seventy (Luke 10:17). If we have been called to this ministry, it is important that we are able to practise it.

Healing is also important for the life of the local church. Where there is regular prayer for healing, the spiritual life tends to deepen, the very church building itself seems more of a place of prayer and pilgrimage. Healing is a sign that the church cares, a sign that can be offered to outsiders just as much as to the regular congregation.

Healing keeps us humble and dependent upon God. We soon discover that slick theologies don't work, and that there is a deep mystery at the centre of it all. Some are blessed in suffering, some are blessed through healing. Some who pray are 'wounded healers', some are whole and wonderfully healthy.

Individual healing may lead us to consider wider issues. As a small local church, my own congregation is deeply committed to a house for the young homeless (with all the difficulties and heartbreak that such work often brings!), and also to the Jubilee 2000 campaign for relieving international debt.

What is important is discovering God's will for us, as individuals, and as a body. If that includes offering prayer for healing, then we must set out on that journey (see chapter 10). It is a journey that will deepen our prayer life, It is a journey which will open us to the Holy Spirit, and increase our love for Christ. It is a journey that will help us discover what Isaiah calls 'the oil of gladness' (Isaiah 61:3), a journey on which we will make many friends. By and large, the most contented (not complacent!) Christians that I know are those deeply committed to this work. Jesus said, 'By your fruit you will recognise them' (Matthew 7:20). Occasionally, the fruit is bad –

proud, arrogant, unloving, self-centred, but usually it is good – humble, loving, selfless, and full of joy.

2) Isn't my illness too small to bother God with?

People are naturally reluctant to seek prayer – either their problems are too great and thus insoluble, or too trivial to trouble God with. The question implies that God is sitting at a celestial telephone line which is quickly clogged by unimportant calls! If we must use modern technology, the fax seems a much better model. Message transmitted, and instantly received!

Often we need to experience God's teaching in small things in order to have faith to pray for greater ones. I find headaches and migraines particularly easy to pray for. Perhaps because I had to tackle a really difficult one early in my prayer ministry, I now tend to have 'faith' in other similar situations.

The healing of Peter's mother-in-law (Mark 1:30) wasn't a great miracle, but it was important for Peter, and it led to many other people coming for healing. The healing of Publius (Acts 28:8) wasn't particularly sensational, but again it led to the whole island of Malta turning up for prayer!

Don Latham tells a nice story to illustrate this (see also p. 324).

He was about to pray at a healing service, when the Lord told him that there was someone in the congregation whose big toe was very painful. Don felt pretty stupid sharing this knowledge, but an enormous Christian Marine hobbled up for prayer. His military career was being ruined by the physical condition of his toe – and he badly wanted it better. This clear healing led to the far deeper work in the lives of others who witnessed the healing and were converted, and Don learned another lesson in trusting the Lord.

One man's small problem (or big toe!) healed, leads to spiritual life for others.

Nevertheless, behind the question may lie a deeper theological question. I remember a doctor coming back, very angry, from visiting South Africa (c.1980). She had heard many testimonies to the healing of backs of wealthy white people. At the same time, she had seen the total lack of even basic medicine in hospitals in the black townships.

At one level this seems totally unjust. Yet I believe that the renewal that the Anglican Church experienced under the leadership of Archbishop Burnett in that period was crucial. Renewal led to theological confidence. This led to the church, instead of being a part of a small, but significant protest movement, as in the days of Trevor Huddleston at Sophiatown, becoming a major broker in the peace movement. The role of Archbishop Tutu in bringing reconciliation in the new South Africa has been absolutely crucial. Small beginnings, like mustard seeds, can lead to great faith.

3) What are the main reasons why people aren't healed?

After the incident of the disciples' failure to heal the epileptic boy (see chapter 3), Jesus gave three reasons – lack of prayer, lack of faith, and the prevailing spiritual climate. I have discussed these at some length earlier. However, I would add a number of other possible reasons – unconfessed sin, especially unforgiveness and bitterness, is a great block to healing. Some need inner healing (see question 9), some may have ancestral problems (question 10). Occult involvement will need to be sorted out first. Often God is wanting to use other methods (medicine, herbs), and sometimes his plan does not include physical healing.[1] Explaining these in a little more detail, we note that many doctors associate physical illness with our psychological condition. It is said, for instance, that rheumatoid arthritis is often linked with bitterness. How this can happen is something of a mystery. If rheumatoid arthritis is caused by a virus, perhaps our immune system doesn't work so well if we are full of anger and bitterness. The epistle of James (James 5:13ff) emphasises the importance of confession before receiving anointing and prayer for healing, as does the often ignored teaching on illness and misuse of the Lord's Supper (1 Corinthians 11:27–32).

Some illnesses stem from personal hurts in the past. An 'unwanted' baby may experience deep self-rejection leading to depression and other problems in later life. Unless the root cause is prayed about, there is unlikely to be healing.

Some illnesses (see question 10) are caused by problems inherited from previous generations (Exodus 20:3–6). Others are caused by occult involvement. Unless these are dealt with first, healing prayer is likely to be unsuccessful. Some plants cannot grow in acid soil – if you want to plant them you will have, at least, to neutralise the soil first! The same is true in the healing ministry.

Sometimes God wants to use different means. I was diagnosed with a very arthritic left hip at the age of thirty-three. For many years, my friend Fred Smith prayed for me. It was never completely healed, but for about twelve years the X-rays showed no deterioration, and even a slight improvement. Then, quite suddenly, it grew worse. It was time to seek medical help, and after an operation, I have felt fitter than for many, many years. Prayer helped, and delayed the need for an operation (important as artificial hips don't last for ever!), but ultimately, God's healing came through the hands of a skilled surgeon.

Some situations don't ever get healed. There is the well-known case of Joni Eareckson, writer of many Christian books, who has been a quadriplegic, confined in a wheel-chair since a diving accident as a teenager. God has used her wonderfully to help and encourage others. She has sought healing, but it hasn't come, but her faith has helped many people suffering from long-term 'incurable' diseases.

The healing ministry needs to be very sensitive to such situations. Before I was involved, I heard Margery Stevens[2] giving her testimony of healing from multiple sclerosis, but I have heard of very few similar cases.

We also need to remember Paul's teaching in 2 Corinthians 4:7–5:5 – put simply and starkly, bodies wear out. Obviously we can pray for people with Altzei-mer's, and their carers, but it is unlikely that we shall see any physical improvement. Much distress is caused to people with long-term illnesses who are constantly bom-barded with well-meaning prayer.

I would add that there is very little evidence of those born with severe mental illness ever being healed. (Of course, as I've seen in my own parish, they may have a very meaningful life surrounded by love, care and prayer.) If this is correct, then it poses sharp questions for the sort of theology quoted in the last chapter (see p. 210) which encourages us to claim healing as a theological right.

4) How important is confession before prayer for healing?

Three main biblical passages spring to mind. Two are well known, Mark 2:10–12, where the healing of the paralytic is preceded by the public forgiveness of his unspecified sins, and also James 5:13–18 (discussed in the previous answer). The third, 1 Corinthians 11:28–30, unfashionably lists failure to prepare oneself before receiving communion with illness and even death. This is clearly important for professing Christians, who need to be in a 'state of grace' if they are to receive healing or any other benefits from the Lord. Confession, whether alone to God, or formally (or informally) before a church leader is healthy medicine. I remember feeling spiritually quite different after confessing a sin, possibly linked to an event way back, to someone leading a healing service. This is particularly important in the deliverance ministry. I remember one girl who needed deliverance struggling to confess her interest in pornography – only for one of the prayer team to make a public confession, and vow to destroy a particular book or magazine on the same subject.

On the other hand, the multiple healings recorded in the Gospels (see chapter 3), and elsewhere in Acts, don't give the impression that there was a time or place for the confession of sins. Non-Christians are more likely to be 'convicted of sin' (John 16:8) after prayer for healing rather than before. However, I would stress that a confession and full renunciation of any occult involvement (see question 11) is essential.

Those praying may be given a gift of knowledge, or discernment (see question 6), which opens up the need for confession or renunciation of evil. Again, I would emphasise the need for wisdom and openness to the Holy Spirit among those who are praying. I once attended a large convention where the phenomena of the Toronto blessing were being encouraged. There was much screaming, laughter, jerking, and a sense of total spiritual chaos. The cry of the leadership was 'More, Lord, more!' Jane and I, who had seen this sort of thing in Zambia, felt that the main need was for repentance, renunciation and deliverance – which all goes to show what very different opinions Christian people can form in identical situations!

A particular trick of the enemy is to plant misplaced guilt on people (Revelation 12:10). We need to help people take a 'sober judgment' (Romans 12:3) of their spiritual state. False guilt is particularly common after tragedies like suicides, but it also hampers the spiritual freedom of many Christians in much more normal situations.

The most significant confession that someone may make will contain words like 'I don't think I'm really a Christian!' The discerning counsellor may say, 'Alleluia!' (because it's the surest sign that the Holy Spirit is working within them, and will soon bring them to faith) or, alternatively, provide words of reassurance, usually pointing to the fruit of their lives (Hebrews 13:15–16).

Healing and evangelism are closely linked. Jesus expected gratitude and obedience (Mark 5:19, for instance) from those he healed. We, too, should not be afraid to point people to Jesus, the author and perfecter of our faith (Hebrews 12:2). Fred Smith's powerful ministry (chapter 7 p. 212ff) was a model, in this respect.

I remember being present in a crowded house in Winchester, where a Christian with a well known healing ministry preached a long, rambling sermon on Isaiah 53. He was trying to bring people to faith. I heard several people mutter, 'Why doesn't he get on with the healing?' When he did, the results were electrifying. Several dramatic healings occurred, including one lady who, in response to a word of knowledge, unbandaged her previously ulcerated legs and found them healed. Then he confronted a spiritualist about her spiritual disobedience. Sparks flew, and the Spirit seemed to be quenched. But at least one person was converted, a number healed, and the preacher, for his part, was accused of theft! Satan does not like being exposed, especially when a respectable nest of spiritualism close to a cathedral is confronted.

5) How do I know if I have a gift of healing?

Other people will often recognise your gift before you do. They will ask you to pray for them, they may even comment on the benefits that they have received.

You will find an increasing compassion for the sick; you will long to help them. You will be drawn to read the Gospel stories of Jesus' healing. You will be challenged by great modern testimonies to healing (I was profoundly moved by reading *The Cross and the Switchblade*). You will hear people speak of these great matters, and you may, to your surprise, be asked to be involved by your local church.

If you are in a church situation where healing is either taboo, or practised so quietly that nobody knows what happens, you may feel the nudge of the Holy Spirit to challenge the leadership.

You will certainly want to pray more, and you may ask God for some sign to show you that he really does want you to be involved. It is fatally easy to be attracted to the healing ministry for the wrong reasons – power, self-fulfilment, pride.

It will take time. Paul went into the desert for three years (Galatians 1:18), Dorothy Kerin[3] had years of quiet preparation between her own dramatic healing and her public ministry. Many others would tell the same story.

You may find some strange phenomena when you pray – transference of pain, trembling hands, the gift of knowledge. Don't be alarmed by these, neither be put off by the lack of them. If you have a true gift of healing, you will be eminently teachable, flexible in theology, you will leave the results to God, and be prepared to put yourself under authority. If you have a self-centred (natural) gift of healing, you will be dogmatic, independent, results-oriented, and anxious for personal acclaim.

Jesus taught his disciples to heal in pairs. James told the sick person to summon the elders of the church. We need teamwork. We need the support of other people. Working in pairs means that the glory goes to God, and prevents people from saying, 'I was healed by the rector.' Occasionally, circumstances will dictate, especially for church leaders, that we pray on our own, but that should be the exception and not the rule.

Finally, if you have a gift of healing, you will see people healed! You may have to wait for a while (John Wimber prayed for many people before seeing any positive results), you may find encouragements come in clusters and in certain places, but you will see God at work. If no one is ever healed when your team prays, ask the Lord why, and be prepared to serve him in other ways.

If God wants you to be involved, he will put you in the right place and at the right time.

I shall never forget the first person for whose physical healing I prayed. My mother-in-law had had a word from the Lord that a lady who was to visit us that day would be healed of a back condition. I fervently hoped that we wouldn't be called on to pray. All this sort of thing was very new to me. But at the end of the day, our visitor suddenly complained about her back. 'Mummy, your back's a bore!' her ten-year-old daughter said, whereupon her mother withdrew in tears to the kitchen. I followed her, and rather reluctantly, I said, 'I think my mother-in-law has a gift of healing, would you like us to pray?' To my horror she agreed! As soon as we started to pray she was healed. To prove it, she jumped up and down. Naïvely, I expected her and her family to become Christians then and there. But none of those present did, although they were appreciative and moved. The person who was challenged, and changed, was me!

6) How important is fasting, for those involved in prayer for healing and deliverance?

Jesus said, 'This kind can come out only by prayer (and fasting)' (Mark 9:29). Fasting is an important spiritual discipline. Jesus preached it regularly. He condemned its misuse, but gave instructions as to how to fast without showing off (Matthew 6:16f). It is probably better that fasting should be part of our regular spiritual discipline, then carried out on the day of a healing service, or before a deliverance. Different people can cope physically with different levels of fasting. We need to take advice on what is suitable. Fasting from newspapers, TV, particular food or drink, sex (1 Corinthians 7:5), may be valuable, but the primary Gospel meaning of fasting is abstinence from food. I used to find this a terrible burden; now I find it a little easier. More regular practice has helped my body accept this discipline without so much internal screaming.

Fasting gives us more time for prayer, it sharpens our spiritual awareness, it reminds us that much of the world fasts involuntarily because of lack of food, and it follows the pattern of Jesus and his saints throughout the ages.

Probably the most helpful modern book is *The Celebration of Discipline*.[4]

7) What other gifts of the Spirit are important in healing and deliverance?

The most important thing is to be 'filled with the Spirit' (Ephesians 5:18). This, as the Greek makes clear, is to be a continuous process. We were not called to be stagnant ponds from which others may drink occasionally, but lakes, into which rivers flow and from which rivers leave.

'Whoever believes in me, as Scripture has said, streams of living water will flow from within him' (John 7:38). That said, particular gifts are very valuable. Some find praying in tongues helpful (1 Corinthians 12:10, etc.). 'In the same way, the Spirit helps us in our weakness. We do not know what we ought to pray, but the Spirit himself intercedes for us with groans that words cannot express' (Romans 8:26).

Paul may not be specifically referring to praying in tongues, but such prayer falls into this category. We do not know how to pray, so we let the Spirit lead our praying. I remember one lady with a back problem, beseeching me to pray in tongues as it was more effective. I had previously held back, because I thought it might seem strange to her and be a block, but in fact, it was what she needed.

The gift of knowledge (1 Corinthians 12:8) is widely used. Some churches, and individual preachers, use this gift. God tells them, either through a silent voice, or a definite pain, what sort of things he's going to heal. Such gifts, if correct (!), are a great help to faith. Sometimes, in a more personal way, the gift of knowledge enables the healing team to unlock a particular situation. It isn't easy to ask someone if they've been involved in incest, but it may be necessary. A particular biblical verse has sometimes been given to me, usually in difficult deliverance situations. (See chapter 1 for examples.) More recently, one of our healing team had a curious picture of someone coming into our church wearing dark glasses. Rather diffidently, she shared this with the group, and a week later with the church. A lady who was only present because in the intervening week I had urged her to come, was much encouraged. Among her problems was a dislike of bright church lighting, hence her desire to wear dark glasses. Although she hasn't been healed as yet, the picture opened up the possibility of a considerable amount of prayer and care.

The gift of distinguishing between spirits (1 Corinthians 12:10) is self-evidently important. Prayer for healing will be useless if deliverance is needed. Prayer for deliverance will be harmful if no evil powers are involved. This needs discernment. Often people need reassurance that they are not demonised. Usually a simple prayer for release from spiritual attack is all that is needed.

The gift of faith (1 Corinthians 12:9) is very precious, and misunderstood. The word 'faith' is used in at least three different ways in Scripture. 'Since we have been justified through faith' (Romans 5:11) expresses what is commonly called *saving faith*. We need this gift of faith in order to believe and to respond to the gospel. Later in the same epistle, Paul writes, 'Everything that does not come from faith is sin' (Romans 14:23). Here, Paul is saying that the Christian life must be based on faith. We are called to exercise faith continually throughout our discipleship. James (1:2–7) illustrates this very clearly as he writes about persistence in trials, the need for wisdom, and praying in faith.

In the morning, as they went along, they saw the fig tree withered from the roots. Peter remembered and said to Jesus,

'Rabbi, look! The fig tree you cursed has withered!' 'Have faith in God,' Jesus answered. 'I tell you the truth, if anyone says to this mountain, "Go, throw yourself into the sea," and does not doubt in his heart, but believes that what he says will happen, it will be done for him. Therefore I tell you, whatever you ask for in prayer, believe that you have received it, and it will be yours. And when you stand praying, if you hold anything against anyone, forgive him, so that your Father in heaven may forgive you your sins.' (Mark 11:20–26)

The faith Jesus is talking about here is exceptional – he has just cursed the barren fig tree! It is the faith that Paul experienced at Lystra (Acts 14:9) when the lame man was healed. It is the faith that has been expressed in many of the stories in this book. It is a faith which is based upon an inner certainty that God will act. I have experienced it quite often in evangelism – it is possible to sense God working in someone's life long before they acknowledge Jesus as Lord. I have experienced it occasionally in healing (chapter 1, p. 18) for instance.

My old friend Fred Smith (see chapter 7, p. 212ff) used to tell how one afternoon he sat drinking a flask of tea looking down on the city of Bath where he was to preach, and pray for healing, that night. He asked for the 'gift of faith' so that *everyone* might be healed. God heard his prayer, and he never looked back.

Most of us do not attain this level of faith, or anything like it. Do not be discouraged. We are called to pray with as much faith as we can, and not to try to screw ourselves up to believe what we can't believe. We may be grateful to the father of the epileptic boy: 'I do believe; help me overcome my unbelief' (Mark 9:24).

As to the faith of those being prayed for, I would re-emphasise that Jesus frequently commended the faith of others, and reserved his rebukes for the disciples and unbelieving cities and territories. He did not leave people feeling condemned because they hadn't had enough faith. We should be careful to follow his example. The burden of faith lies with the praying group, not with the people that we pray for. Obviously their faith is helpful, and usually there has to be faith somewhere, either within the sick person, or their friends.

Often the gift of wisdom (1 Corinthians 12:8) is important. It can lead to suggestions about change of diet, habits, and circumstances, that can be vital to healing. It is a much neglected gift. The Book of Proverbs is full of it.

'Trust in the Lord with all your heart and lean not on your own understanding; in all your ways acknowledge him, and he will make your paths straight. Do not be wise in your own eyes, fear the Lord and shun evil. This will bring health to your body and nourishment to your bones.' (Proverbs 3:5–8)

These verses brought a much needed smile to my lips when suffering severe spiritual delusions, the reaction to anaesthetics, after my hip operation.

Many people in the healing ministry exercise these gifts without relating them to 1 Corinthians 12. Some people's theology distances them from these 'charismatic gifts', but their practice includes them!

8) Can we pray for someone to be healed of homosexuality, or other sexual matters?

A valued friend, gay, celibate, and a Christian leader, commented, 'Gay people see their sexuality as something to be affirmed – not changed.' He also commented that he had seen many casualties from healing and deliverance ministries – Christians wanting to be changed, struggling to be changed, told that they ought to be changed, but that the invariable result was heartache and no change.

A similar viewpoint was expressed by the evangelical writer and theological college lecturer, Michael Vasey.[5]

Many homosexuals feel sufficiently threatened, or even undermined, by such ministry to distance themselves from it. Nevertheless, as it is, perhaps, the most divisive issue in today's Anglican Church, and as many people want to pray, we must consider the matter in more depth.

Most people see sexual orientation as a continuum. People's inclinations, homosexual and heterosexual, are formed partly by their genes, and partly by their experience. At one pole, there are people whose heterosexuality is so strong that they find the whole idea of homosexual love, let alone physical relations, repugnant. At the other pole, there are people so homosexual that they are repelled, sexually, by people of the other sex. In days gone by, some married, and could only have any sort of physical relationship with the aid of often degrading outside stimuli. In the centre are many people whose sexuality is ambivalent. If male, when young, they will often have passed through a homosexual phase, and then moved on to a 'normal' heterosexual relationship. Elizabeth Moberly[6] writes in detail about this. Her thesis is that male homosexuality is caused by an over-close relationship with the mother. She locates the source of the emotional insecurity that prevents a person attaining their intended heterosexual orientation in an unresolved deficit in the person's relationship with their same-sex parent. Consequently, she is able to suggest a therapeutic programme for gay people wishing to change their orientation. This programme, underpinned by prayer and counselling has, according to Vasey, been well received by many gay people. It takes their pain seriously, and offers a realistic hope.

It is, of course, totally unacceptable to those homosexuals who see their sexuality as 'God given'. To such people, I believe that the Church must offer acceptance and love, not rejection and the offer of ministry. If, for reasons we cannot fathom, God has created them with this nature, it is not for us to interfere. The Bible doesn't condemn a homosexual orientation as more fallen than any other. Sometimes people point out that Jesus doesn't mention homosexuality in any of the Gospels. However, the Jewish culture of the day was such that this was one issue on which he probably felt it was unnecessary to speak. When the Church moved out into Greek and Roman culture, the issue became important (see 1 Corinthians 6:9–11 'and that is what some of you were.') Scripture does condemn homosexual acts just as it condemns lustful looks and adultery (Romans 1:26f; Matthew 5:27f). The biblical choice appears to rest between celibacy (greatly exalted by Jesus in Matthew 19:11–12 – and *not* just for gay people), and seeking healing. Gay people, however, want to be allowed to form stable, loving relationships without constantly being challenged about the physical nature of their relationships.

Some churches have offered counselling and prayer for the healing of gay people. They would claim some success, and also feel that they had failed if they didn't offer people a way out of a sexual mire into a better, more creative state. This is a costly ministry, causing outrage to homosexual groups who feel judged and degraded by such ministry.

My limited experience in this field suggests that many homosexuals do not rejoice in this aspect of their nature. One well known to me struggled through an almost sexless marriage, while practising homosexuality whenever possible. He found the path of faith difficult. 'God has weighted the scales against me', though, ultimately, he made a deep peace with God. His marriage was outwardly successful and exhibited a deeper friendship with his wife than many more normal relationships achieve. His world fell apart when his wife died at quite a young age. He, certainly, fell into Elizabeth Moberly's category – a difficult, distant father and a powerful, tempestuous mother who had had a far worse heterosexual relationship that ended in divorce and suicide.

Another gay person rebelled against his biblical upbringing, pursued an active homosexual relationship, and although released of this and restored to faith, has found the prospect of marriage more difficult because of his past. He, too, I think, fits Elizabeth Moberly's basic thesis.

A gay couple told me of their (obvious) relationship. They were regular members of the church that I used to lead. I expressed my disapproval (probably more decisively than I would now). I didn't enquire as to the extent of their physical relationship, but said that if their consciences permitted, they were welcome to take communion. I added that I wouldn't be able to use them in the leadership of the church. I have taken a similar position with heterosexual couples living together unmarried, and with divorced couples who have been in Christian leadership, but whose relationship has been a major factor in the break-up of their previous marriages.

One young man thought he had been released from homosexuality. He felt called to evangelise in the 'gay' bars of Oxford. We tried to dissuade him, but he didn't listen. Soon he returned to his active homosexual ways, and he had to leave his paid position in a prominent church in a cloud of mutual recriminations.

Homosexuals, and lesbians, feel aggrieved whenever Christians take a 'biblical' stand.[7] We are accused, sometimes justly, of being judgemental, insensitive and obsessed with sexual sin. They want to stress that loving, stable, single sex relationships can enable them to serve their fellow beings creatively and spiritually. This view is powerfully supported by such leaders as Archbishop Tutu of South Africa, and Bishop Jim Thompson of Bath and Wells.

It's a view I would like to support, but I feel that an unbiased (and who is unbiased?) reading of Scripture doesn't allow it. Here I must agree to differ with some of my homosexual friends, but unless they ask, I shall not pray for their healing, or change of sexual orientation. We are not called to judge, but we are all called to stand, unflinchingly, for what we see as the truth. But let the truth be tempered with genuine love and compassion – which means trying to see the other person's point of view from *their* perspective.

There is nothing to stop Christians of the same sex living together – this frequently happened in the past, and happens now in religious communities. The biggest danger, apart from contravening the natural interpretation of Scripture, of rejoicing in one's 'God given sexuality', is that it may encourage others, of a bisexual nature, to turn in a homosexual direction. It is very doubtful whether that can be helpful either socially or spiritually.

As to healing from other sexual problems, prayer is obviously possible and desirable. One of the most difficult and, sadly, common situations is the need to pray for Christians after divorce, due mainly to their own adultery. What do you do faced with a couple who have been in Christian leadership whose adultery has broken up two households? The question of forgiveness, when they were apparently enlightened (Hebrews 6:4–6), is so much harder. I was greatly helped in one such case by the loving attitude of one ex-partner who said in effect 'They need your help. Pray for them and with them.' Incidentally, I found this far harder than any acceptance of homosexuals, however much I might disagree with them. Adultery harms so many people: loving stable, one-sex relationships harm no one – except, perhaps, the biblical witness of the Church.

In these deep waters, we need to remember the double challenge of Jesus to the woman taken in the act of adultery: 'If any one of you is without sin, let him be the first to throw a stone at her' (John 8:1–11). And later, to the woman herself, 'Then neither do I condemn you. Go now and leave your life of sin.'

9) What is meant by the healing of the memories (or inner healing) – is it scriptural?

A key scripture would seem to be Isaiah 61:1–4, especially 'they will rebuild the ancient ruins', as well as Hebrews 13:8 which is always quoted. Some techniques in this area are much less obviously acceptable. Reliving one's birth experience seems to have no scriptural foundation, and some healing of memories practitioners encourage us not only to see Jesus in the hurts of the past, but also to imagine those who have hurt us differently in the light of Jesus' presence. This seems a downright perversion of the truth and is to be avoided. Some of the classic books of healing recommend this sort of approach and should be steered well clear of!

St Paul presents the idea in Romans 6:4 that the past is

buried in baptism. The problem, as he knows (see Romans 7:17), is that this doesn't happen easily. People who have suffered abuse, rejection, lack of love in their early life, especially in the years which they cannot remember, or even before birth, will be very vulnerable and need the sort of prayer described above to bring them to freedom.

Marks of needing this prayer can include recurring mental problems and disturbing dreams (occult involvement can also cause this), hatred and resentment towards God and other people, very poor self-image, humiliating practices (eating problems, sexual perversion, compulsive gambling, self-mutilation, etc), frozen emotions, and a lack of any sort of balanced Christian life.

Praying in these areas needs training and knowledge. Healing teams should *not* get involved in this, but seek help from those who have some real knowledge.[8]

I received, as a result of a request in the diocesan newspaper, a warning testimony. One lady, who had lost a son at birth, had at the time been told to forget about it. 'God takes his own' was said to her. Sixteen years later, the arrival of a vicar interested in the healing ministry encouraged her to release her buried memories. She attended a Eucharist, led by an experienced clergyman, named the child, but didn't really feel at peace. A few years later, through her GP, she found the details of her stillbirth, visited the cemetery and wrote her daughter's name in the book of remembrance. She joined SANDS (Stillbirth and Neonatal Deaths Society), and received great help from a consultant specialist. She says: 'I have written in because I would like to hope that other mothers, bereaved long ago, can benefit from my experiences. There are many steps needed to be taken rather than leaving it all to God.'

This testimony acts as a warning. It should remind us all what a complex matter healing is, and the necessity of professional medical skill in many situations. Our prayer team would not feel competent, nor called, to pray through most of these sorts of problems. However, we can be used to ask the right questions, and to set people in the right direction to receive the healing that they need. Sometimes God acts sovereignly, sometimes he uses Christian counsellors, often he uses professional medical channels.

The important thing is, as Jesus said, 'You will know the truth, and the truth will set you free,' (John 8:32).

I have included a number of other testimonies in chapter 10, pp. 336ff. I believe that Psalm 139 is particularly appropriate to help people who suffer from a deep sense of inferiority. If they can come to believe not only that God has made them, but that he has made them for a purpose, much healing can begin.

On a more profound level, there is a real need for much healing of past place memories. This can involve praying in haunted houses, praying at sites of atrocities. We have prayed in Shepton Mallet market place where local citizens were hanged after Monmouth's rebellion in 1688, and in Shepton Mallet Prison where many executions took place, especially of American troops in the 1939–45 war.

Michael Mitton, deputy director of ACORN, told a moving story of this sort of ministry at the 1998 Lambeth Conference of Anglican bishops. The day after the conclusion of the difficult debate on homosexuality, a Japanese bishop was asked to celebrate the Eucharist. The date, 6 August, was doubly significant. Not only was it kept as 'The Feast of the Transfiguration', but it was also the date of the dropping of the atomic bomb by the Allies in 1945 on the Japanese cities of Hiroshima and Nagasaki.

The preacher was a daughter of the late Bishop Wilson of Birmingham. In the war, Wilson as a young man was captured by the Japanese. His amazing courage, and his Christian demeanour in terrible circumstances, so impressed one of his captors that he became a Christian. This man was ordained a priest, in the Anglican Church of Japan, some years later, by Bishop Wilson.

It is these sort of actions which are so needed, and which can help to bring healing to deep national wounds.

10) What is meant by the healing of the Family Tree[9] – is it scriptural?

The scriptural basis is the warning (Exodus 20:3–6) centred in the ten commandments that spiritual disobedience can affect future generations. Many people recoil in horror from this idea, yet there is solid experiential evidence that people can be badly affected, especially by occult activity, suicide and murder, by their direct ancestors.

The Bath and Wells Diocesan Healing Group, of which I am glad to be a member, has taken this seriously enough to publish a pamphlet of guide-lines and to include a suitable service.[10]

I have often used this approach. I have found it especially helpful with a young ordinand in deep depression, clearly affected by attitudes and events in previous generations. I have found it helpful with a very young person seriously talking about suicide, who was unaware of many suicides among his ancestors. I think it will be helpful for the family of a young woman who has recently killed herself in an identical way to that used by her father many years earlier.

There is plenty of evidence of occult and white-magic influence descending from one generation to another. Near where I was brought up, there was a stately home. The family had been cursed long ago, and each eldest son had died tragically for many generations. I met one female member of the family, a former heroin addict, now converted and wanting to help others. Sadly, her brother didn't share her faith, and some years later I read of his suicide – leaving an illegitimate baby boy as his heir. Such a curse could, and should, be broken in the name of the Lord.

I remember long ago handing over what I sensed would be a difficult deliverance case to Michael and Rosemary Green. The spirit spoke through the young man claiming to have lodged in successive members of the family since the reign of Charles II.

Here is a more detailed example. A fairly recently converted Christian businessman came to see me, seeking prayer for healing from a persistent stomach disorder. He shared with me a tremendous bondage to superstition which he felt affected his business and family life before he became a Christian. For example: 'Decision making depended upon the omens being right – one magpie seen on the road spelt bad luck, fingers had to be crossed the right number of times, wood had to be touched, and so on. Failure to apply these rituals in the right way generated great fear of the consequences.'

After his conversion, intellectually, he had accepted Christian teaching on superstition and the occult. He renounced the rituals and accepted instead the protection given to every Christian. Nevertheless, a deep-seated fear invariably surfaced whenever one of these rituals was broken.

At a distance it all sounds quite trivial, but that wasn't how it felt as, on a hot July afternoon, we went for a walk to discuss the problem. It quickly became clear to me that it was substantially an ancestor problem. He had been brought up in a notoriously haunted pub, and claimed to have tape-recorded the resident ghost when a teenager. He had traced a history of 'white magic' back on his grandmother's side of the family tree. As we walked, we came to a fork in the path. To the left I saw a man with a net, evidently taking his bees. Intrigued, despite my fear of bees and wasps, I suggested we went left. The hives were about twenty metres off the path, but the bees were in great quantity around the bramble blossoms. We hastened by, and my companion was stung twice on the ear. I was very embarrassed! When we were safely in the next field, I put my hand on his ear and prayed with minimal faith for his healing. To my immense surprise, and his relief, the pain instantly went.

'They swarmed around me like bees, but they died out as quickly as burning thorns; in the name of the Lord I cut them off' (Psalm 118:12) seemed an appropriate commentary on our experience. It also helped to confirm to me that God did want me to pray to cut off his problems which had arisen from the white magic and other spiritual disobedience in his family tree. I made it clear, as I always do, that we are not judging the ancestors. Their spiritual state is between them and God. But we are, in the name of the Lord, cutting off any negative spiritual influence which they have left behind.

We held a simple communion service in the village church near the family pub. I prayed for complete release for him and his family, and future generations, from any such spiritual bondage. There was a great sense of peace, and a general sense of God's love. The man testifies that, when he awoke on the morning after the service, he felt as if a physical burden had been lifted from his shoulders, as well as a dark cloud lifted from his mind.

More recently, a lady sought help for her schizophrenic

son. There were certain dark influences from previous generations, and some spiritual disobedience in the present. She brought a friend, and we had a simple communion service with the intention of praying for her son's healing. Very soon afterward, she noticed a significant improvement in his attitude to life, and we continue to pray for his full recovery.

11) What are the marks of those needing deliverance?[11]

A good opening question is to ask people whether they have been involved in any occult practices – attending seances, reading tarot cards, and playing with Ouija boards are the most common. In practice this is usually denied, only for the answer to be reversed later on. If the answer is 'no', then I ask about the practices of parents or grandparents. Sometimes the person doesn't know, more often they do.

Once, in Zambia, I was getting nowhere praying for a woman very obviously demonized. It was only when I established that her husband had strong connections with witchcraft that the source of her problem, and the possibility of freedom, became apparent.

I am dubious about praying for deliverance for people unless it is established that they, their ancestors, or their partner(s) have been involved in occult practices.

There do seem to be examples of extreme forms of selfishness, sexual sin, or deep anger, allowing demonic influence to disturb a person's life (see James 3:13–16). I am very cautious, because scripture mainly speaks of the sins of the *flesh* (Galatians 5:19f) which had to be confessed, with the full assurance of God's forgiveness (absolution), and not dealt with by exorcism.

Confession can seem a daunting prospect; yet it is

remarkably liberating – not unlike deliverance in its spiritual effect.

There are, of course, degrees of demonisation – complete possession is very, very rare. Just as Jesus says in John 14:17 of the Holy Spirit, 'he lives *with* you and will be in you', so many people are troubled by the presence of evil, but not demonised. Others may be demonised, but still fully co-operative in helping in the process of deliverance. We need to avoid any theology which even hints that it is normal for people to suffer from demonic problems. The New Testament doesn't do that. Quite the reverse, the few demoniacs react violently to the presence of Jesus or his disciples (see Mark 1:23 f, and Acts 8:7), whereas many others wait quietly for healing and teaching.

I was preaching once on Acts 8:7. We were in a remote Zambian village, and a member of the Mothers' Union fell out of her pew screaming (see p. 119). This is a clear sign that there is a problem! Such people may react, often violently, against the sacraments. Sometimes they will be unable physically to receive communion, they will dislike blessed water (a reminder of baptism and the cross), and object to holy oil. When freed, people who have previously violently resisted anointing now receive it gladly.

A third mark is that of unusual physical symptoms. Temporary deafness, an inability to recite the Lord's Prayer, strange, distraught eyes (Matthew 6:22–23), also inordinate strength (Mark 5:4) are all quite common marks of a problem. Many times, I've seen people's eyes clear after prayer. Quite often, people refuse to look into my eyes, complaining of their brightness.

A fourth mark is deep fear or mocking laughter. Both are designed to prevent the person from being prayed for. Demonised people are very reluctant to receive prayer, and often say vehemently that it won't do them any good.

A fifth mark is speaking in an unknown tongue, and speaking words that the person would never normally say, or doesn't know (see chapter 1, p. 33, for example).

I am fully aware that most, if not all, of these symptoms can be displayed by the mentally ill, and/or those suffering extreme forms of stress. Interestingly, however, most of the psychiatrists I've talked to have less of a problem about prayers for deliverance than many priests.

A sixth, but much less reliable mark, is that the person thinks that they have a demonic problem. Psychiatrically ill people often attribute their troubles to the devil, and other people are looking for a convenient cure.

If the diagnosis is correct, prayer is relatively simple. Cyprian (who lived in North Africa and died in 258), says, 'Yet these (spirits) when adjured by us through the true God, immediately withdraw and confess and are forced to go out of the bodies which they have possessed.' While elsewhere he comments that demons might leave slowly or rapidly depending on the faith of the sufferer and the grace of the healer.[12]

12)   How do we pray for deliverance?

The first answer is that we don't. If we are Anglican, we shall be under authority, first of the parish priest, secondly of the bishop who will have appointed a diocesan exorcist. The diocesan official should be contacted in all but the most minor cases. This gives the praying team 'cover' both in prayer and in the sense of being shown to have acted responsibly. There have been enough disasters in this area to prevent well-meaning people from blundering in.

Secondly, we use the gentlest approach possible! Encouraging someone to retake their baptismal vows both opens the way to a new or renewed commitment to

Jesus (and without this the warning of Matthew 12:43 applies), and also contains the great question 'Do you renounce evil?' which, in these cases, I would take first. I would encourage them to renounce everything connected with the occult in their own experience and in their family. Often at the beginning of the interview they will deny any involvement. About an hour later, the truth seems to emerge. This would be a typical prayer: 'I renounce tarot readings, fortune-telling, the yoga mantra that I was given, and my grandfather's involvement in Free Masonry. . . .'

At the end, I would pray for them to be filled with the Holy Spirit, anoint them with oil, and ask them how they felt!

A typical recent case was of a woman who, with great reluctance, told me that for about half the month she suffered from severe pre-menstrual tension which caused migraines, depression and inability to work. She then reminded me that she had attended spiritist meetings when her husband was involved in 'spiritual' healing. We had a time of prayer, after a church service, with a few of her friends present. She felt an immediate release, and a physical improvement from the time we began to talk about the problem. She also started to grow spiritually into a much clearer commitment to Christ as soon as she asked for help – and was taken seriously.

Thirdly, we encourage the co-operation of the patient! Particularly in Zambia (see chapter 1), when faced with many people who seemed to need deliverance, it was very helpful to ask them to name the spirits, and to pray, themselves, for release. This was usually sufficient for them to feel completely free.

Fourthly, we take authority (see chapter 7 p. 228 for a description of Archdeacon Kaoma calmly at work amid the chaos). If, in rural Zambia, as soon as you pray some-one collapses on the ground doing a passable imitation of the local snake, you haven't time, or the means, to phone the diocesan exorcist. A prayer of command needs to be said: 'In the name of Jesus, leave this person!' It will be helpful to establish the name of the evil spirit, and also to cut off any hold from previous generations, and any chain of command from local spiritist powers.

Such prayer shouldn't take long. Lengthy exorcism sessions are to be avoided. A few minutes usually suffice, and you should certainly stop after an hour.

In difficult cases, I often used local water, blessed (by me!) for the occasion. I realised the importance of this when the woman, whose lengthy exorcism I described in chapter 1, said to Michael Green, 'You can't help me, you haven't got any holy water.' He took a glass to the nearest tap, said a quick prayer, and returned triumphant. When it was sprinkled over her, she reacted violently and was, at least temporarily, set free. Two surprised Evangelicals sought the Scriptures. Colossians 2:15 seemed the best answer. Through his death on the cross, Christ disarmed the powers and authorities. His baptism in the Jordan foreshadowed his death. Similarly, the baptism of a Christian is linked to Christ's death and resurrection. Consecrated water is a reminder of baptism, and is thus linked to the cross – hence its efficacy against the powers of darkness.

The person will usually know if they are free, and they will look different. Physical healing of stomach pains and headaches often accompanies deliverance.

Before you begin, pray for protection for your team, your household, and the building in which you are praying. Similarly, pray for the patient's family. Afterwards, challenge them to renounce and destroy any charms, occult books, etc.

Interestingly, the ministry is almost identical in rural Zambia and central Oxford! Judging by what I've read, it is very similar to that offered by the Early Fathers. It is not a '*cultural*' matter, but a deeply spiritual one. It may be more common in Zambia, because many people seek healing and protection from witch doctors, but the means of release and the symptoms of the problem are identical. Surprisingly, healing services that I've held in Uganda showed, at most, two such problems out of several hundred who asked for prayer. Perhaps the East African revival in the 1950s rooted out these spiritual problems for that part of Africa.

13) Can prayer for healing and/or deliverance do harm?

Yes! Prayer for deliverance of non-existent evil spirits will do much harm, and tends to leave people frightened, perplexed and dependent upon those who have ministered to them (see also p. 15 for a personal failure).

Certain types of deliverance ministry are potentially very dangerous. At a recent conference, an Anglican bishop spoke of the dangers of so-called 'interior ministries'. This is a process of anointing which anoints all the potential exits from the body which a demon might use. This is a peculiarly horrible and totally unscriptural approach which has apparently led to legal action in some cases.

Prayer for healing can also do harm if it leaves the patient feeling guilty that he/she hasn't been healed. People who come for prayer are often very sensitive and vulnerable. Great care must be taken to lay the 'burden of faith' on those who pray. Jesus commanded faith in those he prayed for, and deprecated its lack in the disciples and in some localities, notably Nazareth (Mark 6:6), Korazin and Bethsaida (Luke 10:13).

Prayer in highly emotional meetings can lead to 'apparent' healing. People get up and walk, but sadly, they are often back in their wheelchairs two days later. People who appear to have received great blessing need very careful follow-up to help them hold on to what they have gained.

Healing of memories (see question 9) is another potentially dangerous area. Some fashionable books have encouraged people to relive past experiences, bringing Jesus into them (see Hebrews 13:8), and imagining him transforming the situation – changing the abusing father or whatever. Such a technique has no scriptural basis, and seems to be encouraging people to act out a lie.

Equally dangerous are some forms of regression therapy. In secular circles these have caused children to make often unfounded accusations against innocent parents, thereby causing unbelievable distress. Occasionally, the Christian gift of knowledge (see question 7) may be used to unlock a deep past history, but it needs to be done with immense sensitivity and pastoral care.

14) Can I pray for people who don't know that they are being prayed for?

Yes, Jesus did so (John 4:46f, etc.). Fred Smith tells one such story.[13]

> I never normally stopped to pick up hitch-hikers, but I sensed that God wanted me to stop for this man. As I drew up beside him, and he climbed into the car, I noticed that he was wearing a clerical collar. I had picked up a vicar! I told him

it was rather unusual to find a vicar hitch-hiking, and asked if he was a local man, and where he wanted to go. I told him that I was on my way to Oxford for a prayer meeting, and could take him as far as that. The vicar told me that he was from Coventry, but he was on his way to visit a young girl from his congregation who was in hospital in Birmingham with a tumour on the brain. She was going to have an operation the following day, and the doctors had told her parents that there was only one chance in ten that she would pull through. Her parents had asked the vicar to give their daughter Holy Communion the night before the operation, and he was on his way to the hospital now. I told him that I was on my way to a prayer meeting. 'We regularly pray for the sick and see God heal them, and if you would like we will pray for the sick girl tonight.'

About ten days later I received a letter from the vicar:

'Dear Fred,

Thank you for praying for the girl in my church with the tumour on the brain. She did not have her operation after all. When they came to prepare her for the operation on the morning after I met you there was no sign of the tumour. I am writing to you from the office at church, and downstairs the children are having a party. I can hear the shrieks of joy as I write. At the moment, the girl for whom you prayed is leading them in a game of Follow my Leader!'

I think it is better that people should know that they are being prayed for, as then they are more likely to attribute their recovery to the right source!

15) When and how should anointing be used?

Anointing for healing occurs twice in the Bible (Mark 6:7–13, and James 5:13–20). The generally agreed practice is that anointing for healing should, after preparation, be for serious cases of illness. Nevertheless, it sometimes seems appropriate to anoint at healing services – usually for long-term persistent illnesses, and after any sort of deliverance ministry – this acts as a sort of litmus-paper test that the person is now free, as well as providing an important sense of well-being in the presence of the Holy Spirit.

Bishops, following ancient tradition, but without any scriptural authority, often bless three types of oil at a special service on Maundy Thursday. One is used[14] for baptism and exorcism, another at confirmation, and the third for healing. As so often, the Church has complicated what Scripture makes simple.

The Old Testament phrase 'the oil of joy/gladness' (see p. 63) is rather lovely. I think that anointing often brings great blessing. At a recent cathedral healing service, I was given the task of anointing a number of people. It was a great joy, and many were very obviously touched by the Holy Spirit.

It is also a great privilege to visit people in their homes and to take part in a service which includes anointing. In cases of lengthy illness, this should be repeated as often as seems appropriate.

Francis Macnutt makes it clear how many parts of the Roman Church have recovered the idea of anointing for healing rather than in preparation for death. He helpfully explains how the confusion arose owing to the Vulgate (the Latin Bible) using the same word for both salvation and healing (see Chapter 7, p. 221).

16) What about alternative approaches to healing such as homoeopathy?[15]

This frequently asked question is really too big for a short section in this book. However, because it is so often asked,

I shall attempt a brief answer. A physical cure, from a Christian perspective, can be seen as positive, neutral or negative. Some things clearly bring glory to Christ and are the work of the Holy Spirit (John 16:14). Christian healing prayer, a Christian hospice, a Christian doctor or surgeon, are likely to bring glory to Christ – provided, of course, their work and practice are of the highest standard.

We shall look at some of the negative, unhelpful approaches in the next two sections. Always remembering that if people are cured physically, but harmed spiritually, this is doubly unfortunate. The effect of such a cure is inevitably to cause spiritual bondage. We are aware that a very few Christians (see chapter 7, p. 208) don't use conventional medicine, that rather more are wary of psychiatry – foolishly, in my view – but the usual basis of this question is uncertainty about homoeopathy, acupuncture, yoga, aromatherapy, herbal medicines and the like.

Some Christians are particularly wary of homoeopathy because of the alleged occult involvement of its founder. They are also unhappy that something so obviously unscientific as a substance diluted a million times could be efficacious. It all smacks of magic or gobbledegook. The problem is that there is considerable evidence for its working. It seems to help animals, and there are Christian homoeopaths who dispense the remedy without using any curious incantations. I have to admit that my wife's chilblains and circulation have greatly improved since taking a homoeopathic remedy, and that I was once released from tennis elbow after taking homoeopathic medicine. Nevertheless, if you are worried, don't take it! Don't confuse homoeopathy with herbal remedies where natural herbs are used to help the body and mind from cancer, depression, and many other illnesses.

Acupuncture is especially controversial. Our local

surgery offers it, and people have benefited. Some Christians won't use it because of its origin in Chinese religious thought. Archdeacon Trevor Nash[16] records a friend saying to him that 'as soon as the skin is punctured, devils can enter in'. However, many Christians believe that it has a sound medical basis. Perhaps we should adopt the strategy of Gamaliel (Acts 5:34f) and leave people to make up their own minds unless it appears to be doing them any obvious spiritual harm.

Yoga exercises bring relief to many, and seem like harmless 'keep-fit' exercises. The problem is that participants are usually given a 'mantra', a Hindu prayer, to repeat. A young lady in my last parish, a near neighbour, suddenly arrived in my home announcing that God had called her to be a nun. She wasn't, at that stage, a Christian. After professing conversion, and being confirmed, she physically couldn't take communion. She had practised yoga, and her 'mantra' took over when she tried to receive communion. After prayer, she was set free. She never became a nun, despite various attempts, but remained a faithful worshipper in the local church.

Aromatherapy is likely to be spiritually harmless, and in practice is often beneficial. As with other 'alternative' approaches, probably the most important thing is the spiritual standing of the practitioner.

Herbal medicine is, of course, the basis for all our pills and potions! Digitalis heart pills are based on the natural healing power extracted from foxglove leaves. Perhaps there is a little parable here – foxgloves are highly poisonous, but rightly used they provide wonderful medicine!

All in all, we would be wise to affirm the general grace of God in healing, and less eager to draw up hit lists of things attributable to the Devil. God is the creator of all things, and he knows how they can be used for our benefit.

17) When is 'healing' spiritually dangerous?

As we shall see (Question 21), virtually all Christians gladly accept medical and surgical help. Such help, whether from Christian doctors or not, is likely to be spiritually positive, and certainly not in opposition to God's general purposes and provisions for humankind.

Psychiatry presents a greater problem to some Christians. Personally, I have received nothing but help and courtesy when consulting psychiatrists either about patients or personal problems. Obviously we might have strong reservations about techniques which involved hypnosis, or other forms of regression therapies, just as searching questions might be asked of certain aspects of the Christian healing ministry (Question 13).

What is far more problematical, and very challenging to the Christian healing ministry, is the rapid growth of alternative healing through people who channel their natural, or psychic, gifts to help others. Some of it may be spiritually neutral, but much of it is based on, or inherited from, occult sources.

'Faith healing', which is often portrayed as being from God, presents a particularly subtle problem. It has become very fashionable, and writing in 1999, I am aware of a rising crescendo of newspaper articles, radio and TV discussion, and general media interest in the subject.

It affects every strata of society. High society is attracted to fashionable healers like Jack Temple (see below), football fans are intrigued by, and sometimes infuriated with, the beliefs of England managers, and ordinary folk rush off to healing centres to buy their crystals and to have tarot readings.

Christians are caught in a vicious double bind. If 'faith healing' is ridiculed, then God appears to be dishonoured – 'after all, healing is such an important part of the Bible, Vicar!' If 'faith healing' is approved and apparently successful, then God, the Bible and the cross of Christ are bypassed and even despised.

Alternative healers present a sharp challenge to the Christian Church. The octogenarian Jack Temple[17] is a typically attractive example. With a combination of diagnosis and direction by pendulum, use of crystals, homoeopathic remedies, the power of stone circles, and advice from deceased healers, he effects some remarkable cures. His book cites well-known names such as the Duchess of York, the late Princess Diana, the model Jerry Hall, and hosts of ordinary clients who have benefited from his techniques. He travels miles to find suitable healing plants, invariably using his pendulum to guide him to their location.

He believes strongly in reincarnation, and sees many people's problems as due to faulty DNA inherited usually, via reincarnation, from thousands of years earlier. Clearly his methods, and personality, are attractive to New Age thinkers. He, himself, having been ill for many years (uninsurable at fifty), is now a remarkably healthy eighty year old, expecting to live for many more years.

In looking for the Christian response, we might cite 'whoever is not against us is for us' (Mark 9:40). The context of this often misquoted saying is interesting – the man who the disciples tried to prevent exorcising was driving demons out *in Jesus' name*. Their objection was merely that he wasn't one of them!

The ministrations of Jack Temple, and people like him,

are probably effective at a physical level – just as the magicians of Egypt could sometimes match Moses and Aaron (Exodus 7:11). But what is the spiritual cost? If we are healed by someone using a pendulum for divination, crystals, and believing in the power of ancient stones, and reincarnation, we are likely not only to absorb some of their beliefs, but also to be affected by their psychic energy. Many people are totally unaware of the occult powers that lie behind the pendulums and of the spiritual dangers that they open people up to. An experience of this sort will inevitably turn people away from Jesus. The answer for the Christian Church is to rediscover Christ's healing gift, and not give people cause to turn to such spiritually dangerous remedies.

As I finished writing (March 1999), there was a considerable furore in the English press caused by the views of Glen Hoddle, then the national football coach. Already ridiculed for his use of a faith healer, Eileen Drewery, as a solution to some of the team's physical problems, his exposition of her views on reincarnation 'that a lot of people come back to earth to suffer' was highly distressing to the disabled and their families. This interpretation of part of the popular theory of reincarnation was deemed so insulting that the luckless Mr Hoddle was sacked from his post.

What is sad, apart from the very real offence caused to some, and the self-righteous intolerance of the media, is that a man who at times has been thought to be a 'born again' Christian could hold such views.

Reincarnation (mathematically impossible without the constant creation of 'new souls'), denies the uniqueness of the human being, removes the efficacy of the cross, and sidelines the resurrection. Not surprisingly, it is popular in various forms, as it deals conveniently with sin and suffering, and avoids looking to Jesus as the source of healing. It is desperately sad that the Christian Church was unable to help Hoddle and show him that there is a Christian ministry of healing which avoids all these pitfalls.

As with Jack Temple, above, it is highly likely that Eileen Drewery's methods are sometimes effective – but at what spiritual and, in this case, material cost? According to *The Times* (5 February 1999), Mrs Drewery had a one-to-one with God which prevented England from scoring a vital goal in a World Cup qualifier – in order to avoid a riot in Italy after the match. 'The lady doth claim too much for her powers, methinks.'

Hoddle's successor seems to be open to the same paths, and the popular press shows signs of hounding both him and his wife.

At a more local level, I've experienced a number of problems. People who go to spiritual healing centres seem to lose their Christian convictions, experience spiritual difficulties, cause confusion to others, and are often very difficult to pray for. It is as though a veil (2 Corinthians 4:3) has clouded their innermost being. Likewise people who come for spiritual help after involvement with faith healers are particularly difficult to help.

Often people get drawn in without realising that there is any danger.

Here is a testimony which illustrates the subtlety of it all. My correspondent's helper sounded safe, but proved to be otherwise.

Fifteen years ago, a young lady (twenty-eight years old) took herself to a professional woman counsellor, due to feeling a great lack of confidence in herself, and general depression. At first she felt helped, but as sessions continued she realised that the method was connected with spiritism – especially when listening to the tape she was given for guidance. She felt a sensation of being strongly attacked by an evil force – physically (hands round her neck, squeezing), and emotionally – giving her no peace of mind and enormous distress. She and her mother were always closely bonded. Her mother had gone forward at a Billy Graham campaign a year before, but she could not release her daughter, nor could any other of the Christians she sought out.

Her parish worker, and others, felt that her reaction showed marks of hysteria and doubted the reality of any evil attack. However, she came, with her parish worker, to a healing service in Shepton. As usual, we took her through a low-key type of ministry, praying to cut off the effects of the past. As a result of this, she was able to make a real commitment to Jesus, but still felt under some bondage.

A while later she returned, again with her parish worker, to a healing service which I was leading and at which Fred Smith was preaching. This time she reacted violently to prayer, screaming and falling over. Very quickly, we took authority over the evil spirit, and she was completely freed.

She is now happily married to a Christian and they often lead services together at an old people's home. Her husband preaches and she sings – quite a transformation from the depressed young lady of the past.

It may be that some healing is 'natural' – after all, the use of conventional and herbal medicine is, for the most part, spiritually neutral. But it needs to be approached with great caution. An interesting test is when such healers want to turn to Christ, are they willing to renounce and release their healing powers? If they are, they are often given them back, redirected and strengthened. If they are not, then like Simon Magus (Acts 8), their heart is not yet in the right place.

Recently, an aromatherapist has become a Christian and joined our church. The aromatherapist (see p. 304) was marvellously converted and now uses her oils with great Christian grace. One member of our congregation testified recently of her dramatic physical improvement as a result of receiving this treatment.

The whole area of 'faith healing' presents a considerable challenge to the Church. If only the Church had her own house in order, and proclaimed Christ's healing love with greater confidence, many of these subtle alternatives would fade away.

18) What is wrong with spiritism?

Quite simply, it is forbidden in the Bible. Numerous Old Testament references include Deuteronomy 18:9f and Isaiah 47:12. In the New Testament, the exorcism of the girl with a spirit of divination, and the burning of the magic books in Ephesus, make the same point.

It is easy to see the attractions. Recently, a mother whose daughter had just committed suicide asked me about it. How tempting to try and make contact. But what a delusion – if the contact is genuine (and 1 Samuel 28 suggests that it may be), there is ever-increasing hunger for more. Besides, there will always be the uncertainty, is the truth being spoken? Is it all a deception?

One great friend of mine told me this story from his teenage years. It shows the depth of knowledge available to those who practise occult things and, more importantly, helps to explain why this man, an innocent victim of the prediction, didn't really turn to the Lord for over fifty years.

Over fifty years ago, my mother was visiting an aunt who occasionally took in paying guests. It was late evening, when there was a knock on the door. It transpired that two people, a Madam Zelda and her husband, unable to find accommodation anywhere, had been directed by the police to my aunt's house. She was unable to help, and feeling sorry for them, my mother offered to put them up for the three days required. Madam Zelda was a professional palmist and was resting between appointments. During her stay, two friends of my sister called. Madam Zelda agreed to read their palms. During one reading, she suddenly turned very pale and almost fainted. We rushed around getting smelling salts and a glass of water. Having recovered somewhat, she said to the girl whose hand she had been reading, 'Go straight home, my dear, it is important.' After the two girls left, Madam Zelda said, 'That girl's sister has just met with an accident near here. I am afraid it is serious.' It transpired that the sister was on her way to our house when she was knocked down by an ambulance and was found to be dead on reaching the hospital.

On her last day, Madam Zelda read my mother's hand. As she was leaving, she gave my sister an envelope with instructions not to tell my mother its contents, but to read the note and act accordingly. The note stated that on a certain day, in the distant future, my mother would meet with an accident, connected with a piece of rope, or a dog lead, and that on that day my sister and I should be on our guard. My sister put the note away and, in due course, we forgot it. About two years later, I returned from work to find the house in darkness. My mother was lying on her bed where she had been all day. She told me she had gone to my room to change the bed linen, when she tripped over the earth lead of my radio set, attached to a low water pipe. She had hurt her ankle. It had taken her nearly two hours to reach her room, and she was exhausted. We summoned the doctor who discovered she had broken her ankle. Because of a heart condition, he decided that she go at once to hospital. The following day she was given an anaesthetic and the ankle was set. The operation was unsuccessful, and during the second attempt to set the ankle, she died under the anaesthetic.

After the funeral, my sister remembered Madam Zelda's prediction. I asked her where the envelope was. After a considerable search we found it. The date on the note was the day on which the accident occurred.

How such predictions work, I have no idea. That they have a very negative spiritual effect is certain. During adult confirmation classes, after quite a spiritual struggle, my friend came to faith. He then told me this story! We had to pray to cut off its effect from him, and to set him free to worship the Lord for the remaining years of his life. Madam Zelda, herself, would doubtless have been horrified to discover the negative effects of her 'predictions'. Satan is very skilled at hiding the end results from his often unwitting dupes.

This story had an unexpected sequel. I was preaching in one of our small village churches. I was expecting the children to arrive for the talk, but they didn't come, so I needed to preach an adult sermon. We had just sung Bob's favourite song. Reminded of him, I told the small congregation of about twenty about Madam Zelda. At the end of the service, one leading member of the church told me of past dabblings into spiritism. We had quite a battle in prayer over the next few days before there was complete freedom.

Another story illustrates the dangers of any sort of divination.

Recently, after a parish dinner at the beginning of a weekend of teaching about the healing ministry, I prayed with a young woman who had just married a divorcee. They were both Christians, but she was challenged by a talk that I gave which included reference to the dangers of divination. She had had readings from both a fortune teller and tarot cards. The significant thing was that she had been told she would be involved with one child which was not her own, and have another which would die. Her husband had a child by a previous marriage, and she had had a miscarriage.

She had a strange spiritual experience as we prayed. I wanted to pray to cut off the effects of their predictions, but she was unable to look into my eyes, complaining that she could see nothing but brightness.

As she explained afterwards, she felt all right with me until I called her husband over to join in the prayer. As I looked into her eyes, all she could see was my eyes – no face, no lips, just an absolute nothingness. She began to feel very frightened, she felt that I was a fake, and longed to get away.

I have encountered this sort of thing before, and was anxious to avoid any sort of spiritual battle. We were in a public meeting, and in my limited experience, the enemy likes nothing better than long drawn out, exhausting battles. I felt it right to turn away; I then asked her to pray aloud, renouncing her involvement with these occult things, and to join us in saying the Lord's prayer. When we had finished, I turned back, looked her in the eyes, and all was well.

My praying partner (and how essential it is to have the support and insight of others on these sort of occasions), then pointed out to me that she would now begin to feel grief and guilt about the miscarriage. So it proved, and the next thirty-six hours were times of much weeping and darkness. Thanks to my partner's discernment, we were able to handle this, and the darkness passed. When I last saw them, she and her husband looked radiant, their marriage set free from all Satan's potential cobwebs.

In a subsequent letter, she described how the whole incident had brought a new awareness of the Lord, and the spiritual battle, into her life, and how at times she and her husband feel overwhelmed by God's love.

The problem is not when the predictions are false, but when they are true. The problem is not when physical healings don't take place, but when they do. Satan appears as an angel of light, and simple people think that all is well. A simple illustration of the dangers of fortune telling occurred during marriage counselling many years ago. A Christian couple were struggling with their marriage. There were obvious issues such as the wife's reluctance to have children (she had a good career, better than his, in prospect). But the key factor proved to be the husband's admission of visiting a fortune teller who predicted that he'd be married more than once! When he renounced this prediction, we made rapid progress. Years later, his career has blossomed, and they have a large family and a happy marriage.

I was very surprised when a young man came to our evening service saying that he was interested in healing, but had been involved in spiritist healing and was dissatisfied with what he'd experienced. He joined an Alpha course, formally renounced spiritism, turned to Christ, and was welcomed into our healing team. His journey was surprisingly painless, but I venture to wonder whether it would have been if he hadn't been able to find a local church with an openness to God's healing grace.

19) Why do some people fall over when prayed for – and does it matter?

Some people use the rather horrible term 'being slain in the Spirit' which ought to be reserved for the unfortunate

Ananias and Sapphira (Acts 5). More seriously, when people are prayed for, usually standing, there is a tendency after a time for them to sway very gently and quietly subside to the ground, 'resting in the Spirit'. It is normally a peaceful, healing experience where the Lord can bring healing uninterrupted by the prayers of his servants.

The problem is that it looks curious, it seems undignified, there is no real biblical precedent, but it does happen.

One night in our church, the healing advisor was praying for people to be filled with the Spirit. I sensed that many would fall over, and gave a gentle explanation to any who might be bewildered or put off. I closed by saying, 'If you want to be safe, come over to the Lady Chapel and I will pray for you.'

You can guess what happened. I only had to look at someone, start to pray, and they fell over . . . the Lady Chapel was strewn with peaceful people resting in the Spirit. But it doesn't happen very often when I pray, and I'm quite relieved. I don't believe that it confers any extra blessing, except perhaps a deeper sense of peace and God's presence. Come to think of it, that's a rather large 'except'!

20) Is there a time to stop praying for people for healing – especially when they're dying?

Yes! But it's such an important issue, I'm going to devote a short chapter to it (see next chapter, especially p. 315).

21) What about the relationship of the healing ministry and the medical profession?[18]

Bishop Maddocks writes of what he calls a 'tragic polarisation between church and medicine'. He cites various Catholic councils which distanced monks from visiting the sick, studying medicine, and which prohibited churchmen from practising surgery.

In 1566, physicians were ordered to enforce penance on the sick! In many ways worse has followed. At one extreme, occasional Pentecostal refusal to use medicine (chapter 6, p. 208) has combined with Catholic opposition to contraception, to make the division potentially sharper than in the Middle Ages.

Fortunately, there are signs of hope. At a national level in England, the Church's Council for Health and Healing has tried to build bridges. Elsewhere, at houses of healing, or diocesan healing groups, and in local churches, there has been an increasing dialogue between medicine and church. On the one hand, a greater humility on the part of those involved in the healing ministry has been matched by a greater openness to other approaches by many in the medical profession.[19]

Holistic medicine – the realisation that the patient needs to be treated in body, mind, and spirit, is widely accepted. The hospice movement, which has helped so many cancer sufferers die with dignity, sprang from Christian roots (see also chapter 9, p. 305).

Practically, this means co-operation wherever possible. Hospital chaplains are a valuable part of the National Health Service, paid for by the state. Doctors and nurses are part of local healing teams wherever possible. Dialogue, not confrontation, is the order of the day. Most priests have good lines of communication with local doctors. A few practices make counselling and prayer a real possibility (from a Christian point of view, a difficulty is that the most acceptable therapies had to be of a 'New Age' variety, and not Christian – reflecting, no doubt, the general sympathies of the practice).

Prayer for healing is in co-operation, not confrontation,

with medicine. I remember some years ago, a leader of a local free church asking to see me urgently. I saw him immediately. Apparently he had listened to me talking about healing at a lunchtime service. Subsequently he got his elders to anoint him for healing, and stopped taking his insulin for his diabetes! I asked him if he was healed. He said he was beginning to feel quite ill! Without hesitation, I demanded that he started taking his insulin again, and not put God to the test. There was a happier outcome. He was not healed, but his sugar readings, which had been very erratic, levelled out, and he felt rather better.

That story is quite a warning. Teaching on healing and deliverance acted upon in ignorance, or blind faith, can cause chaos. No wonder the medical profession sometimes looks on with considerable distrust.

By contrast, I received a Christmas card in 1998 with a line of thanks from someone who said they were completely well and enjoying their Christian discipleship. This particular friend was first directed to the church by *a local doctor*. She was suffering from an acute persecution mania which caused her to think that everyone was trying to poison her. After some counselling and prayer she was baptised on Ascension Day in 1988. Gradually her condition improved, and her faith grew. Quite soon, she was completely well.

Although referrals from the medical profession are rare, they are only possible when a real measure of trust and mutual confidence has been established.

22) Is sickness caused by the devil?

'The reason the son of man appeared was to destroy the Devil's work' (1 John 3:8). 'Should not this woman, a daughter of Abraham, whom Satan has kept bound, be set free?' (Luke 13:16).

But it's not quite as simple as that. In the Old Testament, God warns that disobedience will lead to disease – for instance, Miriam's leprosy (Numbers 12:10). Elsewhere, Satan seeks permission to harm Job and his family (Job 2:1–8). In the New Testament, the writer of Hebrews speaks of the Lord's discipline (Hebrews 12:4–11), and the next verse – 'Therefore, strengthen your feeble arms and weak knees!' suggests that this discipline can include physical suffering. As we've said earlier, God allows Satan a great deal of freedom (p. 100), but ultimately, he is in control. God brings prosperity and creates disaster (Isaiah 45:7).

The awesome struggle at Gethsemane, concluded on the hill of Calvary, shows the intensity of the spiritual battle, a battle that involves the very heart of God. It is not a question of 'the Father on his sapphire throne awaits his own anointed son',[20] but that 'God was reconciling the world to himself in Christ' (2 Corinthians 5:19).

It is too simple to say that sickness is caused by the devil, or by sin. Sickness is part of life's tapestry. Our bodies have been given an amazing programme which involves natural healing – blood clotting to stop a wound is a simple example, but they also have an inevitable tendency to decay and death.

Satan will interfere and speed up this decaying process where he can. 'He's such a pest', as one retired lady describes him in our prayer meetings. Ultimately, God has a better plan. The earthly caterpillar must slough its skin, pupate in the shroud of death, and rise gloriously to its new life.

To attribute all sickness to Satan makes prayer straightforward, and makes all healing prayer a sort of exorcism;

but that is too simple, and doesn't recognise the complexity of scriptural teaching and experience. Modern psychiatry, and drugs, can bring relief to many conditions where symptoms are similar to those of demonic possession. My experience of working with psychiatrists has been that they are very courteous and often quite open to the possible efficacy of prayers for deliverance.

Occasionally, sickness is very obviously caused by Satan. I remember a missionary telling me that an embarrassing, and painful, vaginal rash was caused by an aunt deep in witchcraft. I was very doubtful, but I said, 'If you're right – then there will be a rapid healing when we pray.' I rebuked the illness, and she was soon completely better. Her later life has been marred by Alzheimer's disease, brought on at a very early age. That, I believe, is a natural illness. Why it should happen so soon, thereby causing much distress to her mother and family, I don't know, but it seems theologically safer to accept it as part of our mysterious fallen world, rather than praying desperately for Satan's hand to be withdrawn.

23) Can a Christian be demonised?

Years ago, when the late David Watson frequently visited St Aldate's, Oxford, he and Michael Green were going to have a theological discussion on this subject. I was going to attend to listen in. Sadly, it never took place, but the subject remains controversial.

Some of the problem concerns terminology. The New Testament usages include being affected by a demon (eg the daughter of the Canaanite woman, 'My daughter is suffering terribly from demon possession', Matthew 15:21–28); having an unclean (evil) spirit (the Gadarene man, Mark 5:1–20); and being crippled by a spirit (the woman in the synagogue who had been ill for eighteen years, Luke 13:10–17).

In addition, the forces of the enemy can attack the believer. Hence Paul's instruction 'take up the shield of faith, with which you can extinguish all the flaming arrows of the evil one' (Ephesians 6:16). Paul, himself, suffered from Satan's influence. He writes, for instance, 'For we wanted to come to you – certainly, I Paul, did, again and again – but Satan stopped us' (1 Thessalonians 2:18).

Satanic influence ranges from *external* prevention of a Christian's plans right through a spectrum which ends with an *internal* possession that was so strong that the Gadarene man lived a completely wild life. Sometimes he was bound up, then he would break free and roam among the tombs and on the mountains. The woman 'crippled by a spirit' falls somewhere in the middle. She was spiritually alert enough to attend the synagogue, Jesus describes her as a 'daughter of Abraham', and it is far from clear at what level, apart from her physical state, that Satan affected her.

In the Old Testament (1 Samuel 19:9), an evil spirit came upon Saul, and in the New Testament (Acts 5:3), Satan so filled the heart of Ananias that he lied to the Holy Spirit and suffered dreadful consequences. Unfortunately, neither case proves anything – Christians have argued for ever about the spiritual state of both Saul and Ananias, and the degree of Satan's influence upon them. What we can say with certainty is that both appeared to be believers, both were severely plagued by evil powers, and both fell away sharply from their earlier apparent states of grace. Saul went further spiritually downhill, consulting a medium (1 Samuel 28) just before his death, and Ananias died suddenly after hearing Peter's stinging rebuke.

I think we may conclude[21] that the biblical evidence is unclear. There are, of course, two extreme points of view. The traditional Evangelical view is that the Holy Spirit and an evil spirit simply cannot co-exist. Many texts support this view (1 Corinthians 6:10; 2 Corinthians 5:17; Romans 6:3–4, etc). At the other extreme, some books based on theologies such as those I described in chapter 5, p. 147, which use Luke 17:37 in a strange way, teach that it is normal for a Christian to be demonised. I don't believe that there is a single New Testament text which supports this view, and St Paul's teaching on the sin of the flesh (Galatians 5:19–21) and Jesus' teaching on what lies in our hearts (Mark 7:20–23) totally repudiate this.

Nevertheless, pastoral experience does suggest that it is possible for people to believe and to profess the faith, and yet to be severely troubled by evil spirits. The main reason for this would seem to be either that they have received inadequate teaching at the time of their conversion, or that they have inadvertently touched something deeply occult.

The testimony of a young lady (see question 18 of this chapter) who went unwittingly to a spiritist counsellor illustrates the problem. She was able to profess conversion after our first prayer session, but wasn't set free from the demonic influence. Similarly in Zambia, I had great difficulty in praying for a woman who showed all the obvious signs of demonisation, and yet seemed to have done nothing wrong. Eventually, I discerned that her husband came from a family with a history steeped in witchcraft. Her physical union with him was sufficient to give the dark powers a point of entry into her life. Once this was discerned, her freedom came very quickly.

Similarly, the story in chapter 10, p. 342, illustrates how a young man was converted, but not taught to renounce his spiritist past. Inevitably, there was a spiritual collision, but the problem didn't really surface until he was trying to grow spiritually.

Christians can obviously be affected by demons. While St Paul doesn't list attacks by demons among his many hardships (2 Corinthians 11:6–29), he does see his thorn as 'a messenger from Satan' (2 Corinthians 12:7). I have twice been present when members of a prayer team have been nearly knocked over by the power of a departing demon (see p. 29 and 344). Recently, I prayed with other clergy in a disused quarry where there were obvious signs of satanic activity. These were so overt that I found it hard to take it seriously and I wondered if people had been fooling around. Yet, shortly afterwards, I felt so ill that I needed prayer to recover. Similarly, when starting to write this book, I felt very much under attack spiritually. However, after asking a few friends to cover me regularly in prayer, things have been much easier, and at times the task has seemed quite enjoyable.

I think it is very rare for a Christian to be controlled by a demon. If they are, their Christian witness will either be very inconsistent, or so low key as to be almost invisible. If past spiritual disturbances, or ancestral problems, aren't cut off in the name of the Lord (see Psalm 118:12), then there will be spiritual fireworks when they seek to grow as Christians. This can especially occur when people, who have not fully renounced evil, are prayed for to be filled with the Holy Spirit. This might explain why the general invocation 'Come, Holy Spirit' in large, highly charged meetings can lead to such an extraordinary mixture of obvious spiritual blessing and unedifying bedlam.

24) Is healing included in the benefits of the atonement?[22]

This theoretical question has deep practical consequences. An affirmative answer, which is the basis of many famous and successful healing ministries,[23] is based on two arguments.

First, two key scriptures appear to support it. 'This was to fulfil what was spoken through the prophet Isaiah. "He took up our infirmities and carried our diseases"' (Matthew 8:17). And, 'He himself bore our sins in his body on the tree, so that we might die to sins and live for righteousness; by his wounds you have been healed' (1 Peter 2:24).

Secondly, sickness is one of the results of the fall, hence sickness is caused by sin; Christ's death removed the guilt and consequences of sin (2 Corinthians 5:21; 1 Peter 2:24; 3:18; 1 John 2:2). Hence, Christ's death delivers people from sickness, and it is therefore right for believers to claim and receive healing from any and all illnesses.

However, any reasonable reading of 1 Peter 2:24 would see that the healing referred to is clearly spiritual *not* physical.

Looking again at Matthew 8:17[24] *(especially Michael Green's theological comment* – see chapter 3, p. 96), we can express the link diagrammatically with Isaiah 53 and 1 Peter 2:24 as follows (see overleaf).

There is *no* obvious connection between Matthew 8:17 and 1 Peter 2:24–25. They are *distinctive* parts of the ministry of the suffering servant. This releases us from seeing healing as a 'right' and returns it to its rightful place as a 'sign' of God's invasion into Satan's kingdom (Matthew 3:23–30; Luke 4:21, 34).

Looking at the second line of reasoning, based on sickness as a result of the fall, we might reasonably add that

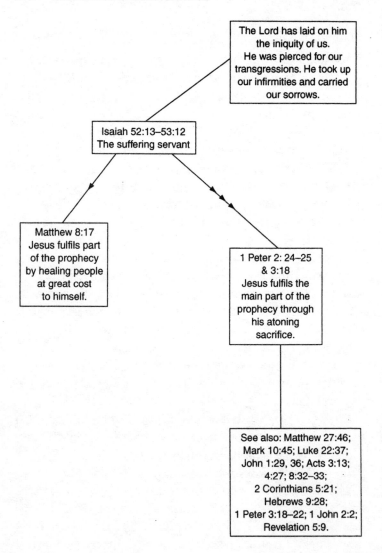

The Lord has laid on him the iniquity of us. He was pierced for our transgressions. He took up our infirmities and carried our sorrows.

Isaiah 52:13–53:12
The suffering servant

Matthew 8:17
Jesus fulfils part of the prophecy by healing people at great cost to himself.

1 Peter 2: 24–25 & 3:18
Jesus fulfils the main part of the prophecy through his atoning sacrifice.

See also: Matthew 27:46; Mark 10:45; Luke 22:37; John 1:29, 36; Acts 3:13; 4:27; 8:32–33; 2 Corinthians 5:21; Hebrews 9:28; 1 Peter 3:18–22; 1 John 2:2; Revelation 5:9.

Scripture sees death as a main consequence of the fall (Genesis 3:3, etc), and no one has suggested that physical death has been abolished by the atonement. Christ's death removed the guilt of sin – but *not* the consequences (see chapter 2, p. 56, and consider again that the consequences of David's adultery lingered on for years, even though he was personally forgiven).

If we do see a healing as a *right*, then it leads to statements such as 'If you'd had more faith your mother wouldn't have died' (as a close relative wrote to me when I began my ordination training). If healing is a right, what does this say to the parents of severely mentally handicapped children? What does it mean for the victims of AIDS (particularly the missionary who died a few years ago from treading on an infected needle).

In conclusion, I believe that it is quite clear that healing is *not* included in the benefits of the atonement. None of the New Testament references to Christ's death makes this point. All refer to the fact that Jesus bears our sins: no more, no less. Also, Jesus clearly taught that although disease could be caused by sin (Mark 2:5), it could also be caused by Satan (Luke 13:16), or for no discernible reason (John 9:2). In other words, although disease is a consequence of our fallen humanity, it is not inexorably linked to individual sins.

This conclusion destroys a simple, tidy theology which, if true, would provide a straightforward theological basis of healing; instead, we have a deep mystery (but is this mystery any different from the whole question of the sovereignty of God in evangelism?).

It is vital that we affirm that all true healing (medical and spiritual) is a sign of God's grace and not a right 'bought at a price' (1 Corinthians 6:20 – which again clearly refers to the forgiveness of sin).

Notes

1. See Francis Macnutt, *Healing* (Ave Maria Press 1974), chapter 18.
2. See Jack Winslow, *Modern Miracles* (Hodder and Stoughton, 1968), p. 22.
3. Dorothy Arnold, *Dorothy Kerin – Called by Christ to Heal* (Hodder and Stoughton, 1965), and many other books on her life and ministry.
4. Richard Foster, *Celebration of Discipline* (Hodder and Stoughton, 1980), chapter 4.
5. Michael Vasey, *Strangers and Friends* (Hodder & Stoughton, 1995). All those concerned in this area of prayer ought to read his moving, gentle book.

   Those seeking prayer ministry would be well advised to go to a professional organisation such as 'Living Water' based on St Michael's, Chester Square, London.
6. Elizabeth Moberly, *Homosexuality – a New Christian Ethic* (James Clarke, 1983).
7. There is, of course, considerable debate as to what exactly is condemned. Evangelists ought to read Vasey, *op. cit.*, chapter 8 before jumping to conclusions.
8. There is much literature on this subject, for instance:

   Jim Glennon, *Your Healing is Within You* (Hodder and Stoughton, 1978), chapter 4.

   Harold Taylor, *Sent to Heal* (Order of St Luke, 1993), chapter 8.

   Francis Macnutt, *op. cit.*, chapter 12.

   Michael Buckley, *Do Not be Afraid* (Darton, Longman and Todd, 1995), especially chapter 12.
9. Dr Kenneth McAll, *Healing the Family Tree* (SPCK, 1982) is the classic book. See also Russ Parker and Michael Mitton *Requiem Healing*.
10. Available from the Diocesan Healing Adviser via The

Old Deanery, Wells, Somerset BA5 2UG. Also helpful is *The Family Tree Journal* obtainable from 67 Old Kennels Lane, Winchester SO22 4JT.

11. See especially Michael Green, *I believe in Satan's Downfall* (Hodder and Stoughton, 1981).

12. R. Kydd, *Healing the Centuries* (Hendrickson, 1998), p. 24, quoting original sources.

13. Fred Smith, *God's Gift of Healing* (New Wine Press, 1986).

14. For a very full discussion see M. Dudley and G. Rowsell, eds, *The Oil of Gladness* (SPCK, 1990), and Francis Macnutt, *op. cit.*, p. 275f.

15. See Dr Robina Coker, *Alternative Medicine* (Monarch, 1995).

16. See Sir James Watt, ed., *What is Wrong with Christian Healing* (The Church's Council for Health and Healing, 1993), p. 43.

17. Jack Temple, *The Healer* (Element, 1998). I am grateful to *The Times* 'Diary' whose rather cynical piece on 29 August 1998, drew my attention to this book. The diarist cites a fee of £40 per forty-five minutes, and claims the Prime Minister's wife as one of Mr Temple's clients. The book mentions neither of these points!

18. See especially M. Maddocks, *The Christian Healing Ministry* (SPCK, 1990), p. 163ff.

19. See, for instance, the bi-monthly magazine *Wholeness* published by Monarch Magazines.

20. See hymn 99 'Ride on, ride on in majesty', *Hymns Ancient and Modern Revised* (William Clowes and Sons Ltd, 1950).

21. See C. Dickenson, *Demon Possession and the Christian* (Moody Institute, 1987), for a very full and fair account of the whole problem. He too regards the

298   HEALING AND DELIVERANCE

biblical evidence as inconclusive, but cites numerous pastoral cases of apparent demonisation of believers.

22. See R. Dunn, *Will God Heal Me?* (Kingsway, 1997), chapter 15 especially, and Michael Green, *Matthew for Today* (Hodder and Stoughton, 1998), on Matthew 8:17.

23. See p. 210 for a brief account of the classic Pentecostal position.

24. ἐβαστασευ the word translated 'bore' in Matthew 8:17 has wide New Testament usage. Dunn, *op. cit.*, p. 171, points out that the word is never used in connection with Christ's bearing our sin. He also makes the point that ἀσθενειας translated 'infirmities', is used by Paul in 2 Corinthians 12:9 as something to glory in. Could Paul glory in something that Christ, on the cross, removed?

9

Healing, Long-term Illness and Death

In this chapter, we look at the difficulties and privilege of praying for those with long-term illness, and medically terminal illness. We look at the mystery of sudden death and accidents; we warn against the use of spiritism to contact the departed. Finally, we wrestle with the question of when to stop praying for healing and to prepare people for a holy death.

Healing, Long-term Illness and Death

Many Christians suffer from long-term physical illnesses, others from severe depression. Often they have sought healing through prayer, but with a few spectacular exceptions,[1] have discovered that God's way usually seems to be rather different.

Long-term illness

'My grace is sufficient for you, for my power is made perfect in weakness' (2 Corinthians 12:9). Joni Earekson, the well-known writer, discovered this after breaking her neck in a diving accident when still a teenager. Her ministry to the disabled, as well as to the physically fit, has been remarkable. Corrie Ten Boom survived Ravensbruck concentration camp, and subsequently had a wonderful ministry for many years, before lying helpless, after a stroke, for several years before God released her.

I have friends with rheumatoid arthritis, multiple sclerosis, Parkinson's disease, motor neurone disease, ME, and Alzheimer's disease. All these conditions are unpleasant, many have received much prayer. All these friends cope with their disabilities with remarkable grace, but there is little sign of physical improvement.

Maybe things will change as faith and expectation grow, but for the moment God seems to be calling them (and us) to bear witness through their sufferings to an unbelieving world which seems increasingly to regard health as a right. Some sections of the healing ministry speak eloquently about God's intentions for the health of his people. The trouble with this approach is that it ignores the biblical teaching about humanity's frailty,[2] raises people's hopes and then often leaves them feeling guilty at their 'lack of faith', and seldom has the results to accompany the theology.

Healings of such illnesses seem to be rare. The man at the Pool of Bethesda (John 5) was one among many long-term cripples present on the day that Jesus went there. But he, alone, was healed.

Mental illness

Depression causes even greater havoc with the faith of Christians and their friends. One psychiatric doctor[3] has written an interesting book about the depressive illnesses apparent in the lives of great Christians such as Luther, the poets William Cowper and Gerard Manley Hopkins, and others. Christians are not immune to depressive illnesses. Many are caused by chemical imbalances in the body, some are inherited, some are caused by spiritual problems. We need great sensitivity when treating and praying for such people. Their faith is easily damaged; yet their witness, and sensitive ministry to others, can be wonderful. Just as with some great artists, dramatists and poets, the pain and darkness of suffering can be used, by God, to bring healing and light to others.

Psalm 139 says many wonderful things. We need the

knowledge that God made us, and understands the very depth of our (flawed) make-up. With that knowledge, we may be able to retain hope in the most trying situations. If we retain hope, we may be able both to absorb and to radiate God's love (see Romans 5:1–5).

An example of severe suffering

Some years ago, a school teacher from Manchester came to Oxford for treatment in the early stages of motor neurone disease. Somehow he had heard of me, and we made contact a number of times. We enjoyed each other's company, especially discussing our teaching careers and the relative failure of our writing projects. During his first visit to Oxford, I teamed up with Fred Smith to pray with him for a real physical miracle. There was no discoverable physical benefit.

Over the next few years, his physical condition deteriorated rapidly. Each time he came to Oxford, we met to talk and to pray. Our prayer gradually shifted away from asking for physical healing to seeking the presence of God. Despite the lack of outward success, Martin experienced a deep peace, and rediscovered his childhood faith. His colleagues were moved, and his funeral and memorial services were powerful acts of witness. As a direct consequence of this, one of his colleagues[4] received a remarkable healing of severe regular migraines.

It would have been wonderful if Martin had been healed, but his approach to death was also very moving. It needed courage and discernment to cease praying for a physical miracle, while still expecting God to do great things.

I am sure that discernment is one of the most important gifts for those involved in healing prayer. Much harm can be done if we continue to pray for a physical miracle, long after God has indicated that this is not his will.

Recently, the diocese of Bath and Wells has suffered from the death of the newly appointed Bishop of Taunton at the early age of fifty-four, and the Cathedral's head server in his forties. Both died of cancer. Both received prayer for healing, both died in faith, and had profound and remarkable funeral and memorial services.

Some years ago, another of my parishioners, Penny, died quite young of cancer. She had been ill for about five years, and during that time I had made several efforts to visit her – always without success. It seemed that God was blocking me from seeing her, or else that she didn't want to see me.

A few months before her death, with some hesitation, I made another attempt. She was in bed, very unwell, but she got up and met me in her kitchen. We had a wonderful talk and prepared ourselves for some prayer sessions which were to include her close friend and a neighbour.

When I returned a few days later, she astonished me by saying that she had been 'born again'! She had visited a local herbalist, and told her that when she died she would go into oblivion. The herbalist, a strong Christian, had challenged this. (How many of us would have meekly acquiesced and have been of no spiritual use?) As a result, she had been shown the way to Christ and was amazingly transformed. Our subsequent prayer sessions were deeply moving. I sometimes felt a deep physical pain, my new friend a measure of peace. One afternoon, I sensed that God was telling me to ask her whether she was at peace about the past. A number of things surfaced which, I believe, she needed to release to God. Knowing how ill she was, yet hopeful of a miracle, I felt that I must trespass on to dangerous ground. Neither of us felt any pain when we prayed, and I left her laughing and happy. Within a day, she had relapsed into a coma and died quickly.

Two deaths and two conversions

For a short time, I felt a sense of frustration and failure. Why had God not raised her up? Did I lack faith? But, quickly, I realised once again, that all of us must accept God's sovereignty in these matters. God's timing is best. He knows what he is doing. He has called her by name.

After her death, I tried equally unsuccessfully to contact her close friend, Mollie, who had helped her so much. Then, years later, to my surprise and joy, Mollie and an older friend, Geoff, appeared on an Alpha course. Mollie experienced a profound conversion, and with a natural interest in healing (she practises aromatherapy and various other natural forms of healing) quickly joined our healing team. It is lovely to see how seeds from one period of ministry bear fruit long afterwards in someone else.

Mollie described her conversion as being surrounded by two deaths. She was quite angry at Penny's deep experience of God (why hadn't this happened to her? She needed just as much help), and moved by Geoff's death soon after the Alpha course.

Specialist ministry to the dying

Most people are aware of impending death. We shall consider later the question of sudden death. Many people don't want to know. Often there is a conspiracy of silence. 'Don't tell him – he couldn't stand it.' 'If he wants to know, he'll ask.' 'Don't visit him, Vicar, he'll think he's dying.'

Modern drugs blur the approach of death. The miracle of morphine releases much pain, it takes much of the terror from death, yet it makes the spiritual side of death harder. It is much easier to allow someone to slip away, pain free, without ever letting them ask what is happening and where they are going.

Prayer and the hospice movement   The hospice movement (which has deep Christian roots), treats death rather differently. People I have been privileged to meet in hospices, whether nurses or patients, seem to have a different approach to death. Here are some moving words from a hospice chaplain, Richard Glover, sometime member of the Bath and Wells Diocesan Healing Group. 'Dying is a process, not an end (as in the call to both Zaccheus and the rich young man, the emphasis lies in what came after the call rather than the call itself). Thus the ministry of healing to the dying is a ministry of healing in order that the person may face what comes after death in a whole state.'

He continues, 'Anger is a natural reaction. It is also the natural action of a hurt animal. In terminal illness the anger is often directed against God. Sometimes it is hidden, sometimes it lies hidden and festers like a sore. Often the healer's task in cases like this is to draw the anger into the open.' As an example of his hospice ministry, Richard gave this example:

There was a lady, whose illness was diagnosed as terminal, who received ministry from a female deacon of her church. The ministry was not going well as the patient remained tight-lipped about anything to do with her illness. The deacon prayed silently to God for help all through the interview, and suddenly began to be aware of the suppressed anger within her friend.

Later, the deacon gathered a prayer group about her who prayed for the healing of this anger. Over the next few weeks, the anger erupted every time the deacon visited her sick friend, and silently, in Christ's name, she received it. Afterwards, in prayer, she handed it over to God.

Eventually, the anger left the patient altogether and she was able to form a relationship with God at a level which she had never dreamed existed. Later she died peacefully and with an inner joy. So she was healed of her anger, and prepared to meet her God.

To me, what Richard Glover has written above is a miracle, and he could multiply such stories. A living testimony to God's grace and presence with the dying. But what of the Gospels? Didn't Jesus raise the dead and heal the dying? Isn't Christian literature full of testimonies from those who, by all reasonable account, should be dead?

Richard Glover, so it happens, is himself such a living testimony. He, himself, was healed of a life-threatening, wasting disease when in his early thirties.

It seems to me that it is always right to pray for a miracle, as long as we understand that God is sovereign, and that such miracles are rare! The Gospels clearly show us that Jesus raised the dead and healed the dying – but I do not get the impression that this was a frequent occurrence. We are told of many multiple healings and exorcisms (Mark 1: 34) but only of a few stupendous miracles such as the raising of the dead or the healing of leprosy (treated with as much fear in the ancient world as AIDS is today).

Sudden death

Of course, not all deaths are expected. A heart attack may be a 'good way to go', but it is very difficult for relatives to handle. Accidents are even harder to bear, and Christians are *not* immune from them.

Occasionally, Christians produce remarkable testimonies to escape from disasters, and guidance to avoid fatal journeys, all of which can leave those who have experienced bereavement from sudden death feeling doubly angry.

One Christmas I received what I thought was a normal Christmas newsletter from a minister whom I hadn't seen for ten years. The newsletter enclosed a photograph of his teenage daughter, taken the day before her death. She was killed in a motor accident. Faith, confidence, love and gratitude for the girl's life, these were the sentiments which shone through a poignant letter.

It is difficult to react to massive tragedies like earthquakes, plane crashes or floods. We may pray, contribute money, talk about them, admire the rescue work, blame human agencies, question providence. Then, quite suddenly, these tragedies become personal. A name leaps out from the paper – a member of a former youth group was among those killed in the King's Cross tube disaster. Some time later, I received a lovely letter from his parents. It showed that they had read my halting words, and responded warmly to them. Once again, I thank God for an utter conviction in the safety of the historic evidence of the resurrection.

I remember Sir Norman Anderson[5] preaching movingly about his faith in Christ, although he had suffered many tragedies within his young family. Sir Norman had examined the evidence. He was, in a real sense, prepared.

Again, I recall the words of Jesus:

Now there were some present at that time who told Jesus about the Galileans whose blood Pilate had mixed with their sacrifices. Jesus answered, 'Do you think that these Galileans were worse sinners than all the other Galileans because they suffered this way? I tell you, no! But unless you repent, you too will all perish. Or those eighteen who died when the tower in Siloam fell on them – do you think they were more guilty than all the others living in Jerusalem? I tell you, no! But unless you repent, you too will all perish.'

(Luke 13:1–5)

Hard words; words which I have felt must be said at some funerals, but words which warn us to have a 'theology of accident' before, and not after, such events.

I remember many other Christian parents, ministers especially, who have lost children at a young age. I remember their grief, their faith – God's rainbow overarching their tears. I remember especially, my joy at the birth of Timothy, overshadowed by the cot death of a daughter of Christian friends the very next day. I remember their faith. The funeral service was an amazing testimony to the resurrection. The parents received a vision of their daughter growing into a full spiritual person with the Lord in heaven.

Countless examples could also be given from the mission field. One particularly poignant example was the death of Freda, the sister of Frank Houghton, former leader of the China Inland Mission. He had put out an appeal in 1931 for 200 new missionaries to China. Freda was one of the first to respond, yet she died within a year of her arrival. Frank could have asked the question 'Why?' Instead he chose to express his faith as follows:

> On Freda's Death
> We do not ask Thee to explain
> Why Thou has acted thus, nor how
> Such seeming loss is turned to gain,
> Eternal gain – but even now
> Acknowledging that all Thy ways
> Are right, we offer Thee our praise.
>
> Others may count Thy dealings strange,
> That, with her service scarce begun,
> Thy Voice should call her to exchange
> Great tasks for heaven's greater one,
> But good is all that Thou hast planned
> We do not seek to understand.
> We do not ask Thee to explain,
> We do not seek to understand,

We know He needed her again
Who gave her, and at His right Hand
She shares His joy for evermore
Whom we in steadfast faith adore.[6]

Intellectually, we want to ask, 'How could God have guided a young woman to her early death on a foreign mission field? What good did it do the cause?' Surely the potential converts must have said, 'Where is now thy God?' Surely the missionaries must have been discouraged?

The China Inland Mission, and many other missions, were born out of that sort of suffering. Just as the Apostles faced great trials, dangers and death (see, for instance, Paul's classic statement in 2 Corinthians 11:22–29), so Christians are not immune from 'the changes and chances of this fleeting world'. What is different is that the Christian has a real hope beyond death. How we Christians approach our own deaths, and how we react to other people's, is a vital part of our witness to the world in which death is largely unmentionable, unacceptable and profoundly unpleasant.

I write as a grateful survivor. A few years ago, just before a mission in our parish, I was walking on the Brecon Beacons. In the midst of a sudden hail storm I saw a flash of light. For a split second I thought I'd seen an angel (at last!), then I felt a wave of electricity and saw an arc of light bounce from me to my son. We were both unharmed. Passers-by walking in the other direction laughed – my hair apparently stood on end! I do know that one of the missioners, who said that it was a work of the devil, had got his theology totally wrong. 'Praise the Lord . . . lightning and hail . . . that do his bidding' (Psalm 148:7–8).

False guidance and death

Today, spiritism, tarot readings and such like are becoming increasingly popular.[7] These, along with the popular doctrine of reincarnation, present a considerable challenge both to the Christian view of death, and the Christian healing ministry.

The very title of this section seems harsh. But what are we to say of books, talks and testimonies which speak of the afterlife in terms of spiritist visions and reincarnation?

I was given one such book to read recently. It told of a famous medium who had died giving messages to another medium via 'automatic writing'. The essence of the message was that all was well on the other side, the famous were having a splendid time (there was a lot of stuff about the Kennedys and other prominent statesmen), there was a lot of relearning (especially for clergy!), and everyone had the option of rejoining the cycle of life to pay back any 'karma' that needed to be released.

The book seemed to have a number of fatal flaws. There was an extraordinary interest in the 'famous'. The medium claimed a previous incarnation as Lazarus' father, and the writer as Lazarus' unnamed sister. The cycle of reincarnation was designed to improve people, yet there is no evidence that humanity is spiritually any better than thousands of years earlier. Though very religious, and full of quotes from Jesus' teaching, the book totally ignored the central part of Jesus' doctrine of atonement. In consequence, there could be no real doctrine of resurrection. Each soul was an amalgam of many human lives (something which mathematically is impossible, if you consider the present-day population of the world compared with, say, a thousand years ago!).

But what of these all-persuasive 'visions' where people

revert to previous lifetimes and experience things about which they can have no actual knowledge?

The Christian has, I think, two possible responses. The simplest is in 2 Thessalonians 2:9, 'The coming of the lawless one will be in accordance with the work of Satan displayed in all kinds of counterfeit miracles, signs and wonders.' A more complex view may be to see these regressions as experiences similar to some of Dr McAll's[8] patients when he prays for the healing of their family tree. If people can, occasionally, recall the experiences of their ancestors, that would simply explain other regression experiences. We know that butterflies have an inbuilt computer which enables them to retrace the journeys of their ancestors. The Monarch butterfly, in America, will hibernate in the same one square kilometre of Mexican mountain, despite the fact that those which return the following winter are three or four generations later.

In the end, we need not know. What we must realise is that contacting the dead is explicitly forbidden in the Scriptures.[9] However tempting it is to want to know where our loved ones are, we must wait in faith, and in hope, for our own time. (See also chapter 8, question 18.)

The unquiet dead

Here again, we face a considerable mystery. A little while ago I was asked to visit a house because the occupants were being disturbed by tobacco smoke, the sense of a 'presence', and some other phenomena. The owners of the house were ordinary people, neither particularly religious, nor people who dabbled in any sort of spiritism. After some discussion it emerged that no one in the house smoked, that both the husband and wife had independently smelled the tobacco, that one of the children had experienced some curious things in her bedroom, and that a previous owner had committed suicide some years earlier.

A reader and I said some prayers and the situation first improved, and then normalised. This sort of experience is quite common. I cannot offer any clear explanation, but I can be certain that prayers, offered in the name of Jesus, and often a celebration of Holy Communion, are more than adequate to cleanse and release the situation. If there are any 'spirits' present, I tell them to go to Jesus for whatever purpose he may have for them. It seems to me that whatever happens, disobedient or unhappy spirits are better under his authority than continuing to trouble people in their natural life. It may well be that there aren't any 'spirits' present, but that something unpleasant, or at the very least, unquiet, is disturbing the situation. Sometimes the people themselves seem to be able to create the psychic energy which causes the physical problems.

Reverent agnosticism about the cause of these phenomena seems wiser than speculative theories or dubious investigation.

Some people are much more sensitive in this area, and do have a definite sense of evil. They also seem to be able to sense when the atmosphere is clear. This gift is presumably connected with the 'distinguishing between spirits' mentioned in 1 Corinthians 12:10. Personally, I seem 'tone deaf' in this area, which perhaps makes it easier to pray in faith and relatively free from fear.

I have prayed in many such households. Usually a few simple prayers have brought peace and quiet. On a few occasions when they have been ineffective, it has usually been because the present occupants have dabbled in some way in forbidden things, and are themselves the channels which are helping to ferment the very disturbances that they want to be freed from.

The God who surprises

About five years ago, a saintly old lady seemed to be dying. Her niece and I even started to discuss her funeral arrangements. She was in hospital, lapsing in and out of an apparently terminal coma. We didn't pray for healing! Quite suddenly, she recovered, and recently celebrated her ninety-second birthday in our church. There are times when it is very nice to get things wrong!

On another occasion, my aunt's death proved personally helpful. She had lived to be ninety-three and, as my only close living relative outside my immediate family, she was very special. She was my godmother, and years ago had sent me a New English Bible. I remember writing to her once, saying something to the effect that 'if someone sent me a modern translation of the Bible, I might start reading it again'. She responded by return of post! After her death, I preached in Cranmore. It was just after Easter. I preached about the resurrection. But also about my aunt. I talked of her helplessness, I talked of God's grace in her, and her choice of funeral hymn:

> God be in my head, And in my understanding;
> God be in my eyes, And in my looking;
> God be in my mouth, And in my speaking;
> God be in my heart, And in my thinking;
> God be in my end, And in my departing.[10]

In particular, I said that I would remember her as she had been in her prime, a gracious, godly woman who had experienced suffering and yet found fulfilment in her life, and not just as the mere shadow that I had known in the last few years.

One visitor was strangely moved. A Norwegian lady,

visiting a friend in Cranmore, had an old father who was dying. She had found the church at home unhelpful. Here, in a strange land, with a strange form of service, with a strange speaker, God spoke words of comfort. I can't be certain, but I don't think that I intended to speak about Aunt Hilda's death when I entered that church.

Ingrid stayed on in Cranmore! She married one of our churchwardens, enjoying a wonderful wedding and a happy marriage. She had been a lapsed communicant in Norway, but became a regular worshipper in our little village church. God certainly spoke to her, and that was a great encouragement to me.

> 'Where, O death, is your victory! Where, O death, is your sting?' The sting of death is sin, and the power of sin is the law. But thanks be to God! He gives us the victory through our Lord Jesus Christ. Therefore, my dear brothers, stand firm. Let nothing move you. Always give yourselves fully to the work of the Lord, because you know that your labour in the Lord is not in vain.
>
> (1 Corinthians 15:55–58)

That is the challenge. Whether in life or death, in response to physical miracles or otherwise, we are to remain steadfast and firm in our faith. It is my belief that the healing ministry, exercised with a godly caution and discernment, can bring much glory to God, and act as a considerable sign of hope even in the face of death, or long-term illness.

Miracles may be rare, but they will occur. Spiritual blessing through such prayer will be frequent. Many a family is deeply influenced by sensitive ministry to the dying – ministry which accepts that death is a natural part of life, while remaining open to the God of surprises!

To pray, or not to pray for healing?

One last great question remains: when do we switch from praying for healing to praying for a holy and peaceful death? I see the agony of a devout Christian couple with a severely brain damaged child. The little girl, now eight, has had no life – just brain-damaged misery from medical mistakes at birth. Can we not pray for her death? And yet she is so important to her mother, so valued, so precious. What should I do, and say, and pray?

My colleagues sense that our dear former secretary is seriously ill. He's still working for us, counting the money every Tuesday, writing and signing cheques, but the signs are that his skin cancer has spread. I arrange to go and see him on the day before Easter, but that night he dies in his sleep. A happy and a holy death. He'd even said goodbye to one member of the parish, sensing that his days were numbered. We can only rejoice and give thanks for his life. If he'd been alive on the Saturday, how would I have prayed? What would I have said? Perhaps it might have marred a happy relationship. Cyril was a very private man, and he might not have welcomed my enquiries.

It takes courage to warn people to prepare for death, especially if they are surrounded by believers still praying for a miracle. I believe that if God is intending to use us to pray effectively for someone who is, in a medical sense, terminally ill, we will be given clear encouragement (see chapter 1, p. 18). Otherwise it will be far better to recognise that God's ways are not ours, and to seek to prepare them for a holy death. It doesn't help anyone to pray for them, and possibly to hold on to them in this life, if they are ready to cross the river. To continue praying for healing can cause false hopes and prevents the person who is dying from settling their affairs on earth. Occasionally,

God may give a word and someone will have the gift of faith to pray for a physical miracle, but far more often the miracle is in the spiritual changes that a realistic approach to death can bring to a whole family.

An important part of this, I believe, is *always* having the honesty and integrity to let one's loved ones know the true state of their physical condition. The conspiracy of silence – 'If he wanted to know, he'd ask' – makes real prayer and counsel very difficult. How can we pray intelligently if we know, but the sick person doesn't know, what is really wrong?

One dear friend, nearing the end of life, was particularly concerned that her death might be a good witness to her family and neighbours. Her prayer was granted, and she died peacefully after admission to the local hospital. Her funeral bore triumphant witness to both her life and her holy death.

Notes

1. See, for instance, Jennifer Rees Larcombe, *God's Unexpected Healing* (Hodder and Stoughton).
2. 2 Corinthians 4:16–5:5, Psalm 90, etc.
3. Dr Gaius Davis, *Genius and Grace* (Hodder and Stoughton, 1992).
4. John Woolmer, *Thinking Clearly about Prayer* (Monarch, 1997), p. 231.
5. See Sir Norman Anderson, *A Lawyer among Theologians* (Hodder and Stoughton, 1973).
6. Frank Houghton, *Faith Triumphant* (OMF International, 1973).
7. See chapter 8, question 18.
8. Dr Kenneth McAll, *The Healing of the Family Tree* (SPCK, 1982).
9. Deuteronomy 18:11.
10. *Hymns Ancient and Modern Revised*, no. 332 (William Clowes and Sons Ltd, 1950).

10

The Local Church – A Place of Healing?

This chapter takes us through the joys and sorrows of my own parish as we seek to establish a healing presence with the congregation and in the wider community.

The Local Church – A Place of Healing?

This chapter is an account of a healing ministry established within an ordinary Anglican parish. I shall look at some of the encouragements, some of the problems, and some of the thinking, and hope that this may be an encouragement to other churches.

I have written elsewhere of the wider healing of society that is so desperately needed.

In our own parish, our SHAL project[1] for homeless young people has been a small but significant attempt to help a deep social problem. There have been some 'successes' resulting in the reuniting of young people with their families, and there has been a time of trauma resulting in the closure of the house for a period after it was trashed by disaffected residents. Spiritually, as yet, it has borne little obvious fruit; but it remains a vivid reminder to our church and town of the healing that society needs – especially when we remember that most of the young people needing our help have arrived largely because of broken homes and other aspects of twentieth century social failure.

When I was appointed rector of Shepton Mallet in 1982, I had charge over the parish church in the market town of Shepton Mallet (population in 1982 about 6,000) and three small villages (combined population about 1,000). In an interview with the local newspaper, I had mentioned my interest in healing. The newspaper received an anonymous letter saying, 'We don't want Shepton Mallet turned into Lourdes'! The parish found my interest in healing quite strange, although there was a small prayer group in the smallest village, Prestleigh, praying along these lines. However, I was quickly given encouragement to teach and to practise this part of my ministry.

Healing as a normal part of the church's prayer ministry

I stated then, as I would now, that I believed that healing should be seen as a *normal* part of the church's wider ministry of prayer. It was important because it was part of the gospel message, a sign of the kingdom proclaimed to an unbelieving world. It was important because it could help a wide variety of people experience something of God's touch – both those within the church, and without. It would help evangelism (the dramatic conversion recorded on p. 349 illustrates this). It would encourage the ministry of lay people, whom I would gladly train to share this work.

Of course, there were fears – spoken and unspoken. These fears hold many churches back from launching into such ministry. Won't there be great disappointment, and spiritual disillusion, if people aren't healed? How will you get the right people interested in such a sensitive ministry? Aren't there more important things to be done? What will the local doctors, and others in the medical profession, think?

Over the years, the healing ministry built up quite

slowly, and still after sixteen years has a long way to develop. We began in two ways. We had occasional healing services, on a weekday evening, in the tiny Prestleigh church, and with one leading lay member of the congregation, I offered prayer once a month during an evening communion service in Shepton. Years later, we have a monthly evening service with a large team, usually five pairs of people available to pray, and we offer prayer during the administration of communion at our morning services in Shepton. In one of our villages, we have about three healing services a year, and throughout the parish prayer is offered through house groups, parish visiting, and sometimes members of the healing team make regular visits to particular people.

Results and questions

The results have been encouraging, though seldom spectacular, and have, I believe, deepened the faith of those privileged to lead the prayer, and those who have received. Obviously, we've prayed with many who have died, or who have not received any physical benefit, but in nearly all cases, prayer has enabled people to talk more freely about their illness, about their fears, and to receive a real measure of God's peace. The testimonies given later in the chapter are some of the clearer examples of God's healing touch in people's lives. A number of people have been converted, or feel their faith greatly deepened, through such ministry. Some right outside the church have been healed, with, as in the Gospels, varied spiritual fruit.

In many ways, healing and evangelism are very similar. Both pose the same theological problems – why is X healed, and Y apparently isn't? Why is A dramatically converted, while B remains apparently unmoved? Both present similar opportunities. In the beginning, I had to do a lot of the front-line work in both areas. Gradually, over the years, many others have come to share the ministry. Parish visiting is one of the joys of the Anglican ministry. It is a great privilege (and an impossible task) to have access into almost every home in the parish. Opportunities for offering healing prayer abound, and we need discernment as to when such prayer will be helpful, and when it would cause embarrassment or rejection.

Healing Testimonies

At one of our earliest healing services in the little village church at Prestleigh, one of the older ladies suffered from considerable pain in her shoulder and back. Now over eighty, she writes as follows: 'Some years ago I wrote in the *Shepton Mallet Journal* about healing. Having experienced great pain myself, I went along to a healing service in church, where our rector John laid his hands on my shoulder and back. My back became warm, and gradually the pain went. It really was incredible.' This was a great encouragement to all involved, especially to the prayer group in the village.

Testimonies of healing from church members and outsiders

Visiting a local doctor, semi-retired, but still working as a consultant in local factories, provided a challenge and an opportunity. He was lying in bed, in a Bath hospital, suffering with severe back pain. Although he came to our early morning communion service, I didn't know him very well, and had no idea about his views on healing. I felt the inward spiritual nudge that I should offer to pray. He agreed very readily. Later that day he felt dramatically better, and was soon out of hospital. Not long afterwards, his wife who was suffering from tinnitus (a very trying 'buzzing' in the ears), asked for prayer. She, too, was healed and, importantly, has encouraged others to seek prayer for similar complaints.

Pam, at that stage an occasional attender at Cranmore Church, had a major cancer operation. As a result of breast treatment, and radiotherapy in her lymph glands, she was very depressed, in great pain, and had little movement in her shoulder. After prayer, she became dramatically better, and many years later is still very well. She has grown spiritually, becoming a leading member of the local church, and occasionally involved in praying for others. One of her sons, when quite young, came to the church and received healing of severe and persistent migraines.

Suzette, living in the same village, has suffered a great deal from Crohn's disease. While never completely healed, she has felt great benefit from prayer, both when at home and during two long periods in hospital. Her faith was greatly increased by one dramatic event. She was diagnosed as suffering from an ovarian cyst, large and painful. After coming to a healing service in Shepton, she felt much better. A few days later, she went for the operation. When the operation started, no cyst could be found. Apparently, her medical notes say something to the effect, 'Prayed for, operation unnecessary.' One of her children has suffered from a considerable problem in his hips. He, too, has been prayed for and has made remarkable progress after a complicated operation. These incidents illustrate, to me, the complementary nature of prayer and medicine. Occasionally, God intervenes dramatically, and no medical treatment is required, but usually prayer and medicine work hand in hand, hopefully bringing wholeness and healing.

One lady came with her fiancé for wedding preparation. She writes of the unexpected developments as follows:

> I would like to share my experience of healing. My story begins when myself and my fiancé approached the local rector with regard to being married in the church. During discussions regarding the marriage ceremony, it was mentioned that marriage meant the creation of new life – children. I asked the rector not to mention in the service the part relating to the creation of children as I had been informed some thirteen years previously that this would be out of the question for me. Mr Woolmer suggested healing and prayer. He laid his hands on us and prayed with us on several occasions leading up to the marriage. The marriage ceremony took place and my husband and I went on our honeymoon. We came back expecting our first child! I have since been blessed with another child and now have two healthy boys after over thirteen years of trying. This is the true power of healing, and I am very grateful.

Sometimes prayer needs quick thinking! Arriving at St Aldhelm's, Oxford, I noticed the tall figure of Ron descending the steps from the belfry. He was hobbling badly, and I had forgotten that he had severely strained a ligament in his knee three months earlier. My reader had already begun the service (I had come up from Shepton, inevitably arriving just after the start). My instant offer to pray was accepted. We prayed in the churchyard, very briefly. The next day I visited Ron, and he was significantly better and able to drive his car for the first time for a while. This initiated a series of times of prayer, and steady healing progress, where before there had seemed to be very little.

Norman was another person whom we prayed for at home. His wife, Gwen, is a regular church-goer, and member of the Mothers' Union. Norman was finding life very difficult, much depressed by constant pain in his knees and feet. Although he has never been healed, he felt such uplift from prayer that his whole life became much more positive, and he was confirmed in his own home in a special service by a visiting bishop. He has become a regular home communicant, and seems to have much more zest for life since he has received prayer. It is a great joy to visit him, and to see how the original prayers have had such a releasing spiritual effect.

Over the years, we have seen many people come for prayer. Some, during or after our normal services, some at special healing services, some when we've had distinguished visiting speakers. Many problems have been shared, many things much deeper than physical needs have been opened up (though by their very nature, they are much less easy to write about), and all sorts of things have happened. A steady trickle of people from further away have visited us seeking prayer. I remember, in particular, one young woman very tired and stressed by Crohn's disease, who came up from Exeter to several healing services. Her condition improved so much that she was able to go and work abroad in Greece, something that would have been unthinkable before prayer.

A visitor experiences a miracle

One of our regular visitors is Don Latham.[2] In his book he mentions an incident at Shepton Mallet.

> Sitting at my desk one day, my meeting with my brilliant woman Head of Computing was interrupted by a telephone call from a doctor in Somerset. I asked if I could take the call, pressing the button so it came through on the speaker.
> 'Don Latham?' he said.

'Yes.'

'My brother came to hear you at Shepton Mallet Parish Church last week at a healing service. He became a Christian and was completely healed of his cancer.'

'It was rather a good night,' I said, rather tamely, trying not to look across the desk. I never impose my faith on people, especially at work, but in my experience it is impossible to keep good news quiet.

It would be interesting to know who the doctor was, and what happened to the brother. Alas, such information is often fragmentary, and we have to rejoice at least in what appears to have happened. Betty, one of our readers, suffered for a long time from a very painful shoulder. This was dramatically healed when Don prayed with her. The consequences of this were interesting. Her youngest daughter, Janet, suffered greatly from eczema. Encouraged by her mother's healing, Janet, in her twenties, a fairly definite non-church-goer, came to talk to me about prayer for healing. She writes as follows:

I have suffered with eczema from birth. I was treated by doctors throughout this time with steroid creams and emulsifying ointments. When I was seven my condition became so bad that I spent four months in a special children's hospital run by the St John's Hospital for Skin Diseases. On leaving hospital my condition seemed greatly improved. Unfortunately, this did not last and my eczema became so bad again that I spent two more spells in hospital in London before coming to live in Somerset.

The eczema continued to affect my life, and at the age of twenty-one I was once again admitted to hospital for treatment. After each spell in hospital there was an improvement in my skin condition. The treatment given to me dealt with the infected skin area, but I was always left with very dry, red, itchy skin.

Often my clothes would stick to my skin where it was weeping so badly, and also my hair would be stuck to my face when I woke up in the morning. The eczema was affecting my life in other ways. I suffered from a lack of confidence due to the reaction I sometimes got from other people. I also found it difficult to join in PE at school or go swimming with my friends. The eczema had taken such a hold on my life that I was increasingly becoming depressed and felt there was no hope for a normal life.

My mother suggested that I should visit the local rector who had some experience with healing. Although sceptical I decided to go. At this stage I would have tried anything. I visited John Woolmer at his house. We talked and he said a prayer for me. After about two days I called to my mother to come and see my arm. The eczema had gone from this one place. I visited John Woolmer several more times and each time he would pray for the part of me that was most affected.

The eczema disappeared from different parts of my body until it had gone. This happened approximately twelve years ago and I am still clear of the eczema and able to lead a normal life, something I thought I would never be able to do.

Some years later, she and her husband came to see me about a chronic and painful condition that was affecting his ability to work. They came to several healing services, but there was no discernible result. This is one of the mysteries of such ministry. As yet, despite her mother's prayers, there has been no obvious spiritual response to such a dramatic healing. I had hoped, and expected, that her husband would also be healed and that would really open the way for a spiritual change.

Surprised by healing

Phil is a former choir member who has suffered quite a lot of illness, mainly arthritis in hips and knees. He has a robust, down-to-earth attitude to life. He writes:

My story starts in 1993. I had been helping raise money for the church's restoration fund by singing the Psalms of David nonstop.

The last non-stop singing effort was to be for eight hours, so a couple of months before it was due to take place, I thought I would treat myself to a new pair of glasses. I went to the opticians for an eye test, during which he said I had big problems. I had glaucoma in one eye which was very advanced, and he said that if nothing was done I would be blind within two years. He told me he had a new machine coming in a few weeks, and to come back when he would test again.

When I attended church, John, the rector, said I seemed a little worried, so I told him what had happened. He said to come to the back of the church for a few prayers, but that was all – nothing happened! I must say that I did not believe in healing and thought it to be a lot of hogwash.

The following Sunday, I attended a healing communion service. John said to come up for prayers, and he laid his hands on my head. To my surprise my head felt on fire – very strange!

A couple of weeks later I went back to the optician for another test on the new machine. He said that he could not understand it. The glaucoma had completely gone and now, nearly six years on, I still only use glasses for reading. Thank God!

Recently, Phil returned for another eye test, and again received the 'all clear'. When we first prayed, I did rather sense his view of the whole matter, which made it quite difficult to pray in faith!

It seems to me that it is for people like Phil that the healing ministry is particularly important – the reality of God's power has a very remarkable effect on people's thinking, expectations and outlook on life. This also affected one of Phil's grandchildren. His grand-daughter,

Kim, was diagnosed in Bristol by neurologists as having a brain tumour, and she, too, was losing her sight. Two of our prayer team, Jean and Maureen, prayed each week with her for quite a while. She regained what sight she had lost, and is in good health some five years later.

Karen, who organises a busy doctor's practice, came to our church when Jon Peters from St Paul's Onslow Square was leading an evening during a mission. Already a Christian, and having in the past received some effective ministry to cut off some spiritual darkness, she went forward, with others, in response to his sermon. Jon prayed, quite simply, for the Holy Spirit to touch them all. Karen felt a great power, fell to the ground and experienced a deep sensation in her head. She had asked for prayer for her persistent migraines. When she went home she looked in the mirror and gasped. Her eye, which had endured many unsuccessful operations to cure a childhood squint, was normal! Her husband and her optician were most impressed. Other relatives, and some medical people with whom she works, found it rather less impressive. This wonderful experience has given her and her husband confidence to testify to Christ in magazines, on local radio, and in their everyday life. Such healings are a very powerful testimony to God's grace (see 1 Peter 3:15).

One evening, a young lady, a relative by marriage of our verger, came forward for prayer. She told me, and my praying partner, that she was suffering from a serious cancer. Both of us felt a surge of faith that gave us an expectation that God was going to do something special. Nothing particular seemed to happen, but about two weeks later, she awoke with a tremendous sensation of fire and light in her body. She felt much better, and her next visit to a doctor confirmed a dramatic change in her condition. She is still well, about eight years later. She, too, has apparently been untouched spiritually by the dramatic physical change.

Transformed by healing

By contrast, one old lady, who seldom came, but often seemed critical of the modern church, came to one of our healing services. Some months later, I met her. She fixed me with a beady eye and said, 'Vicar, I came to one of your healing services.' I waited for the inevitable criticism! Her next words astonished me.

'Vicar, I felt a presence that I'd never felt before.' It was a transforming experience. She wasn't healed of her illness, but she knew God's love for the first time. When she faced a terminal illness a few years later, she faced it with great bravery, humour and faith. One brief moment at a village church healing service seemed to give her spiritual hope and comfort.

Robin hobbled up for prayer at a healing service. He was in plaster and using a crutch. X-rays had shown that his knee was in a bad state, and he was about to have an operation for a cartilage problem. He was in great pain. After prayer, there was a clear improvement. By the end of the service he was so much better that his wife carried his crutch out of our church. When he saw his consultant three weeks later, the doctor was greatly puzzled and kept saying, 'It can't have happened. It's not possible.' No operation was needed, and he has remained free of pain. This remarkable healing caused Robin deep theological problems. He had seen others, notably a small baby, apparently untouched. He continues to agonise over the question 'Why me?' Which again illustrates how complex and varied the spiritual results of such services can be.

Testimony from a member of our team

Over the years, we have had many members in our healing team. We meet once a month, the week before our monthly healing service, to pray and to exchange information, and to think theologically. Our present team has about a dozen members, including one nurse. For a short time, we had a local doctor as part of the team, and it has always included our readers. Some members of the team are particularly available to visit people in their own homes. Jean, who has suffered a lot herself with illness in her own life and in her immediate family, seems to be used a lot by the Lord. She was involved in many of the incidents about which I have already written. I add a few other examples from her testimony.

She writes first of a healing from the New Wine Conference, on the showground just outside Shepton Mallet.

> I have been involved in the healing ministry for about ten years, and although obviously I don't call myself a healer (or allow anyone else to do so), I do feel I am used by God as a channel for his healing power and that of the Holy Spirit. The healing that stands out from New Wine was that of a sixteen-year old girl called Annie, who was born, as were her brother and father, with deformed hips. Her walking was not good and she had been under an orthopaedic surgeon all her life. Annie and her mother, a nurse, came to New Wine and I prayed with Annie several times during the week. Several months later she had a riding accident and went to see her surgeon. X-rays showed considerable *new growth of bone* where the deformity had been, and the surgeon had no explanation at all for this.

Another very moving case was of a brain-damaged baby, who some years later is making very encouraging progress.

Jamie was first brought by his mother, Julie, to a healing service. John was away, but Don Latham and I prayed for Jamie before the service as he was crying so much. I think it was our curate, Dale, who suggested I might follow up the case. I visited their flat at Hillmead weekly. Jamie was badly brain damaged. He was six months old and blind. After a time I felt very strongly that Jamie would see one day, and I took along a mobile which Julie (rather reluctantly) put up over his cot in the sitting room. I remember saying to her, 'Julie, one day Jamie is going to gain his sight and he'll want something to follow on.' Sure enough, Jamie *did* gain his sight.

Jean writes about a very different healing.

Some years ago, a young woman, Tracey, came to see John about her problem with endometriosis, a condition which was extremely painful, and difficult to treat. Her doctor was seriously considering recommending a hysterectomy. I joined John for prayer, and we saw some improvement. For a long time, I visited Tracey weekly in her dinner hour. As a result of the gradual improvement, sexual relations became possible, and she conceived. Her husband left her during this remarkable pregnancy, and in due course Hannah (see 1 Samuel 1 for choice of name) was born. It was a great joy some years later to attend Tracey's second wedding, taken by John, at which I read a lesson. All of which was very much better than when we started praying years earlier.

Time and space preclude more than the briefest mention of other notable healing experiences. We have had some particular encouragements with children, including a little boy who lived in a local pub. He was literally covered with eczema, but after several visits from members of our healing team, he improved so dramatically that his father could often be heard entertaining his customers with his son's story. This healing took place as a result of our being asked to pray through the pub because the children found great difficulty in sleeping peacefully. (There is a strong tradition that a former criminal who was hanged lies buried under the pub!)

Another young child, a regular worshipper at the church, suffered from very bad hearing problems. She had to sit at the front of her class in school, and was having real learning difficulties as a result. After a brief time of prayer, including the laying on of hands, she seems to have had a dramatic improvement that has helped her relate to people far better, and be much more involved in life. She, too, will have a testimony to share with friends as she grows up.

About fifteen years ago, a young boy was in danger of dying due to his inability to make platelets. These blood-clotting agents were essential to his health. The outlook was poor. His grandmother had a strong faith, and asked for prayer for him. He made a dramatic recovery which certainly surprised his doctors and family.

I have received many other testimonies from members of our congregation testifying to healings received at the earlier stages of their lives. It is good to know how wide-spread the work of healing is. Most of it has happened quietly, and largely unrecorded, in churches and chapels, though some have taken place at big rallies and large healing services.

Ministry to children

It isn't always possible, or desirable, to pray directly with the people who are ill. This is particularly true when praying for children. We have prayed, usually with parents, for a number of children. Nightmares, inability to sleep due to involvement with ouija boards, disturbance due to 'psychic' healing with a pendulum, have all been healed without the children concerned being aware (until afterwards) of the prayers being offered.

Praying down the telephone can be particularly effective. Of course, that is no substitute for personal contact; but both the Gospels and Christian history abound with testimonies to absent healing, and we should be prepared to use any opportunities to pray for those who are ill.

Medicine and healing

In this country, with our excellent medical facilities, we experience healing of many illnesses which over fifty years ago would have seemed unthinkable. There should be no conflict between healing and medicine. Medical people, rightly, get fed up with healing testimonies which seem to be exaggerated, or even untrue. Those involved in prayer sometimes find the degree of proof required by medics impossible to provide. There is a necessary balance between faith and testimony on the one hand, and evidence and caution on the other.

Here is one testimony to a remarkable surgical result:

Having crossed the threshold of the door marked 'cancer', I live my life conscious that I have been protected and healed.

During my 1992 illness, I was wonderfully supported by prayer. Not having any suspicion that I had cancer, I had been spared any build-up of fear and anxiety, but even when the diagnosis was clear (and I knew from the experience of others how very serious ovarian cancer is), I do not recall any panic – just a deep thankfulness that I should proceed with the chemotherapy, a deep thankfulness that I was part of a believing community, gratitude for all the help that was available to me, and that my operation and treatment had been so timely.

Reading (from the Lectionary) during my stay in hospital,

my prayer diary of those first few days includes, among others, the following texts that inspired: 'On my bed I remember you; I think of you through the watches of the night. Because you are my help I sing in the shadow of your wings' (Psalm 63). 'And even the very hairs of your head are all numbered. So don't be afraid; you are worth more than many sparrows' (Matthew 10:30). 'Praise be to the Lord God, the God of Israel who alone does marvellous deeds. Praise be to his glorious name for ever . . . Amen and amen' (Psalm 72). 'He said to the man, "Stretch out your hand." So he stretched it out and it was completely restored, just as sound as the other' (Matthew 12:13).

In retrospect, however, it is Hosea 10:12–13 that has meant the most. 'Sow for yourselves righteousness. Reap the fruit of unfailing love, and break up your unploughed ground for it is time to seek the Lord until he comes and showers righteousness on you.'

I seemed to be being told that I still had work to do! It wasn't obvious at first, and I had to get well, but as time has passed and as I have remained healthy, I do regard my work with SHAL (see p. 318) as my unploughed ground! My conviction sometimes wavers and panic sets in, and it all seems impossibly full of immovable rocks! More than once at these times the verse from Hosea has been brought back to me in readings or other messages.

Trying to express this experience is difficult. It's such a delicate matter! One asks 'Is this really so, or is it just fancy?' But nonetheless, there it is. Others, I know, have succumbed to cancer in the years since my illness, and I cannot help but ask why I should have been spared and have suffered so much less than they. At the very least my special verse provides the beginning of an answer.

Very recently, some six years after the original trouble, Joan's cancer recurred. We continue to pray, confident in the knowledge that an operation has been possible.

I have written extensively in chapter 8 about healing

prayer and the approach of death. I have received many testimonies in this area, and I would just re-emphasise in this chapter on the ministry in the local church, of the importance of such prayer, ministry, and support both for the one who is dying and for their immediate family.

It is very moving to take the funeral service of people who through their illness have become friends, who through their courage have helped the faith of their nearest and dearest, and who through their death have become witnesses to the great hope given us by the resurrection.

This is an important and vital part of the ministry of the truly local church, and is far removed from the unrealistic triumphalism of some wandering, peripatetic, healing ministries. Such funerals are, of course, a considerable challenge to the local healing prayer team who are inevitably faced with questions of guilt, lack of faith, and general failure. As the team matures, these questions can be turned round, and death can be seen, for what it is – the gateway to eternal life.

A deep puzzle

Praying for healing can, however, cause unexpected problems. Let me give one painful example. Some years ago, a married couple came for prayer. They had been married for some years, but had been unable to have any children. There was no obvious medical reason. At one healing service, the wife mentioned some of the unusual circumstances of her own birth. The lady praying with me had a 'visionary' experience which seemed to confirm the birth trauma. We all felt the strong presence of the Lord, and were all encouraged.

Very soon afterwards, she became pregnant. They made my Christmas by sharing the news with me on Christmas Eve. By the end of January she had lost the baby. They were both deeply hurt, and believe that this was a major factor in the break-up of their marriage. They both remain regular worshippers, but have gone their separate ways. I still feel the acute pain of the whole incident. Why did God seem to bring a wonderful answer to prayer, only for the whole situation to dissolve in tears and disappointment?

My editor asks, pertinently, what lessons do you draw from this incident? I remain deeply puzzled. I am a little comforted that Norman Anderson's faith survived the death of his children (see p. 307); that Selwyn Hughes[3] wrestled with his wife's illness and death, but remains committed to praying for healing.

C.S. Lewis[4] raises many of the same questions when writing about the apparent answers to prayer for his wife's healing, only to find that the respite was very temporary, and that her death was again imminent.

For my part, it increases my certainty 'that now we see through a glass darkly, then face to face' (1 Corinthians 13:12, AV). I, like many others, have to bow my head before the sovereignty of God; and say, in faith, I don't know – mine not to reason why.

Inner healing

Doctors, psychologists, counsellors and those involved in the healing ministry soon discover that many illnesses, both physical and emotional, often seem to stem from deep hurts in the past.

I remember very well praying with a fellow clergyman who had very little self-confidence and a low opinion of his own work and ability. Much of this could be traced back to a traumatic moment when, in his early teens, he was told that he was adopted. The shock of this un-expected disclosure, coupled with the inevitable feelings of rejection and insecurity that he would have picked up from his natural mother before, during and just after birth, and around the time of his adoption, had left him with a deep-rooted insecurity.

'Jesus Christ is the same yesterday and today and forever' (Hebrews 13:8). This key text, combined with Romans 8:8, and Isaiah 61 (see pp. 258ff) form a biblical basis for praying about people's past. Often there is a tremendous need to forgive others – parents, brothers and sisters, school teachers, marriage partners, and a need to forgive and love oneself.

The great command, quoted by the lawyer in the encounter with Jesus which led to the parable of the good Samaritan is, 'Love the Lord your God with all your heart and with all your soul and with all your strength and with all your mind; and, love your neighbour as yourself' (Luke 10:27). Without loving oneself, we cannot really get very far in loving God or our neighbour. Many people have a great desire to serve and to pray for others, but sometimes this stems from deep personal insecurity. We subconsciously feel that if we help others, they will love and accept us, and this will help our own inner problems. This can be particularly true of members of healing teams. The phrase 'the wounded healer' can apply both physically and emotionally. Such people are valuable and sensitive members of healing teams; but they, themselves, will often need a lot of spiritual and practical support. Loving oneself ultimately depends on accepting what God has done for us. It depends on trusting his free grace, and believing that his Holy Spirit is continuing to work within us for our own sanctification.

Healing from a painful marriage

Here are some examples. The first is from someone who

has become a very sensitive and caring person, well able to pray for and to help others. This testimony is particularly important as it shows the healing work of the Spirit acting sovereignly with very little human ministry:

The year after my husband died, the vicar of the church where I worshipped led a Saints Alive course during Lent. The final session was set aside for individuals to receive prayer. He was assisted by my house-group leader – a lady. When I went through to them the atmosphere was heavy and dead, and he finally sent me on my way with nine words – 'I think this is tied up with your marriage' to which I had replied, 'So do I.'

Two days later, while drying up after lunch, I suddenly put the towel down, grabbed some paper and a pen and made two lists. A long list of negatives, and a short list of positives about my marriage. The sobs that then came from me were not from ordinary crying, they were quite horrendous. When I quietened down, I tore the list up and praised God. I could not remember what I had written. I do not believe a human counsellor could have unearthed what the Holy Spirit did.

Later in the week, I had on a Fisherfolk tape and found myself dancing round the room – that is not a normal thing for me to do! I stopped suddenly and experienced a very supernatural sensation, quite impossible to describe. After a while I telephoned my house-group leader and simply said, 'What we were expecting to happen the other evening has just happened.'

Clearly, God knew that a deep healing needed to take place before I could receive the baptism of the Holy Spirit.'

What really excites me about this story (which took place before she joined our church) is how this healing released her from what could have been the most terrible bitterness, both against her late husband, and even God himself. Her husband, a church leader, had caused her great pain which she has minimalised in her gracious testimony. This story also helped us greatly in a subsequent time of prayer for her daughter, who had also been affected by the family situation.

Healing from childhood abuse

Here is another example from someone who has been freed from the traumas of the past into a deep faith which is expressed in many ways within both church and workplace.

> For years after the birth of my first child, I became haunted by memories of sexual abuse by a friend of the family that I had experienced in early childhood. The trauma of the abuse had distorted relationships within the family early on, leading to a turbulent adolescence, unsuitable and hurtful relationships with men, and cast a darkness over the time before I met my husband.
>
> The healing has taken many years as the layers of hurt have been peeled away. I have always had a strong faith, but at times where forgiveness seemed an impossibility in these circumstances, I had reckoned without the grace of God. At a crisis point we brought the subject to light as a family – an extremely painful process, and decided to report the crime to the police. As a policewoman took my nine-page statement in my sitting room one afternoon, we both became aware that we shared a common faith in Christ – she was a very gifted person who, in her gentle way, made me realise that this was the right thing to do. It was decisive action, and the first stage of the healing process.
>
> Forgiveness came unexpectedly one day in the middle of a Sunday Eucharist. One of my sisters had given me a word of scripture from the sermon on the mount (Luke 6:27–28), where we are urged to 'Love your enemies and pray for those who abuse you'. It suddenly seemed so easy, and I left the church free of the bitterness and hate that had been consuming me for so long.

A further period of time elapsed, during which a good deal of healing took place in the family. My sisters who had also been affected were able to move forward and begin to put the events behind them. One evening, during a healing service, I knew I needed God's healing touch for myself at a deeper level if I was to journey further with Christ and to build on my loving relationship with my husband. I had been puzzled by the many different ways the childhood traumas had affected my adult life, and had begun to develop unnatural and exaggerated fears for my own children. In the next few weeks, as I received the counselling I needed and was at last ready, I knew that through God's love and purpose for me I could break free of the bondage and slavery of the sin that had been done to me. Images of chains being cut and, above all, of myself as a new creation, washed in the blood of Christ, became my assurance that I could break away from the past, leaving it behind and cast aside from my daily thoughts.

Here, the healing included a lovely combination of God working through a normal church service, a key text of scripture, and effective prayerful counselling to bind up the wounds and set her free. As a result her faith has grown dramatically, and she has been blessed by God in leading a very difficult area of ministry.

Healing from feeling worthless

My third example is from another church leader who has a great gift for serving and helping others. She, particularly, needed assurance of her self worth.

During a joint healing service held at the local Roman Catholic Church in 1998, the rector came and spoke about some spiritual barriers to God; one of them included a low self-esteem. This spoke loudly to me and when the opportunity came to go for prayer, I went to the couple sitting nearest to me. We spoke together of sharing this feeling, and then both of them prayed for me. It was during the husband's prayer, when he spoke of how God had made me 'special', that I began to feel a lightening within myself.

After I left the service, I spent some time thinking around that 'special part of me that God had created.' So, I may not be as bright, intelligent, logical as another person, but this special part that God has given me is unique to me, and God has given it especially to me to reflect that part of his nature to others, in the hope that people might be drawn to him through this uniqueness that he gives all his followers. These experiences have led me into a deeper relationship with God, a greater understanding about his loving nature, and a stronger desire to worship, obey, serve and to listen and learn more about him.

In her letter, she describes herself as having a background of faith which did not include present-day healings, something that has changed with this and other experiences.

You don't get involved in the healing ministry for long before problems of a more sinister nature emerge. To these we now turn.

Deliverance for people and places

In the local parish ministry, we have adopted a very low-key approach, usually inviting those who feel some sort of spiritual oppression to renew their baptismal vows. From time to time, we encounter the clear signs of demonic interference (see p. 264ff), sometimes the family tree ministry (see p. 261ff) has been very helpful. After prayer I often find that my most important task is to assure someone that they were not demonised, but were, at worst, suffering from some sort of spiritual darkness.

Deliverance without ministry

A clear example of how this low-key approach can be effective came from someone outside the parish who sought help.

A man came to see me about a past spiritual problem which he felt (rightly) was affecting his present Christian life, and disturbing others in his church. Years earlier he had been involved in occult activities and experimented in various other ways at university. Subsequently, he had married, settled down to a good job, become a Christian, suffered a severe breakdown, been substantially cured, moved south to a new job, home and church. All was fairly well, but he couldn't share his faith with his wife – not surprisingly, she'd had plenty to put up with! – and he felt that he was a disturbing influence in Christian groups.

I enjoyed meeting him, but felt a real sense of his spiritual disturbance. We went to the church to pray, but as I couldn't find a suitable prayer partner (Jesus sent his disciples out in pairs – and that is a sound guide-line for all of us), I prayed a holding prayer, like a dentist's temporary dressing. I asked him to come to our cathedral day of healing two days later. I planned to pray for him there, in the greater atmosphere of faith, and to ask him to be anointed with oil after we had cut off any evil powers that were troubling him. I was unusually confident that God would set him free.

During the service in the afternoon, I was greatly occupied in prayer. My contact arrived – looking different. 'What's happened to you?' I asked. 'Whatever it was left me last night,' he replied. I met his wife on the cathedral steps after the service. She looked a bit shattered when I tried to explain what had happened, and how important her own commitment to Christ would be. A short time later, she turned to the Lord, and the family was able to experience God's healing power in a fresh way! For me, the wonderful thing was that God brought about the healing without any direct ministry, and then used it to bring someone else to faith.

I think that over the years, a significant number of people have benefited from this sort of ministry which is, of course, much less memorable and less clear cut than some of the dramatic incidents that I have written about earlier.

I always mention ministry in this sort of area when explaining the question 'Do you renounce evil?' to families bringing children for baptism. It is surprising how often this opens up an interesting conversation, and occasionally leads to significant ministry to a member of the family.

At first sight, ministry to disturbed places seems less scriptural, yet as we showed in chapter 2, p. 67, places where spiritual disobedience had taken place were a constant source of conflict in Old Testament times, and in Acts 19, Paul's ministry in Ephesus led many to burn their magic scrolls and to confess their occult deeds.

Over the years I have prayed in pubs, private houses where past tragedies had taken place, or disturbed people had dabbled in occult things. Such prayer has usually been effective, although Jesus' sharp warning (Matthew 12:43–45) seems to be just as applicable to buildings as to people. Such ministry requires repentance, and a turning to Christ by those who live there if it is to be truly effective.

Deliverance for a property

Here is a clear example which had a sequel a number of years later. It is written by a close friend, Anne Goode:

In worldly terms, the house was a challenging buy. Basically an attractive early eighteenth-century building, it had been both neglected and subjected to ugly and inappropriate alterations. The property was overpriced and, moreover, right opposite the site of an annual pop festival which was to become the largest event of its kind in Europe. Work on the place proved exceptionally difficult, and I became aware of an atmosphere of menace. The effect on my family was grim. My academically brilliant husband began behaving oddly, displaying signs of early dementia; my musically gifted son was severely bullied at school by the son of a woman I hardly knew, but who unaccountably began spreading malicious stories about me in the village; my daughter spent all her time like a ghost child, pale and withdrawn, in the stables; and I was prone to uncontrollable outbursts of rage which upset the whole family.

In spiritual and emotional disarray, I sought the help of John Woolmer whose recently published book *Growing up to Salvation*, contained a chapter on the occult which I had read with surprise and relief. During prayer with the laying-on of hands, I experienced liquid light flowing through my whole body, and I found that I was totally free of the dark fear which until then had been gripping every area of my life. Problems with the house remained to be dealt with, but I was no longer afraid and family life improved. The church began using the house for staff days, but I knew that the place needed deeper ministry than the simple blessing it had received from a friend.

After the mysterious death in the field of one of my daughter's horses, John Woolmer decided, during a staff day, to perform a full-scale exorcism of the premises, complete with a large jug of holy water. My daughter and I were particularly troubled by unpleasant graffiti on the stable walls which seemed to imply a rather sinister use by previous occupants. I felt that the evil presence in the house predated the previous owners and had been around for a very long time. When it came to the stable previously occupied by the dead horse, the assembled staff stood in a semi-circle outside while John entered, praying in tongues, and finally tipping half a jugful of water out on the straw. One of the staff members, not usually sensitive in these areas, reported that he had almost been knocked over by 'some force' coming out from the stable.

From that day, the atmosphere in the house and lands changed dramatically, and it was not long before we erected a thirty-foot high cross at a high point in a field where there have been many gatherings of prayer, praise and worship. One of these was featured on national television in contrast to demonic scenes at the pop festival. After one celebration of Holy Communion, a huge cross was observed in the sky, formed by the floodlit shadow on a unique cloud formation. The house has become a centre for prayer and hospitality, not only during the pop festival when scores of Christians from different fellowships gather, but also throughout the year at significant times. Visitors invariably comment on the peace and loveliness of the place.

Some years later, Anne again sought my help. Following the death of her husband, she was being troubled by horrendous nightmares during which she felt physically attacked in a most unpleasant way. She had recently moved bedrooms, and was sleeping in the room which she felt the instigator of the stable graffiti had occupied years earlier.

I have to confess that I prayed in a slightly desultory and low-key way. But as we finished, my Bible fell open at Nehemiah 13. Rather disinterestedly, I picked it up and suddenly noticed vv 4–9, especial v.8: 'I was greatly displeased and threw all Tobiah's household goods out of the room.' Feeling exceptionally foolish, I asked Anne, 'Do you still have any furniture owned by the previous occupants?' As she had lived in the house for over ten years, I didn't expect the reply, 'Yes, the bedside table and the carpet in *this* room.' We prayed harder, and determined to get rid of the offending articles as quickly as possible.

Immediately the nightmares ceased. This house, incidentally, has become my main venue for regular prayer mornings and writing which is a rather nice sequel to the whole story.

It was very unusual for me to undertake such ministry on my own. On this occasion, Anne's recent bereavement and my own scepticism that the nightmares were really a spiritual problem, led me into deeper waters than I had expected. Normally, I would take a lay member of the congregation with me, whether praying for people, buildings, or both. Such ministry bears deep spiritual fruit. Recently a very simple prayer of blessing in a house where a new member of our church had experienced spiritual disturbance has led her to join a confirmation class, and hopefully will soon lead to a clear Christian commitment.

Sometimes the praying team are quite adversely attacked by such ministry. Talking, writing or praying in this area can be dangerous. We need to put on the full armour of Christ (Ephesians 6:1–10), resist the devil (James 4:7) and seek immediate help if we are badly affected. Symptoms can include extreme tiredness, irritability, depression and loss of sleep. People who are prayed for invariably feel very tired, and should be encouraged to go and have a long rest. They need careful follow-up and nurture over the next few days.

Prayer and preparation

I was very impressed when visiting Holy Trinity, Leicester. I attended their time of 'listening prayer'. About twelve people prayed for about half an hour, sharing themes and particular 'words'. On this particular Sunday, the theme of rejection seemed important, and various particular words were given – one of the team had an unexpected pain in the left arm. These were mentioned half way through the service. After communion, about twenty people came for prayer, many responding to the particular topics or illnesses mentioned in the service. I felt that this church had an effective ministry which God was blessing. Of the few people that I was privileged to pray for, in one case both my prayer partner and I felt there was need for deep, future ministry. Independently, we sensed that we were only touching the surface of a deep spiritual iceberg. I shall be interested to hear how it works out.

There are obvious dangers in such teams! If the wrong people join them, it is very hard to ease them out without deep hurt. Also, the existence of a team may give the impression that everyone else can forget about healing and leave the experts to get on with it.

But we mustn't leave this ministry just to an 'elite' prayer group. The whole body of Christ is called to this work. That means that we can all pray for other people – in the house group, over a cup of coffee, after the church service. There are just a few conditions – we need a measure of faith, and ideally we shouldn't be on our own. (Jesus always sent people out in pairs! It releases us both from the spiritual burden of 'failure' and the awful spiritual pride of 'success'!) We should be right with the Lord, and we shouldn't rush in blindly. As with evangelism, ill thought-out, unasked-for prayer for healing can do a lot of harm. We would be wise to pray along these lines, 'Lord, if you want me to pray with my neighbour, please give me some clear indication. May she ask me to pray, and will you please show me how to pray and what to pray for?'

What about spiritual warfare?

Prayer in difficult places

Within the parish, we haven't been very successful in this field. A small prayer group ran into considerable personal difficulties when praying against what were perceived to be local spiritual influences from the past and the present. These included the area around the market cross where a number of citizens had been publicly executed after Monmouth's rebellion in 1685; the prison where, in particular, a number of American soldiers were executed in the recent World War, often for questionable offences; the area where a local highwayman was hanged. We also prayed constantly about what we all felt to be the low self-image of the town and many of its citizens.

The prayer in the prison, again an ecumenical venture, seemed quite effective, and certainly there were a number of conversions soon afterwards. Ecumenical prayer at some alleged sites of 'worship' around the edge of the town was good for relationships, and we have certainly learnt from the spiritual toll taken among our first group of intercessors.

Probably this is something that shouldn't have been undertaken without much clearer leading, although there have been some signs of recent 'successes' for the town, and some of the churches involved have experienced a real measure of spiritual encouragement.

Very recently, we received a wonderful encouragement. For many years, Jean White had prayed for husband Laurie's conversion. Laurie was very supportive of Jean's important work as our Sunday Club leader, but firmly unbelieving. He and I had many intellectual arguments, from which I, invariably, left feeling bruised and out-argued by his gentle, but razor-sharp logic. Early in 1997, Jean had a serious skiing accident. Her knee was severely damaged. Laurie was very impressed by the care shown by many parishioners to his wife. In May 1998, they came on a parish holiday in the Wye Valley.

One of our prayer team was watching the bubbles on a stream, noting how they arrived separately and then often united. She felt that she should show this to Jean who burst into tears, and said that they showed her how she and Laurie would be united in faith. Encouraged by this, a group of people prayed for Laurie's conversion; emboldened, I spent an evening debating the faith with Laurie. As usual, although his attitude was different – 'I'd like to believe, but I can't' – I was routed. He even agreed to pray 'to the unknown God'. He wanted a sign. I said these usually came after belief, not before.

A remarkable conversion

Later in the summer, our churchwarden's elder daughter smiled innocently at him and said, 'Laurie, why don't you come to church?' He made some excuse. Just before our parish fête, our parish prayer group marched around the churchyard praying on all the sites of the stalls. It was quite a 'warfare' prayer, claiming the ground for God.

On the afternoon of the fête, I found myself beside Laurie at the secondhand book stall. My heart quickened as I noticed an almost new copy of *A Doctor Investigates Healing Miracles* (see p. 192 notes 42–44). I turned to him and said, 'If I buy this book for you, will you promise to read it?' He agreed. Later he met the churchwarden's daughter who repeated her question. Laurie said afterwards that he felt 'another's eyes looking at him through hers'.

He read the book, and found it intellectually convincing. There was no doubt that God did heal – here was medical proof. He didn't like the selectivity and described himself as having climbed out of the sea of unbelief onto a rocky island detached from the mainland. He said that he needed a sign. I replied that he was unlikely to get one – until he committed himself to Christ.

A few weeks later, crossing the Atlantic by plane, he looked at Jean and said, 'I've become a Christian!' At the end of the flight, he turned to Jean, expecting to need to help her stand freely. She had been suffering from severe back problems connected with the accident of the previous year. But Jean got up and lifted down her own baggage – she had been healed! Laurie had received his sign, and they had a truly wonderful holiday.

Confirmation, if any was required, was given to Laurie at our evening healing service a few weeks later. One of our new readers shared a picture that had come to him in prayer. He began with characteristic modesty, 'I am not given to seeing pictures, but I had a tremendous sight of autumn leaves, not symbolising death and winter, but rather of their beautifully changing colours in the sunlight, with the whole picture overarched with a rainbow.' Laurie and Jean had travelled to America to appreciate the fall, and their trip had indeed been crowned with a rainbow.

This story illustrates the inter-relationship of interpreting nature (the bubbles and the leaves), spiritual warfare (praying in the churchyard), the innocent testimony of children (like the famous conversion of St Augustine), the importance of persistent prayer, the wonderful evidence of healing, and above all, the mysterious, providential sovereignty of God. Despite the rather temporary nature of Jean's healing, Laurie's faith has continued to grow.

How should we pray?

There are, not surprisingly, many different approaches. The more 'Catholic' way is to lay hands upon people silently, and leave what happens between God and the person. This is quite similar to the 'Toronto' approach when the Holy Spirit is invoked with some prayer like, 'Come, Holy Spirit', and the results are left between the person and God. The difference is, perhaps, one of expectation!

Many people find it helpful to ask why someone has come for prayer (most people, in my experience, expect this and are helped by this sort of enquiry) and then to pray as seems appropriate. But how should we actually pray with those who come for help?

How, when and where to pray

It is important that each person prayed for is given time and enabled to relax. A long queue of people in a prayer line, waiting to receive brief prayer from a visiting expert, needs very careful handling. They need to be talked to, given some idea of how long they will have to wait, and receive proper follow-up afterwards. Obviously, a visiting speaker can have only a short time with individuals; back-up teams to follow up, and if necessary continue in prayer, are important.

More normally, prayer will take place in a quiet corner of the church, a study, or a home. The person asking for prayer often brings a friend, and usually there will be a pair of people praying. I find that one person usually leads the prayer time, the other mainly listens – for a word of knowledge from the Lord, a key question, or just observing what seems to be happening as a result of the prayer.

There is often a marked physical improvement that is an

encouragement to pray more. If there is no improvement, it is usually best to cease, and enquire later how they are. Occasionally the person feels physically worse, which is usually a sign of some quite deep spiritual disturbance. Following James 5, I sometimes anoint with oil. This can be done formally, following liturgy provided by the Church of England, or more informally. It seems appropriate for persistent illnesses, depression, migraines . . . and also as a follow-up to any sort of deliverance prayer.

Mistakes we've made

I must also mention two mistakes that we have made. One is insufficient prayer cover for the prayer team, especially before, during and after any form of deliverance or especially complicated prayer. Some people are particularly vulnerable and feel great pain or disturbance when praying for others. Perhaps, because I am fairly insensitive to evil (a form of spiritual tone deafness?), I have underestimated this need. People in prayer teams are very vulnerable to spiritual attack, and need to be looked after better than we have sometimes managed.

Another mistake has been in the failure of our follow-up. It is difficult when someone comes for prayer during a service to know if they require, need or expect follow-up. But we have failed people by failing to seek them out and offer further friendship and prayer. This is especially difficult when a visiting 'expert' is leading the prayer ministry, and there are always the essential boundaries of confidentiality to be observed.

Sometimes, healing prayer takes place without any physical contact, or even the knowledge of the person prayed for (Luke 7:1–10). When I was recovering from a hip operation in the spring of 1991, someone gave me an article written in the *Evening Standard* by Archbishop

George Carey just before his enthronement. He described his belief in the efficacy of prayer and recalled how he was struck down by a migraine at a particularly busy time, just before Pentecost 1988, when he was hosting a very special day in Wells Cathedral. He remembered that the Rector of Shepton Mallet, hearing about his problem, rang up and prayed down the phone. Apparently, the migraine left.

My memory is of ringing up and offering 'to come over and pray.' Bishop George politely, but firmly, said he was too busy! In desperation, and to be honest, with a tinge of annoyance, I offered an immediate prayer over the phone. I had no idea it was efficacious until I read the article nearly three years later!

Some questions about ministry

Different forms of healing prayer

How important are the actual words which we use? Obviously, we need to choose our words very carefully. They express our theology, our level of faith in the particular situation, our compassion and our love. Silence can be golden. Nevertheless, different people pray very effectively using different words, or sometimes none at all, from differing theological perspectives. Some people, Agnes Sandford for instance, use the model of Jesus' cursing of the fig tree (Mark 11:14) to curse cancers. Some rebuke illnesses, using the model of Jesus' prayer against Peter's mother-in-law's fever (Luke 4:39). Some see much illness as demonic. Fred Smith, for instance, saw all cancer as demonic, and prayed appropriately.[5] Some pray in tongues, remembering that 'the Spirit himself intercedes for us with groans that words cannot express' (Romans 8:26).

I have sometimes been asked to pray in tongues on the grounds that 'your prayers seem more effective when you pray in tongues'. I only pray in tongues with someone if I've asked their permission, I don't want to confuse them with a completely different theological issue!

What is reasonably clear is that no one approach is right. I may disagree with my dear friend Fred Smith when he assumes that all cancers need a form of exorcism; what I cannot deny is that God greatly honoured his prayers – far, far more than anything that I have experienced (see p. 212ff).

I believe that God is looking for faith, faithful prayer in the name of Jesus, and is able to overlook the imperfections of our theology.

After verbal prayer, it is good to continue to pray silently, with our hands *gently* on or close to the person's forehead.

Strange phenomena sometimes associated with healing

Some people experience strange phenomena – a strong sensation of heat, a transference of pain, a gentle power which causes the prayed-for person to fall over . . . None of these is essential, or even important, but they do happen. Jesus had some strange experiences; power left him (see Luke 8:46), and he did see strange things (see especially Mark 7:33; 8:23). The best thing we can do about such happenings is to relax – neither to seek them, nor to try to quench them.

Some people like to touch the painful area on the person's body. Obviously, this has to be done with extreme care, and often would be totally inappropriate. Namaan's comment (2 Kings 5:11) is interesting: 'I thought that he would surely come out to me and stand and call on the name of the Lord his God, *wave his hand over the spot* and

cure me of my leprosy.' This can be helpful. I have sometimes felt the pain, particularly of headaches, migraines
and bad backs, at quite a distance. It certainly increases
my faith, and occasionally helps to discern a problem.

Recently at the cathedral healing day, several people
asked for prayer to be 'filled with the Spirit' for their
own future ministry. Twice, I felt pain as I gently placed
my hand on their forehead. When I asked them if they
suffered from migraine, they seemed very surprised, but
their *faith was increased*, and I believe that our prayers
were more effective as a result.

People being prayed for need space and time. We must
learn to *listen*, and when praying not to crowd them. I've
too often experienced prayer that feels more like being at
the centre of a rugger scrum than in the peaceful presence
of the Lord.

Usually, coming to receive prayer is just the tip of a
spiritual iceberg. Discerning prayers, led by the Holy
Spirit, often uncover unexpected needs – for conversion,
for release from the occult, for the ability to forgive others,
for deep inner healing. For instance, I believe that an old
lady was brought to a real faith and discipleship as a result
of her experience at a small village healing service.

The great joy of the 'Toronto experience' is that a few
minutes, or several hours, flat out before the Lord often
bring effective healing that would otherwise have taken
hours of counselling. The danger appears to be an uncri-
tical acceptance of 'phenomena' – many of which certainly
cause me, and others, to believe that people are more in
need of deliverance rather than encouragement to shake,
shout, scream or whatever.

We need to prepare ourselves in prayer. It is not always
practical just before a service, but it is the responsibility of
each team member to make sure that they have plenty of

time with the Lord before praying for others. *Leaders, too, need to receive prayer.* I always remember Colin Urquhart saying at a Good News Crusade, 'Leaders, if you want an effective healing ministry in your church, be prepared to be prayed for publicly by your own people!'

The joy and the privilege of ministry

It is a great joy, privilege and challenge to be involved in such ministry. I believe *every* parish would benefit (as many have in recent years) for stepping out into these waters. There are tremendous benefits to those who are prayed for, often this is their first link with the church, or real experience of God. There are great benefits for those who pray – the privilege of seeing God at work in healing and deliverance (especially when it all happens with virtually no human involvement) is amazing. Of course, there are risks, and we will make mistakes, but Jesus always seems to encourage us to make the fullest use of whatever gifts he has given us (Matthew 25:14–30).

I would want to encourage every church to start praying and *thinking clearly* about their possible involvement in such a beautiful work.

How do we begin a healing ministry in our local church?

It goes without saying that without the full co-operation of the leader and his pastoral team, little can be achieved. Healing, although it may be part of the experience of the every-member ministry described in Ephesians 4:11–13, is essentially a matter for the leadership. The well-known passage in James 5:13ff supports this as does 1 Corinthians 12:28–30.

How to get started

A leader desiring to make healing part of his church ministry might well adopt this strategy.

1) Get well informed. Read biblically and widely (including books whose theology you don't think you will be comfortable with!).
2) Preach and teach about healing.
3) Have a parish conference for those who are interested, and those who, reluctantly, or willingly, feel called to this work.
4) Train and build a healing team which is open, accessible and accountable. Concentrate on building good relationships and friendships within the team. Such teams will need to be open to changing membership. There is great danger, and little blessing, in becoming a holy clique.
5) Make healing prayer a normal part of church services, as well as, or instead of, holding special services.

   At Shepton, people are available to pray, in a specially set aside area, while the congregation receive communion. Such prayer may be appropriate before or after receiving communion. Inevitably, it will be quite brief, and certainly should not develop into a counselling session. Follow up, when necessary, is vital.

   After non-eucharistic services, prayer is always available. At special healing services, a large team is available, and the prayer time may be rather longer (say up to twenty minutes). It is helpful if the choir sing 'Taizé' style music, or something else that is quiet and worshipful.
6) Review what has happened – honestly and fearlessly!

The result may well be that many people can relate to the words of the Apostle John, 'I pray that you may enjoy good health and that all may go well with you, even as your soul is getting along well' (3 John 2).

Notes

1. SHAL, Shepton Housing Association Limited, is a house for the young homeless set up largely by the church, staffed professionally, funded by government grants and benefits and private giving. Homelessness is a very important problem. See also John Woolmer, *Thinking Clearly about Prayer* (Monarch, 1997), p. 204.
2. Don Latham, *A Faith that Works* (Terra Nova, 1997), p. 87.
3. Selwyn Hughes, well-known author of *Every Day with Jesus* and books on healing and evangelism.
4. C.S. Lewis *A Grief Observed* (Faber and Faber, 1961).
5. See chapter 8, question 22.

11

Towards a Theology of Healing and Deliverance

The final chapter glances at the wider issues of the healing of society, and then looks at the importance of serious thinking about spiritual warfare. We summarise our theology and practice in both deliverance and healing. We face the call for all churches to take the risk and get involved in these areas.

Towards a Theology of
Healing and Deliverance

The healing of society

We have already seen (p. 148f) that Oscar Cullman makes the surprising point that εξουξιαι, the word usually translated 'angelic powers' (eg Colossians 1:16) has the same meaning in Romans 13:1 where Paul is writing about secular governments: 'Everyone must submit himself to the governing authorities, for there is no authority except that which God has established. The authorities that exist have been established by God.'

If Cullmann is right, there is a strange synthesis between the liberal scholars who want to demythologise the devil and see demonic power as represented most clearly by apartheid, fundamentalism, multinationals, the World Bank . . . and charismatics who want to challenge the principalities and powers in spiritual warfare.

Taking stock of society can be depressing. In England, the last quarter of the twentieth century has seen the appearance of a real underclass, an increase in homelessness, especially among the young, a seemingly less effective health service, many more one-parent families, increasing use of dangerous drugs, severe food scares such as BSE with its dramatic effect on the farming industry.

Overseas, the attempts to repay even the interest on loans so freely given in the 1970s are crippling most Third-World economies. The scourge of AIDS is cutting a terrible swathe through Africa and many other nations, and corruption and dictatorship are rife, especially in the poorest countries.

There are, of course, signs of light – the collapse of the Berlin Wall and the end of Marxist tyranny has (at a great economic price) brought freedom to millions; the peaceful collapse of apartheid in South Africa has been hailed as a miracle; there is a glimmer of hope in Northern Ireland, and the Jubilee 2000 campaign is a mighty effort by World Aid agencies and church leaders to tilt at the windmills of the World Bank, IMF, and to relieve Third-World debt.

Liberals and Evangelicals have often argued as to whether society is best healed by individual conversion or corporate action. The success of the early Methodists in rescuing a huge segment of society from a hopeless existence ('drunk for a penny, dead drunk for two pence'), was based first on individual conversion, and then on the Methodist class system – giving the new believer a much-needed support group. In the nineteenth century, evangelical-led social action tackled the evils of the slave trade, and other social ills of the industrial world. In the twentieth century (Christian) socialist ideals created the Welfare State, the National Health Service, and created a climate in which poverty was supposedly (!) to be eradicated. Human nature knew rather better. Socialist utopias seldom recognise the power of original sin. The sexual revolution may have freed many women from the

362   HEALING AND DELIVERANCE

drudgery of impossible marriages, but it has led to the break-up of far too many homes which has helped to create the underclass of the long-term unemployed and the young homeless.

Overseas, missionary societies have turned from evangelism to aid. Development projects aim to teach the locals how to fish rather than supply them with tins; education is a priority, health care another. All of these worthy aims are somewhat defeated by mushrooming populations, and the devastating effects of civil wars, corruption, the re-emergence of killer diseases such as malaria, and the effects of AIDS. The healing of society still seems a distant dream.

A hopeful case – a nation transformed

The recent changes in South Africa have been some of the most encouraging in the whole international scene. Obviously, huge problems remain, but the difference between the oppressive, doctrinaire governments of the past, and the new South Africa with its emphasis on 'truth and reconciliation' is dramatic.

Two outstanding books show, from very different perspectives, how this was achieved. *Long Walk to Freedom*[1] is the autobiography of Nelson Mandela without whose courage, and graciousness towards former enemies, little could have been achieved. *A Witness Forever*[2] tells the fascinating story of preparatory meetings, including deep theological discussions, of men and women from very diverse organisations, and of an intense time of prayer, especially in the weeks preceding the elections in April 1994.

Liberals will see the dismantling of apartheid and the beginnings of democracy as a triumph for international trade sanctions, sporting boycotts, and the emphasis on reconciliation by Nelson Mandela before, during and after the elections.

Charismatics will see the witness of a mighty prayer battle, with a number of miracles acknowledged even by hardened reporters. John Simpson, of the BBC, made a typical comment, 'It was the Jesus Peace Rally which tipped the scales'.

Miracles in South Africa A month earlier (23 March 1994), a South African policeman, Colonel Johan Botha, was praying in English, something he had never done before.

> I was asking the Lord in all sincerity, 'God, what is it that you want from us, what do you want from South Africa?' At that moment the whole extraordinary thing happened. An angel stood before me, bathed in a brilliant, indescribable light which hid his face, and answered, 'I want South Africa on its knees in prayer.' At that moment a light appeared with the word *gebedsdienskettings* (chains of prayer services) spelled out. I asked when we must do these things and the angel told me, 'You have fourteen days. Go to the highest authority if it is necessary.' 'Would you then give us peace?' I asked, to which the angel responded, 'You will experience the wonders of my workings.'[3]

Johan was overwhelmed and almost struck dumb with the awesome presence. How could he convey any angelic message to the whole country? The notion was absurd. He would be laughed out of court. He bumbled out excuses, 'The people will not believe me, I don't have the courage. I shall cry if I have to recount what is happening to me now.'

He was able to take his message even to President de Klerk. Many, many prayer rallies took place fourteen days later, on Founders' Day – a significant date in the South African calendar. A few days later on 17 April, the great Jesus Peace Rally took place. Michael Cassidy, who had arranged it, collapsed tired and exhausted at the end of the day. He writes:

'Utterly played out, I sat disconsolate under my juniper tree like Jonah. But there was more than weariness and stress. There was a tremendous oppression and sense of blankets of heaviness. I sat in my study and stared at the floor. I pleaded with God to forgive me for letting him down. If only I could have seen three incredible encounters going on right then in three very different corners of South Africa.

Then, says my journal, dictated late that night: 'I must record an astonishing thing which happened this evening, because about 9 pm I suddenly had a sense of a tremendous cloud, burden and oppression lifting. And as it did so, I seemed to hear the Spirit of the Lord within my soul saying: 'The stronghold has broken and has been pulled down.' I do not understand the full significance of that except that I believe something in the heavenlies has taken place and we can rejoice and be glad.[4]

Behind all the necessary political efforts, and the vital praying, lay the sovereign purposes of God. Years earlier, Nelson Mandela, in the infamous Rivonia treason trial, faced a probable death sentence.[5] Yet, somehow, it didn't happen. The terrible sentence of life imprisonment on Robben Island gave life to the future president, and time for apartheid to run its evil course. Was this the direct hand of God (as with Joseph in Genesis 37ff) bringing healing to the nation?

A hopeful case – healing in society

My second daughter, Susie, has just finished working for eight months in the rural south-west of Uganda. Many things impressed me on a brief visit – the wonderful vibrant cheerfulness of a people with very little in the way of material goods, their faith, their concern for the environment (conservation of mountain gorillas and butterflies). But something that was very special was to see the co-operation between TEAR Fund and the local community.

When she arrived, Susie had to walk about 300 metres, mainly down a steep slope, to a water point. Now, thanks to TEAR Fund, there is a fine new tap just 100 metres away on the level. All over the school complex, and throughout the area, taps have arrived, the foundations built by hard local work, and the finance and expertise provided by TEAR Fund.

Compassion in Uganda On a Saturday, Susie usually spent the day with Compassion, a TEAR Fund local organisation, run entirely by two employed Ugandans and many volunteers, who look after 250 orphaned or single-parent children. There is a little teaching, craft instruction, a health check, games, good food, and prayer. Behind this lies a child sponsorship scheme which helps pay for the children's education, clothing and food. Each child helped, helps one very poor local family, each family helped eases the burden on the community. Such schemes can seem like a drop in the ocean, but in Nuryahanga this seems like many drops forming a lake, and bringing hope to the whole community reeling under the scourges of AIDS, malaria and other diseases.

Jubilee 2000

Of course, if the Jubilee 2000[6] campaign were successful, this would have an even bigger effect on countries like Uganda and its much poorer neighbours.

Jubilee 2000, supported by British Prime Minister Tony Blair, has been spearheaded by churches and charities of many different theological persuasions. Here real political action, backed by intense prayer, is doing more than tilt at windmills as it tackles the World Bank, and International Monetary Fund, challenging them to do more to alleviate the scandal of Third-World debt.

However, our discussions (pp. 225ff) about spiritual warfare on the mission field cannot be ignored. Much can be achieved by sensible political action and intercessory prayer, but there are darker, more intractable situations. Michael Green[7] has alluded to the probable occult influence on the early Marxists, and more certainly on the German Third Reich leaders.

Let me offer a parable from nature.

A butterfly and its enemy   Each year in May, I look for Holly Blue butterflies flying around the big holly tree in our churchyard. Most years, I notice a small number, occasionally I see more. In 1998 there were many. Often I could see a dozen or more, and there seemed to be a very large colony, perhaps over a hundred. I captured a few females, and released them after they had laid some eggs. I farmed about a dozen caterpillars, protecting and feeding them. Most days, I would pick a small amount of holly to feed my captive caterpillars. One day, I noticed a small wasp, with a long ovipositer, lurking on a branch that I had picked. I identified it as a parasitic wasp which survives solely by laying its eggs inside the caterpillars of the Holly Blue butterfly. Adult wasps emerge from the dead pupae of what should have been emerging Holly Blue butterflies.

The Lord seemed to give me an interpretation. 'Today's Church is largely built up by the families of believers, carefully farmed and protected from the worst of the world, just as your captured caterpillars are protected. If you want an explosion of new members, you will need to defeat the spiritual powers which are targeting your church and locality, just as the Holly Blue numbers explode in the rare years when the parasitic wasp is largely unavailable to sting the majority of the caterpillars.'

As the Holly Blue colonies only have exceptional years if the wasps have been largely absent, so Christian evangelism depends much on defeating the spiritual powers. One particular wasp targets the Holly Blue, and in order to help the colony you will need to eliminate that wasp. So particular spirits target and control particular regions, and you need to identify them in order to make real progress.

Of course, not all butterflies have such determined individual enemies. To some extent such forces are needed to keep numbers in check, otherwise, as occasionally happens, hungry caterpillars would swarm in a desperate search for ever-diminishing food supplies.

In the spiritual realm things are rather different, and it seems to me that serious prayer is needed to identify the main areas in society that are in need of healing, and that there is enough evidence from Scripture and experience to suggest that spiritual warfare should be on the agenda of far more churches.

I noticed a report in *The Times*,[8] of a church led by a converted Muslim which had grown so much that it had moved into new premises in London which seat 5,000. The key to its growth and life was attributed to 'warfare prayer', and two months a year devoted to prayer and fasting. Why are most of us so slow to grasp the challenge? Why are we so eager to stall, with comments on spiritual warfare like 'the jury is still out'? Perhaps it is because we are afraid of tilting at windmills, because we are unsure where or what the local spiritual enemy is, but how are we to find out if we don't work hard at prayer and listening?

Spiritual warfare needn't be just negative. Many areas, if Origen and Cullmann are right, are not under negative spiritual control. In such places deep prayer may pave the way for revival. Visions, angels, prophecy and spiritual gifts may flow, and the growing, Spirit-led church may transform society as surely as the Methodist movement helped the poorest in eighteenth-century England, and the Welsh revival transformed society in early twentieth-century Wales.[9]

A theology and practice of deliverance

1) Healing and Deliverance are linked

Anyone involved in the healing ministry is likely, from time to time, to step over an invisible line and become involved in praying for deliverance. Fred Smith used to pray against all cancers as evil spirits. Agnes Sandford used to curse cancer, modelling the prayer on Jesus' treatment of the barren fig tree (Matthew 11:14). Others would anoint with oil, or use the laying on of hands. Readers may feel uncomfortable with Fred's theology (I did in this area), but it was certainly efficacious. Testimonies on Radio Oxford and in local newspapers bore witness to powerful healings wrought through his prayers. I, myself, saw a man walk into Oxford Town Hall, yellow with cancer. I saw him walk out apparently completely well. I followed him up some months later and he was still completely well. I don't suppose he was too bothered by the niceties of Fred's theology. In the end, the crucial matter was Fred's faith and his anointing by God to heal (viz Luke 5:11).

In a way, this is all very biblical. As we have seen (p. 94), the healing of the leper (Mark 1:40f) and the healing of the crippled woman (Luke 13:10f) illustrate the close link that sometimes occurs between healing and deliverance. What is vital is that we do not see all healing in this way. The man born blind (John 9:1ff) hadn't sinned, nor had his parents. The miracle there is to display the work of God, not specifically to destroy the revenge of Satan.

2) Towards a theology of deliverance.

Again, I've aimed to steer a positive course between the Scylla of dismissing all talk of deliverance as medieval, and the Charybidis of regarding demonisation as the normal state of the human race.

As a preliminary, I would remind readers that in the Anglican, and other churches, this is a ministry only to be exercised under authority. In most dioceses, the bishop has an appointed adviser on such matters, and his advice (and permission) should be sought before proceeding with such ministry.

Praying for buildings

Problems may occur in buildings, people or both. There is no direct scriptural evidence as to problems in buildings or places. However, the constant cleansing of 'high places' (where idolatrous practices had taken place) in the Old Testament, suggests that the godly kings and prophets understood the problem.

Signs that there are problems in a building may include sighting of ghosts, strange noises (such as footsteps, banging doors, etc.), strange smells, movement of objects, and a sensation of extreme cold. In one extreme case, I visited a house where a poltergeist had terrified various workmen by moving their tools. It had also alarmed the occupants by breaking things, and hurling objects like slippers and knives across their bedroom. All of this may make it difficult for people, especially children, to sleep peacefully, and dogs will often react in a distressed manner. The usual causes are some previous tragedy in the building (often the suicide of a former occupant), or the use of the building for occult practices. Sometimes no obvious cause can be discerned, but ministry is still needed.

Such ministry can be quite simple. A small team, usually just two, can pray through the house – preferably with the occupants present. Any evil powers should be commanded to leave, it may be helpful to sprinkle the room with consecrated water (p. 344), and it is desirable that a simple communion service be held in the main room when the prayers are completed.

This is usually adequate. If it isn't, the spiritual problem is likely to include someone living on the premises. After one 'failure' in a difficult building, we discovered that the owner was 'psychic', and had a history of such disturbances following him wherever he was living.

Guide-lines for praying with people

1) The team should come prepared, spiritually cleansed, under authority, and covered with prayer for themselves, their households, and the person (and their family) for whom they are going to pray.

2) It is unlikely that people will need such ministry unless either they, their partner, or their ancestors have been involved in some sort of occult or white magic practices. Very occasionally, Christians who have undertaken this ministry without proper authority and prayer cover may themselves need to be prayed for, for release from its

effects. (I guess that the sons of Sceva, Acts 19: 14, would have needed some prayer themselves.)

3) The usual sign that there is a demonic problem include strange eyes (Matthew 6:22–23); aversion to prayer, church, Christian symbols and sacraments; sudden deafness, or inability to say the Lord's prayer; hearing voices, and speaking in strange ways; unnatural strength, and general lack of self-control; extreme fear, and general feeling of an evil presence within or around.

4) The simplest possible ministry should be used. For Anglicans, this means that a service involving the renewing of baptismal vows is often all that is necessary. It can be adapted to include a specific renunciation of any occult, or white magic practices that have been mentioned.

5) After such ministry, people should be encouraged either to turn to Christ (see especially the warning in Matthew 12:43ff), or, if already a professing Christian, to receive the laying-on of hands and prayer to be filled with the Spirit (Ephesians 5:18). Anointing with oil is also helpful. It should help to reassure both the prayers and the prayed for that the problem has been dealt with. Demonised people sometimes react to anointing quite violently.

6) It will not always be clear whether the person was demonised, or under attack by some external spiritual forces. What matters is how they are after such ministry. This is far more important than a total diagnosis of the problem.

7) If it is felt that the main problem is ancestral, a simple service for the healing of the family tree should be undertaken (see chapter 8, question 10).

To sum up, evidence from Scripture, church history, and experience, both in sophisticated Western culture, and in the mission field, suggests that the ministry of deliverance is a vital part of the Church's approach to evangelism and healing.

Caution and authority

The right approach is one of cautious authority.

Cautious because it is vital that the diagnosis is correct. Exorcising non-existent demons does great spiritual and psychological harm. Confronting a 'demon of anger' will not only prove futile, but will cause the person concerned to avoid taking responsibility for a sin of the flesh (Galatians 5:20). Nevertheless, wrong emotions are described in James 3:13–14 as earthly, unspiritual, *of the devil*. That means that the ultimate cause of my own envy and selfish ambition is my flesh (the part of 'me' opposed to God's will – see Romans 7, etc.), but behind that lies the influence of the devil. I suppose in very extreme cases envy and ambition could become so all-consuming that they allow an evil spirit access to someone's soul. Lady Macbeth, in Shakespeare's play, is portrayed as being driven to murder by these sorts of emotions, while lurking behind the scenes the witches stir the brew of future trouble with their predictions.

Authoritative, because if the diagnosis is correct, and if the person really wants to be free (it is very rare for a person to be so demonised that they cannot exercise their will in this matter), then the demon(s) will leave after prayer in the name of Jesus. There are no doubts here about God's will – he wants demons out!

We should neither tease the demons (Jude 9), nor send them to hell (for which we have no authority), but release them into the presence of Christ. He will dispose of them, as he alone can (Philippians 2:10).

Our ministry will be gentle and minimal. We shall look for signs of demonisation, investigating the spiritual background of the person, their partner(s), and their ancestors. Without any obvious occult links, or involvement in dubious practices, it is unlikely that a person is demonised.

We must not be alarmed by any physical, or spiritual fireworks. People can display great strength, give words of knowledge, speak in strange tongues, and react in strange and unpleasant ways. As I've mentioned above, after such ministry people need to turn to Christ and/or receive prayer to be filled with the Spirit.

They are usually the best judge that the spirits have left. If there has been a clear manifestation of the evil presence, it may be helpful to challenge any remaining spirit(s) to show itself. If there is no reaction, and the person feels better, then laying-on of hands and anointing with oil will strengthen them spiritually.

Such ministry shouldn't last an excessively long time (one hour would seem to be more than enough). Afterwards the person prayed for may feel very tired, as may members of the prayer team. They will need considerable care and follow-up. Prayer for inner healing or physical healing may also be needed – on another occasion!

Incidentally, before praying for someone to be filled with the Spirit, it is *essential* to ask the same questions. Evil spirits prefer to lie dormant: once active they are easy to deal with, (once you discover a wasps' nest it is reasonably easy to destroy it!) but they cannot stand 'the fullness of the Spirit'. That's why there's such a collision on SOMA[10] trips where a gospel, which includes being filled by the Spirit, may well be being preached for the first time. Similarly, it is why there's such a collision in some healing services. Philip discovered this in Samaria, others have found the same battles in their own experience.

Finally, I do believe that a Christian can be oppressed

by demons, and in extreme cases partially controlled by them (see chapter 8, question 23). At baptism, confirmation or conversion, they ought to have been challenged to renounce evil – then much future trouble would have been eliminated. Ancient services contain clear prayers of exorcism. The Early Fathers wrote much about this. *The Oil of Gladness*[11] gives a number of examples of suitable prayer and practice.

Advice to the prayer teams

I haven't given any sample prayers, as I believe that we all develop our own style of ministry. Perhaps a few guidelines as to the actual praying would be helpful.

The praying team should be quite small, two or three (*never* just one). The person prayed for may be accompanied by a partner/friend. It is wise to begin such sessions with prayer for protection for all those involved, their families and their houses. They should be encouraged to pray and to tell the spirit to depart. I have found recently, especially in Zambia, that people knew the name of the spirits that were troubling them, and were quite capable, after a little encouragement, to pray for X to depart in the name of Jesus. The praying team can back this up by praying to cut off any controlling spirits, and seeking any gifts of knowledge which would help unlock the situation. Sometimes the person being ministered to becomes temporarily deaf, or refuses to open their eyes and/or hands. A gentle but firm prayer to open their eyes is helpful.

Spiritual dangers   The praying team needs to be aware of the dangers of such ministry. The most obvious is some sort of spiritual counter-attack. I used to experience extreme tiredness about a day later. It became so obvious that Jane used to ask me, 'Who have you been praying with?' Michael Green sometimes used to experience psychic phenomena in his rectory until I quoted Psalm 34: 7 – 'The angel of the Lord encamps around those who fear him, and he delivers them', and we took authority over these counter attacks.

It is certainly wise to seek the protection and prayers of others, as I discovered when starting to write this book.

Finally, we should beware spiritual pride, and a sort of unpleasant spiritual hardness which can mar such ministries. We need to keep humble, prayerful and open to advice, and the correction (!), of others.

Towards a theology and practice of healing

A parable from nature

Let me offer another parable from nature. One evening, when working on the first draft of this chapter, I wandered in the gathering twilight through the grounds of Hilfield Friary. It is a beautiful, prayerful place. It was in late spring. In one field primroses and cowslips grew abundantly. Almost inevitably, hybrid oxlips grew. I find them particularly beautiful and intriguing. They vary immensely – some flowers are small and deep yellow, almost cowslips; others much larger and, except for their multiheads, not very different from primroses. It is our wisest course, theologically, to be oxlips. We can draw the best from all shades of theology, and yet become distinctive and beautiful. Remember, too, that hybrids are usually barren. New plants have to be created each year. Theologically, this means that each year our synthesis will have to be worked out afresh, which keeps us alert and prevents us from settling into comfortable theological ruts.

There are, however, some extremes which allow no

synthesis, which must be rejected. We will not allow a 'dispensationalist' view of the gifts of the Spirit. This view is usually expressed by arguing that, with the completion of the canon of Scripture, such gifts were no longer necessary, or alternatively, that such gifts were only given to authenticate the ministry of the first Apostles.

Jack Deere[12] writes eloquently on the theme 'Did miraculous gifts cease with the Apostles?' Serious students should study the classic cessationist arguments of Warfield and others,[13] as well as Deere's lengthy demolition of them.

I have argued at length from Scripture and church history against this view. Nor will we accept a sceptical view which rejects or downplays the miraculous, regards talk of deliverance as medieval, and spiritual warfare as absurd. But we will listen to the hard questions posed by doctors and others who look for real evidence of physical healing, and who caution, rightly, against exaggerated claims.

Here is a typical, very cautious, comment from a summary of a consensus book on Christian healing written by medics and clerics together.[14]

Healings having all the characteristics of those in the ministry of Jesus are rare today. Although in the nature of things complete medical histories are not often available, few cases with these characteristics have been documented in western countries in recent years – some would argue that there is no adequately documented case. More cases are reported from missionary situations in countries of the developing world – although they are even more difficult to verify. Why are such Christ-like healings rare today? Some attribute it to a lack of faith on the part of Christians. Others argue that God in his sovereign purposes is just not often working in that way today especially in countries with well-developed health services.

Nor will our theology accept that 'healing is in the atonement' (see chapter 8, question 24). I have much admiration for the ministries of many who lead the healing ministry, and for whom the belief that healing is in the atonement provides a simple, clear, positive theology. But I have to say that I think that Scripture and experience show that this theology is wrong, and quite harmful, especially to those with serious long-term illnesses whether physical or mental.

So what is to be our theology of healing? It should, I believe, be a synthesis of a theology which expects God to heal and a theology which sees healing as an occasional sign to an unbelieving world.

John Wimber[15] puts the view clearly, stating six principles. He, himself, we should remember was a severely sick man, suffering from both cancer and a stroke, before his relatively early death at the age of sixty-five.

1) God wants to heal the sick today.
2) Corporate ministry is important.
3) Trust in God is demonstrated in action.
4) All Christians are empowered by the Holy Spirit.
5) Loving relationships are important.
6) God wants to heal the whole person, not just specific conditions.

That seems good, though I would want to modify 4 to read: 'All Christians are *potentially* empowered by the Holy Spirit.

On the other hand, if we see healing as an occasional sign to an unbelieving world, we are then both acknowledging that remarkable things do happen (and have happened throughout Christian history), and also being realistic in the face of scriptural teaching concerning the frailty of our bodies (Psalm 90 and 2 Corinthians 4:16–5:5), about long-term illness, problems arising from birth, death, etc. Many Christians suffer potentially debilitating long-term illnesses such as multiple sclerosis, many have children born with some mental and physical problems, and all Christians die, some from painful and difficult illnesses.

The synthesis that I would offer between Wimber's fairly optimistic view and this last rather pessimistic paragraph is as follows:

1) God still gives gifts of healing today to his Church (1 Corinthians 12:9, 28; James 5:13–18; Mark 16:17–18).
2) Healing is a sign that may be expected to accompany the faithful preaching of God's word (Acts 4:29–30; Acts 14:1–3).
3) There is a strong link between healing and deliverance (Luke 13:10–17 is an example of a healing couched in the language of deliverance). Jesus' commission to the twelve and the seventy included commands to both heal the sick and exorcise (Mark 6:7–13 and Luke 10:1–22).
4) Anointing with oil (see chapter 8, question 15) is often helpful, especially in more serious cases of illness.
5) Death may be welcomed (Philippians 1:19–25); bodies will decay (2 Corinthians 4:16–5:3); illness can bring blessing (Galatians 4:13 – see discussion on pp. 139ff). Satan can work miracles 'to deceive even the elect – if that were possible' (Matthew 24:24).

Final thoughts

There are some real dangers in this whole area of ministry to which we must allude. There is the danger of disappointment which can quickly lead to disillusion. There is the danger of spiritual counter-attack which can involve depression, danger or even demonic experiences. There is the more subtle danger of pride with apparent success, or jealousy of the success of others. There is the great danger of judging a person's spiritual standing by their 'results' in this field. Jesus has a deep warning for all of us who are involved: 'Many will say to me on that day, "Lord, Lord, did we not prophesy in your name, and in your name drive out demons and perform many miracles?"' (Matthew 7:22). To overcome all this, we need to know Jesus and show further the eternal qualities of faith, hope and love.

Faith is a vital ingredient for spiritual warfare, deliverance and healing. It is essential somewhere, either in the hearts and minds of those who pray, or in the simple trust of those for whom prayer is offered, or in the general spiritual climate. Good services of worship can bring spontaneous healing and deliverance as Christ is exalted by believing people.

The importance of hope

Hope, a strangely neglected and overtly positive New Testament quality, means that we continue to trust God despite apparently adverse circumstances. 'Against all hope, Abraham in hope believed and so became the father of many nations' (Romans 4:18). Hope sees beyond the present towards eternity. Perhaps to rewrite Tennyson,[16] we might say: 'Tis better to have hoped and prayed than never to have prayed at all.'

There is a vital need for all churches to take the risk and to get involved. All around us people are turning to other means for healing, experiencing at best confusion, and at worst spiritual ruin. If we stand aside, either because of fear of failure, or because we cannot sort it out theologically, we shall be denying hope to many of our people in their time of greatest spiritual need.

But, above all, we need love, expressed most clearly as compassion. Without love, these ministries become concerned with power, status, self-fulfilment, and they become a seed bed for deadly pride. With love, all things are possible, and no situation unbearable.

We see through a glass darkly

'For now we see through a glass darkly; but then face to face: now I know in part; but then shall I know even as I also am known' (1 Corinthians 13:12, AV). I believe that healing and deliverance prayed for with love, compassion and discernment will help both those who pray and those who are prayed for to see something of the glory of God in the face of the Risen Christ (viz 2 Corinthians 4:6).

Prevailing prayer shines through this present darkness. Under God, captives will be set free, ancient ruins will be repaired, and the broken-hearted will be bound up.

Dare we, in the midst of Christ's suffering world, through fear, doctrinal differences or indifference, fail to strive and pray for those great signs of the kingdom of God?

As we enter a new millennium, the greatest gift that Christ's Church could offer his world would be to become truly 'catholic and apostolic'. Catholic, so that our gospel is universal and our witness united. Apostolic, so that our preaching, truly scriptural, can be accompanied with signs and wonders. Then, and only then, people everywhere will take notice, and once again have just cause to complain that their world is being turned upside down (Acts 17:6). Isn't that what Jesus always intended?

> Come, Holy Spirit, to cleanse and renew us:
> Purge us from *evil* and fill us with power:
> Thus shall the waters of *healing* flow through us;
> So shall revival be born in this hour.[17]

Notes

1. Nelson Mandela, *Long Walk to Freedom* (Little Brown, 1994).
2. Michael Cassidy, *A Witness for Ever* (Hodder and Stoughton, 1995).
3. *Ibid.*, p. 160ff.
4. *Ibid.*, p. 186.
5. Nelson Mandela, *op. cit.*, p. 337ff.
6. Jubilee 2000 is an international campaign, spearheaded by churches and relief agencies, to get the international debt of many of the poorest countries of the world released. It is based on the 'Jubilee' principle of Leviticus 25.
7. Michael Green, *I believe in Satan's Downfall* (Hodder and Stoughton, 1981), pp. 163–166.
8. Monday, 24 August 1998.
9. It was said that even the pit ponies were affected by the revival – they were unaccustomed to being well treated, as started to happen when their masters were converted!
10. Sharing of Ministries Abroad (see chapter 1, note 6).
11. M. Dudley and G. Rowell, eds, *The Oil of Gladness* (SPCK, 1990).
12. Jack Deere, *Surprised by the Power of the Spirit* (Kingsway, 1993), p. 229ff.
13. Benjamin Warfield, *Counterfeit Miracles* (Banner of Truth, 1972), p. 235–236.
14. Ernest Lucas, ed., *Christian Healing, What Can We Believe?* (SPCK, 1997), p. 197.
15. John Wimber, *Power Healing* (Hodder and Stoughton, 1986), p. 172ff.
16. Alfred, Lord Tennyson (1809–1892), 'In Memoriam',

''Tis better to have loved and lost than never to have loved at all'.

17. *Mission Praise* (Marshall Pickering, 1990), 698, v.4.

This verse from Raymond Browne's hymn must refer to his own experience in the Lowestoft Revival of 1921 which Mark Stibbe refers to in *Thinking Clearly about Revival* (Monarch, 1998), p. 210–211. It expresses perfectly the link between renewal, deliverance, healing and revival.

Index